Clarence Henry Haring

The Pirates of the West Indies in 17th Century

OK Publishing 2021

Clarence Henry Haring

THE PIRATES OF THE WEST INDIES IN 17TH CENTURY

The True Story of the Bold Pirates of the Caribbean

Published by

MUSAICUM

Books

- Advanced Digital Solutions & High-Quality book Formatting -

musaicumbooks@okpublishing.info

2021 OK Publishing

ISBN 978-80-272-7529-8

Contents

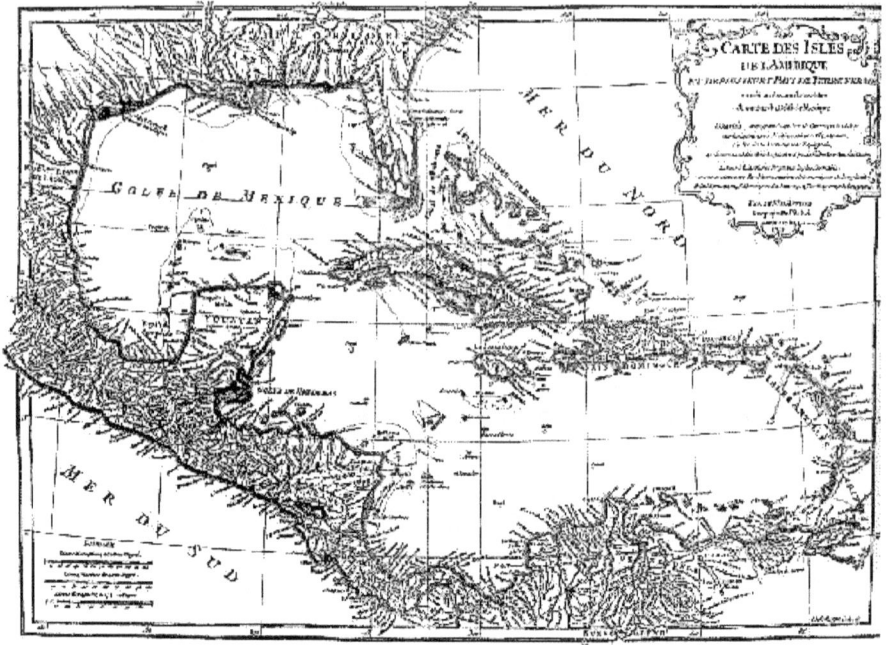

Map of the West Indies

Preface

The principal facts about the exploits of the English and French buccaneers of the seventeenth century in the West Indies are sufficiently well known to modern readers. The French Jesuit historians of the Antilles have left us many interesting details of their mode of life, and Exquemelin's history of the freebooters has been reprinted numerous times both in France and in England. Based upon these old, contemporary narratives, modern accounts are issued from the press with astonishing regularity, some of them purporting to be serious history, others appearing in the more popular and entertaining guise of romances. All, however, are alike in confining themselves for their information to what may almost be called the traditional sources-Exquemelin, the Jesuits, and perhaps a few narratives like those of Dampier and Wafer. To write another history of these privateers or pirates, for they have, unfortunately, more than once deserved that name, may seem a rather fruitless undertaking. It is justified only by the fact that there exist numerous other documents bearing upon the subject, documents which till now have been entirely neglected. Exquemelin has been reprinted, the story of the buccaneers has been re-told, yet no writer, whether editor or historian, has attempted to estimate the trustworthiness of the old tales by comparing them with these other sources, or to show the connection between the buccaneers and the history of the English colonies in the West Indies. The object of this volume, therefore, is not only to give a narrative, according to the most authentic, available sources, of the more brilliant exploits of these sea-rovers, but, what is of greater interest and importance, to trace the policy pursued toward them by the English and French Governments.

The "Buccaneers in the West Indies" was presented as a thesis to the Board of Modern History of Oxford University in May 1909 to fulfil the requirements for the degree of Bachelor of Letters. It was written under the supervision of C.H. Firth, Regius Professor of Modern History in Oxford, and to him the writer owes a lasting debt of gratitude for his unfailing aid and sympathy during the course of preparation.

C.H.H.

Oxford, 1910

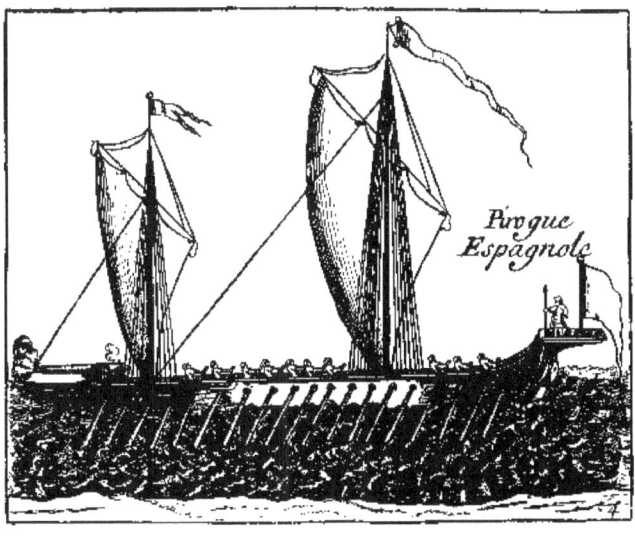

Chapter I
Introductory

I.The Spanish Colonial System

At the time of the discovery of America the Spaniards, as M. Leroy-Beaulieu has remarked, were perhaps less fitted than any other nation of western Europe for the task of American colonization. Whatever may have been the political *rôle* thrust upon them in the sixteenth century by the Hapsburg marriages, whatever certain historians may say of the grandeur and nobility of the Spanish national character, Spain was then neither rich nor populous, nor industrious. For centuries she had been called upon to wage a continuous warfare with the Moors, and during this time had not only found little leisure to cultivate the arts of peace, but had acquired a disdain for manual work which helped to mould her colonial administration and influenced all her subsequent history. And when the termination of the last of these wars left her mistress of a united Spain, and the exploitation of her own resources seemed to require all the energies she could muster, an entire new hemisphere was suddenly thrown open to her, and given into her hands by a papal decree to possess and populate. Already weakened by the exile of the most sober and industrious of her population, the Jews; drawn into a foreign policy for which she had neither the means nor the inclination; instituting at home an economic policy which was almost epileptic in its consequences, she found her strength dissipated, and gradually sank into a condition of economic and political impotence.

Christopher Columbus, a Genoese sailor in the service of the Castilian Crown, wishing to find a western route by sea to India and especially to Zipangu (Japan), the magic land described by the Venetian traveller, Marco Polo, landed on 12th October 1492, on "Guanahani," one of the Bahama Islands. From "Guanahani" he passed on to other islands of the same group, and thence to Hispaniola, Tortuga and Cuba. Returning to Spain in March 1493, he sailed again in September of the same year with seventeen vessels and 1500 persons, and this time keeping farther to the south, sighted Porto Rico and some of the Lesser Antilles, founded a colony on Hispaniola, and discovered Jamaica in 1494. On a third voyage in 1498 he discovered Trinidad, and coasted along the shores of South America from the Orinoco River to the island of Margarita. After a fourth and last voyage in 1502-04, Columbus died at Valladolid in 1506, in the firm belief that he had discovered a part of the Continent of Asia.

The entire circle of the Antilles having thus been revealed before the end of the fifteenth century, the Spaniards pushed forward to the continent. While Hojida, Vespucci, Pinzon and de Solis were exploring the eastern coast from La Plata to Yucatan, Ponce de Leon in 1512 discovered Florida, and in 1513 Vasco Nunez de Balboa descried the Pacific Ocean from the heights of Darien, revealing for the first time the existence of a new continent. In 1520 Magellan entered the Pacific through the strait which bears his name, and a year later was killed in one of the Philippine Islands. Within the next twenty years Cortez had conquered the realm of Montezuma, and Pizarro the empire of Peru; and thus within the space of two generations all of the West Indies, North America to California and the Carolinas, all of South America except Brazil, which the error of Cabral gave to the Portuguese, and in the east the Philippine Islands and New Guinea passed under the sway of the Crown of Castile.

Ferdinand and Isabella in 1493 had consulted with several persons of eminent learning to find out whether it was necessary to obtain the investiture of the Pope for their newly-discovered possessions, and all were of opinion that this formality was unnecessary.[1] Nevertheless, on 3rd May 1493, a bull was granted by Pope Alexander VI., which divided the sovereignty of those parts of the world not possessed by any Christian prince between Spain and Portugal by a meridian line 100 leagues west of the Azores or of Cape Verde. Later Spanish writers made much of this papal gift; yet, as Georges Scelle points out,[2] it is possible that this bull was not so much a deed of conveyance, investing the Spaniards with the proprietorship of America, as it was an act of ecclesiastical jurisdiction according them, on the strength of their acquired right and proven Catholicism, a monopoly as it were in the propagation of the faith. At that time, even Catholic princes were no longer accustomed to seek the Pope's sanction when making a new conquest, and certainly in the domain of public law the Pope was not considered to have temporal jurisdiction over the entire world. He did, however, intervene in temporal matters when they directly influenced spiritual affairs, and of this the propagation of the faith was an instance. As the compromise between Spain and Portugal was very indecisive, owing to the difference in longitude of the Azores and Cape Verde, a second Act was signed on 7th June 1494, which placed the line of demarcation 270 leagues farther to the west.

The colonization of the Spanish Indies, on its social and administrative side, presents a curious contrast. On the one hand we see the Spanish Crown, with high ideals of order and justice, of religious and political unity, extending to its ultramarine possessions its faith, its language, its laws and its administration; providing for the welfare of the aborigines with paternal solicitude; endeavouring to restrain and temper the passions of the conquerors; building churches and founding schools and monasteries; in a word, trying to make its colonies an integral part of the Spanish monarchy, "une société vieille dans une contrée neuve." Some Spanish writers, it is true, have exaggerated the virtues of their old colonial system; yet that system had excellences which we cannot afford to despise. If the Spanish kings had not choked their government with procrastination and routine; if they had only taken their task a bit less seriously and had not tried to apply too strictly to an empty continent the paternal administration of an older country; we might have been privileged to witness the development and operation of as complete and benign a system of colonial government as has been devised in modern times. The public initiative of the Spanish government, and the care with which it selected its colonists, compare very favourably with the opportunism of the English and the French, who colonized by chance private activity and sent the worst elements of their population, criminals and vagabonds, to people their new settlements across the sea. However much we may deprecate the treatment of the Indians by the *conquistadores*, we must not forget that the greater part of the population of Spanish America to-day is still Indian, and that no other colonizing people have succeeded like the Spaniards in assimilating and civilizing the natives. The code of laws which the Spaniards gradually evolved for the rule of their transmarine provinces, was, in spite of defects which are visible only to the larger experience of the present day, one of the wisest, most humane and best co-ordinated of any to this day published for any colony. Although the Spaniards had to deal with a large population of barbarous natives, the word "conquest" was suppressed in legislation as ill-sounding, "because the peace is to be sealed," they said, "not with the sound of arms, but with charity and good-will."[3]

The actual results, however, of the social policy of the Spanish kings fell far below the ideals they had set for themselves. The monarchic spirit of the crown was so strong that it crushed every healthy, expansive tendency in the new countries. It burdened the colonies with a numerous, privileged nobility, who congregated mostly in the larger towns and set to the rest of the colonists a pernicious example of idleness and luxury. In its zeal for the propagation of the Faith, the Crown constituted a powerfully endowed Church, which, while it did splendid service in converting and civilizing the natives, engrossed much of the land in the form of mainmort, and filled the new world with thousands of idle, unproductive, and often licentious friars. With an innate distrust and fear of individual initiative, it gave virtual omnipotence to royal officials and excluded all creoles from public employment. In this fashion was transferred to America the crushing political and ecclesiastical absolutism of the mother country. Self-reliance and independence of thought or action on the part of the creoles was discouraged, divisions and factions among them were encouraged and educational opportunities restricted, and the American-born

Spaniards gradually sank into idleness and lethargy, indifferent to all but childish honours and distinctions and petty local jealousies. To make matters worse, many of the Spaniards who crossed the seas to the American colonies came not to colonize, not to trade or cultivate the soil, so much as to extract from the natives a tribute of gold and silver. The Indians, instead of being protected and civilized, were only too often reduced to serfdom and confined to a laborious routine for which they had neither the aptitude nor the strength; while the government at home was too distant to interfere effectively in their behalf. Driven by cruel taskmasters they died by thousands from exhaustion and despair, and in some places entirely disappeared.

The Crown of Castile, moreover, in the sixteenth and seventeenth centuries sought to extend Spanish commerce and monopolize all the treasure of the Indies by means of a rigid and complicated commercial system. Yet in the end it saw the trade of the New World pass into the hands of its rivals, its own marine reduced to a shadow of its former strength, its crews and its vessels supplied by merchants from foreign lands, and its riches diverted at their very source.

This Spanish commercial system was based upon two distinct principles. One was the principle of colonial exclusivism, according to which all the trade of the colonies was to be reserved to the mother country. Spain on her side undertook to furnish the colonies with all they required, shipped upon Spanish vessels; the colonies in return were to produce nothing but raw materials and articles which did not compete with the home products with which they were to be exchanged. The second principle was the mercantile doctrine which, considering as wealth itself the precious metals which are but its symbol, laid down that money ought, by every means possible, to be imported and hoarded, never exported.[4] This latter theory, the fallacy of which has long been established, resulted in the endeavour of the Spanish Hapsburgs to conserve the wealth of the country, not by the encouragement of industry, but by the increase and complexity of imposts. The former doctrine, adopted by a non-producing country which was in no position to fulfil its part in the colonial compact, led to the most disastrous consequences.

While the Spanish Crown was aiming to concentrate and monopolize its colonial commerce, the prosperity of Spain itself was slowly sapped by reason of these mistaken economic theories. Owing to the lack of workmen, the increase of imposts, and the prejudice against the mechanic arts, industry was being ruined; while the increased depopulation of the realm, the mainmort of ecclesiastical lands, the majorats of the nobility and the privileges of the Mesta, brought agriculture rapidly into decay. The Spaniards, consequently, could not export the products of their manufacture to the colonies, when they did not have enough to supply their own needs. To make up for this deficiency their merchants were driven to have recourse to foreigners, to whom they lent their names in order to elude a law which forbade commerce between the colonies and traders of other nations. In return for the manufactured articles of the English, Dutch and French, and of the great commercial cities like Genoa and Hamburg, they were obliged to give their own raw materials and the products of the Indies-wool, silks, wines and dried fruits, cochineal, dye-woods, indigo and leather, and finally, indeed, ingots of gold and silver. The trade in Spain thus in time became a mere passive machine. Already in 1545 it had been found impossible to furnish in less than six years the goods demanded by the merchants of Spanish America. At the end of the seventeenth century, foreigners were supplying five-sixths of the manufactures consumed in Spain itself, and engrossed nine-tenths of that American trade which the Spaniards had sought so carefully to monopolize.[5]

In the colonies the most striking feature of Spanish economic policy was its wastefulness. After the conquest of the New World, it was to the interest of the Spaniards to gradually wean the native Indians from barbarism by teaching them the arts and sciences of Europe, to encourage such industries as were favoured by the soil, and to furnish the growing colonies with those articles which they could not produce themselves, and of which they stood in need. Only thus could they justify their monopoly of the markets of Spanish America. The same test, indeed, may be applied to every other nation which adopted the exclusivist system. Queen Isabella wished to carry out this policy, introduced into the newly-discovered islands wheat, the olive and the vine, and acclimatized many of the European domestic animals.[6] Her efforts, unfortunately, were not seconded by her successors, nor by the Spaniards who went to the Indies. In time the government itself, as well as the colonist, came to be concerned, not so much with the agricultural products of the Indies, but with the return of the precious metals. Natives were made to work the mines, while many regions adapted to agriculture, Guiana, Caracas and Buenos Ayres, were neglected, and the peopling of the colonies by Europeans was slow. The emperor, Charles V., did little to stem this tendency, but drifted along with the tide. Immigration was restricted to keep the colonies free from the contamination of heresy and of foreigners. The Spanish population was concentrated in cities, and the country divided into great estates granted by the crown to the families of the *conquistadores* or to favourites at court. The immense areas of Peru, Buenos Ayres and Mexico were submitted to the most unjust and arbitrary regulations, with no object but to stifle growing industry and put them in absolute dependence upon the metropolis. It was forbidden to exercise the trades of dyer, fuller, weaver, shoemaker or hatter, and the natives were compelled to buy of the Spaniards even the stuffs they wore on their backs. Another ordinance prohibited the cultivation of the vine and the olive except in Peru and Chili, and even these provinces might not send their oil and wine to Panama, Gautemala or any other place which could be supplied from Spain.[7] To maintain the commercial monopoly, legitimate ports of entry in Spanish America were made few and far apart-for Mexico, Vera Cruz, for New Granada, the town of Cartagena. The islands and most of the other provinces were supplied by uncertain "vaisseaux de registre," while Peru and Chili, finding all direct commerce by the Pacific or South Sea interdicted, were obliged to resort to the fever-ridden town of Porto Bello, where the mortality was enormous and the prices increased tenfold.

In Spain, likewise, the colonial commerce was restricted to one port-Seville. For in the estimation of the crown it was much more important to avoid being defrauded of its dues on import and export, than to permit the natural development of trade by those towns best fitted to acquire it. Another reason, prior in point of time perhaps, why Seville was chosen as the port for American trade, was that the Indies were regarded as the exclusive appanage of the crown of Castile, and of that realm Seville was then the chief mercantile city. It was not a suitable port, however, to be distinguished by so high a privilege. Only ships of less than 200 tons were able to cross the bar of San Lucar, and goods therefore had to be transhipped —a disability which was soon felt when traffic and vessels became heavier.[8] The fact, nevertheless, that the official organization called the *Casa dé Contratacion* was seated in Seville, together with the influence of the vested interests of the merchants whose prosperity depended upon the retention of that city as the one port for Indian commerce, were sufficient to bear down all opposition. The maritime towns of Galicia and Asturia, inhabited by better seamen and stronger races, often protested, and sometimes succeeded in obtaining a small share of the lucrative trade.[9] But Seville retained its primacy until 1717, in which year the *Contratacion* was transferred to Cadiz.

The administration of the complex rules governing the commerce between Spain and her colonies was entrusted to two institutions located at Seville, —the *Casa de Contratacion*, mentioned above, and the *Consulado*. The *Casa de Contratacion*, founded by royal decree as early as 1503, was both a judicial tribunal and a house of commerce. Nothing might be sent to the Indies without its consent; nothing might be brought back and landed, either on the account of merchants or of the King himself, without its authorization. It received all the revenues accruing from the Indies, not only the imposts on commerce, but also all the taxes remitted by colonial officers. As a consultative body it had the right to propose directly to the King anything which it deemed necessary to the development and organization of American commerce; and as a tribunal it possessed an absolute competence over all crimes under the common law, and over all infractions of the ordinances governing the trade of the Indies, to the exclusion of every ordinary court. Its jurisdiction began at the moment the passengers and crews embarked and the goods were put on board, and ended only when the return voyage and disembarkation had been completed.[10] The civil jurisdiction of the *Casa* was much more restricted and disputes purely commercial in character between the merchants were reserved to the *Consulado*, which was a tribunal of commerce chosen entirely by the merchants themselves. Appeals in certain cases might be carried to the Council of the Indies.[11]

The first means adopted by the northern maritime nations to appropriate to themselves a share of the riches of the New World was open, semi-piratical attack upon the Spanish argosies returning from those distant El Dorados. The success of the Norman and Breton corsairs, for it was the French, not the English, who started the game, gradually forced upon the Spaniards, as a means of protection, the establishment of great merchant fleets sailing periodically at long intervals and accompanied by powerful convoys. During the first half of the sixteenth century any ship which had fulfilled the conditions required for engaging in American commerce was allowed to depart alone and at any time of the year. From about 1526, however, merchant vessels were ordered to sail together, and by a *cedula* of July 1561, the system of fleets was made permanent and obligatory. This decree prohibited any ship from sailing alone to America from Cadiz or San Lucar on pain of forfeiture of ship and cargo.[12] Two fleets were organized each year, one for Terra Firma going to Cartagena and Porto Bello, the other designed for the port of San Juan d'Ulloa (Vera Cruz) in New Spain. The latter, called the Flota, was commanded by an "almirante," and sailed for Mexico in the early summer so as to avoid the hurricane season and the "northers" of the Mexican Gulf. The former was usually called the galeones (*anglice* "galleons"), was commanded by a "general," and sailed from Spain earlier in the year, between January and March. If it departed in March, it usually wintered at Havana and returned with the Flota in the following spring. Sometimes the two fleets sailed together and separated at Guadaloupe, Deseada or another of the Leeward Islands.[13]

The galleons generally consisted of from five to eight war-vessels carrying from forty to fifty guns, together with several smaller, faster boats called "patches," and a fleet of merchantmen varying in number in different years. In the time of Philip II. often as many as forty ships supplied Cartagena and Porto Bello, but in succeeding reigns, although the population of the Indies was rapidly increasing, American commerce fell off so sadly that eight or ten were sufficient for all the trade of South and Central America. The general of the galleons, on his departure, received from the Council of the Indies three sealed packets. The first, opened at the Canaries, contained the name of the island in the West Indies at which the fleet was first to call. The second was unsealed after the galleons arrived at Cartagena, and contained instructions for the fleet to return in the same year or to winter in America. In the third, left unopened until the fleet had emerged from the Bahama Channel on the homeward voyage, were orders for the route to the Azores and the islands they should touch in passing, usually Corvo and Flores or Santa Maria.[14]

The course of the galleons from San Lucar was south-west to Teneriffe on the African coast, and thence to the Grand Canary to call for provisions-considered in all a run of eight days. From the Canaries one of the patches sailed on alone to Cartagena and Porto Bello, carrying letters and packets from the Court and announcing the coming of the fleet. If the two fleets sailed together, they steered south-west from the Canaries to about the latitude of Deseada, 15' 30", and then catching the Trade winds continued due west, rarely changing a sail until Deseada or one of the other West Indian islands was sighted. From Deseada the galleons steered an easy course to Cape de la Vela, and thence to Cartagena. When the galleons sailed from Spain alone, however, they entered the Caribbean Sea by the channel between Tobago and Trinidad, afterwards named the Galleons' Passage. Opposite Margarita a second patche left the fleet to visit the island and collect the royal revenues, although after the exhaustion of the pearl fisheries the island lost most of its importance. As the fleet advanced into regions where more security was felt, merchant ships too, which were intended to unload and trade on the coasts they were passing, detached themselves during the night and made for Caracas, Santa Marta or Maracaibo to get silver, cochineal, leather and cocoa. The Margarita patche, meanwhile, had sailed on to Cumana and Caracas to receive there the king's treasure, mostly paid in cocoa, the real currency of the country, and thence proceeded to Cartagena to rejoin the galleons.[15]

The fleet reached Cartagena ordinarily about two months after its departure from Cadiz. On its arrival, the general forwarded the news to Porto Bello, together with the packets destined for the viceroy at Lima. From Porto Bello a courier hastened across the isthmus to the President of Panama, who spread the advice amongst the merchants in his jurisdiction, and, at the same time, sent a dispatch boat to Payta, in Peru. The general of the galleons, meanwhile, was also sending a courier overland to Lima, and another to Santa Fe, the capital of the interior province of New Granada, whence runners carried to Popagan, Antioquia, Mariguita, and adjacent provinces, the news of his arrival.[16] The galleons were instructed to remain at Cartagena only a month, but bribes from the merchants generally made it their interest to linger for fifty or sixty days. To Cartagena came the gold and emeralds of New Granada, the pearls of Margarita and Rancherias, and the indigo, tobacco, cocoa and other products of the Venezuelan coast. The merchants of Gautemala, likewise, shipped their commodities to Cartagena by way of Lake Nicaragua and the San Juan river, for they feared to send goods across the Gulf of Honduras to Havana, because of the French and English buccaneers hanging about Cape San Antonio.[17]

Meanwhile the viceroy at Lima, on receipt of his letters, ordered the Armada of the South Sea to prepare to sail, and sent word south to Chili and throughout the province of Peru from Las Charcas to Quito, to forward the King's revenues for shipment to Panama. Within less than a fortnight all was in readiness. The Armada, carrying a considerable treasure, sailed from Callao and, touching at Payta, was joined by the Navio del Oro (golden ship), which carried the gold from the province of Quito and adjacent districts. While the galleons were approaching Porto Bello the South Sea fleet arrived before Panama, and the merchants of Chili and Peru began to transfer their merchandise on mules across the high back of the isthmus.[18]

Then began the famous fair of Porto Bello.[19] The town, whose permanent population was very small and composed mostly of negroes and mulattos, was suddenly called upon to accommodate an enormous crowd of merchants, soldiers and seamen. Food and shelter were to be had only at extraordinary prices. When Thomas Gage was in Porto Bello in 1637 he was compelled to pay 120 crowns for a very small, meanly-furnished room for a fortnight. Merchants gave as much as 1000 crowns for a moderate-sized shop in which to sell their commodities. Owing to overcrowding, bad sanitation, and an extremely unhealthy climate, the place became an open grave, ready to swallow all who resorted there. In 1637, during the fifteen days that the galleons remained at Porto Bello, 500 men died of sickness. Meanwhile, day by day, the mule-trains from Panama were winding their way into the town. Gage in one day counted 200 mules laden with wedges of silver, which were unloaded in the market-place and permitted to lie about like heaps of stones in the streets, without causing any fear or suspicion of being lost.[20] While the treasure of the King of Spain was being transferred to the galleons in the harbour, the merchants were making their trade. There was little liberty, however, in commercial transactions, for the prices were fixed and published beforehand, and when negotiations began exchange was purely mechanical. The fair, which was supposed to be open for forty days, was, in later times, generally completed in ten or twelve. At the beginning of the eighteenth century the volume of business transacted was estimated to amount to thirty or forty million pounds sterling.[21]

In view of the prevailing east wind in these regions, and the maze of reefs, cays and shoals extending far out to sea from the Mosquito Coast, the galleons, in making their course from Porto Bello to Havana, first sailed back to Cartagena upon the eastward coast eddy, so as to get well to windward of Nicaragua before attempting the passage through the Yucatan Channel.[22] The fleet anchored at Cartagena a second time for ten or twelve days, where it was rejoined by the patache of Margarita[23] and by the merchant ships which had been sent to trade in Terra-Firma. From Cartagena, too, the general sent dispatches to Spain and to Havana, giving the condition of the vessels, the state of trade, the day when he expected to sail, and the probable time of arrival.[24] For when the galleons were in the Indies all ports were closed by the Spaniards, for fear that precious information of the whereabouts of the fleet and of the value of its cargo might inconveniently leak out to their rivals. From Cartagena the course was north-west past Jamaica and the Caymans to the Isle of Pines, and thence round Capes Corrientes and San

Antonio to Havana. The fleet generally required about eight days for the journey, and arrived at Havana late in the summer. Here the galleons refitted and revictualled, received tobacco, sugar, and other Cuban exports, and if not ordered to return with the Flota, sailed for Spain no later than the middle of September. The course for Spain was from Cuba through the Bahama Channel, north-east between the Virginian Capes and the Bermudas to about 38°, in order to recover the strong northerly winds, and then east to the Azores. In winter the galleons sometimes ran south of the Bermudas, and then slowly worked up to the higher latitude; but in this case they often either lost some ships on the Bermuda shoals, or to avoid these slipped too far south, were forced back into the West Indies and missed their voyage altogether.[25] At the Azores the general, falling in with his first intelligence from Spain, learned where on the coast of Europe or Africa he was to sight land; and finally, in the latter part of October or the beginning of November, he dropped anchor at San Lucar or in Cadiz harbour.

The Flota or Mexican fleet, consisting in the seventeenth century of two galleons of 800 or 900 tons and from fifteen to twenty merchantmen, usually left Cadiz between June and July and wintered in America; but if it was to return with the galleons from Havana in September it sailed for the Indies as early as April. The course from Spain to the Indies was the same as for the fleet of Terra-Firma. From Deseada or Guadeloupe, however, the Flota steered north-west, passing Santa Cruz and Porto Rico on the north, and sighting the little isles of Mona and Saona, as far as the Bay of Neyba in Hispaniola, where the ships took on fresh wood and water.[26] Putting to sea again, and circling round Beata and Alta Vela, the fleet sighted in turn Cape Tiburon, Cape de Cruz, the Isle of Pines, and Capes Corrientes and San Antonio at the west end of Cuba. Meanwhile merchant ships had dropped away one by one, sailing to San Juan de Porto Rico, San Domingo, St. Jago de Cuba and even to Truxillo and Cavallos in Honduras, to carry orders from Spain to the governors, receive cargoes of leather, cocoa, etc., and rejoin the Flota at Havana. From Cape San Antonio to Vera Cruz there was an outside or winter route and an inside or summer route. The former lay north-west between the Alacranes and the Negrillos to the Mexican coast about sixteen leagues north of Vera Cruz, and then down before the wind into the desired haven. The summer track was much closer to the shore of Campeache, the fleet threading its way among the cays and shoals, and approaching Vera Cruz by a channel on the south-east.

If the Flota sailed from Spain in July it generally arrived at Vera Cruz in the first fifteen days of September, and the ships were at once laid up until March, when the crews reassembled to careen and refit them. If the fleet was to return in the same year, however, the exports of New Spain and adjacent provinces, the goods from China and the Philippines carried across Mexico from the Pacific port of Acapulco, and the ten or twelve millions of treasure for the king, were at once put on board and the ships departed to join the galleons at Havana. Otherwise the fleet sailed from Vera Cruz in April, and as it lay dead to the leeward of Cuba, used the northerly winds to about 25°, then steered south-east and reached Havana in eighteen or twenty days. By the beginning of June it was ready to sail for Spain, where it arrived at the end of July, by the same course as that followed by the galleons.[27]

We are accustomed to think of Spanish commerce with the Indies as being made solely by great fleets which sailed yearly from Seville or Cadiz to Mexico and the Isthmus of Darien. There were, however, always exceptions to this rule. When, as sometimes happened, the Flota did not sail, two ships of 600 or 700 tons were sent by the King of Spain to Vera Cruz to carry the quicksilver necessary for the mines. The metal was divided between New Spain and Peru by the viceroy at Mexico, who sent *via* Gautemala the portion intended for the south. These ships, called "azogues," carried from 2000 to 2500 quintals[28] of silver, and sometimes convoyed six or seven merchant vessels. From time to time an isolated ship was also allowed to sail from Spain to Caracas with licence from the Council of the Indies and the *Contratacion*, paying the king a duty of five ducats on the ton. It was called the "register of Caracas," took the same route as the galleons, and returned with one of the fleets from Havana. Similar vessels traded at Maracaibo, in Porto Rico and at San Domingo, at Havana and Matanzas in Cuba and at

Truxillo and Campeache.[29] There was always, moreover, a special traffic with Buenos Ayres. This port was opened to a limited trade in negroes in 1595. In 1602 permission was given to the inhabitants of La Plata to export for six years the products of their lands to other Spanish possessions, in exchange for goods of which they had need; and when in 1616 the colonists demanded an indefinite renewal of this privilege, the sop thrown to them was the bare right of trade to the amount of 100 tons every three years. Later in the century the Council of the Indies extended the period to five years, so as not to prejudice the trade of the galleons.[30]

It was this commerce, which we have noticed at such length, that the buccaneers of the West Indies in the seventeenth century came to regard as their legitimate prey. These "corsarios Luteranos," as the Spaniards sometimes called them, scouring the coast of the Main from Venezuela to Cartagena, hovering about the broad channel between Cuba and Yucatan, or prowling in the Florida Straits, became the nightmare of Spanish seamen. Like a pack of terriers they hung upon the skirts of the great unwieldy fleets, ready to snap up any unfortunate vessel which a tempest or other accident had separated from its fellows. When Thomas Gage was sailing in the galleons from Porto Bello to Cartagena in 1637, four buccaneers hovering near them carried away two merchant-ships under cover of darkness. As the same fleet was departing from Havana, just outside the harbour two strange vessels appeared in their midst, and getting to the windward of them singled out a Spanish ship which had strayed a short distance from the rest, suddenly gave her a broadside and made her yield. The vessel was laden with sugar and other goods to the value of 80,000 crowns. The Spanish vice-admiral and two other galleons gave chase, but without success, for the wind was against them. The whole action lasted only half an hour.[31]

The Spanish ships of the sixteenth and seventeenth centuries were notoriously clumsy and unseaworthy. With short keel and towering poop and forecastle they were an easy prey for the long, low, close-sailing sloops and barques of the buccaneers. But this was not their only weakness. Although the king expressly prohibited the loading of merchandise on the galleons except on the king's account, this rule was often broken for the private profit of the captain, the sailors, and even of the general. The men-of-war, indeed, were sometimes so embarrassed with goods and passengers that it was scarcely possible to defend them when attacked. The galleon which bore the general's flag had often as many as 700 souls, crew, marines and passengers, on board, and the same number were crowded upon those carrying the vice-admiral and the pilot. Ship-masters frequently hired guns, anchors, cables, and stores to make up the required equipment, and men to fill up the muster-rolls, against the time when the "visitators" came on board to make their official inspection, getting rid of the stores and men immediately afterward. Merchant ships were armed with such feeble crews, owing to the excessive crowding, that it was all they could do to withstand the least spell of bad weather, let alone outmanœuvre a swift-sailing buccaneer.[32]

By Spanish law strangers were forbidden to resort to, or reside in, the Indies without express permission of the king. By law, moreover, they might not trade with the Indies from Spain, either on their own account or through the intermediary of a Spaniard, and they were forbidden even to associate with those engaged in such a trade. Colonists were stringently enjoined from having anything to do with them. In 1569 an order was issued for the seizure of all goods sent to the colonies on the account of foreigners, and a royal *cedula* of 1614 decreed the penalty of death and confiscation upon any who connived at the participation of foreigners in Spanish colonial commerce.[33] It was impossible, however, to maintain so complete an exclusion when the products of Spain fell far short of supplying the needs of the colonists. Foreign merchants were bound to have a hand in this traffic, and the Spanish government tried to recompense itself by imposing on the out-going cargoes tyrannical exactions called "indults." The results were fatal. Foreigners often eluded these impositions by interloping in the West Indies and in the South Sea.[34] And as the *Contratacion*, by fixing each year the nature and quantity of the goods to be shipped to the colonies, raised the price of merchandise at will and reaped enormous profits, the colonists welcomed this contraband trade as an opportunity of enriching themselves and adding to the comforts and luxuries of living.

From the beginning of the seventeenth century as many as 200 ships sailed each year from Portugal with rich cargoes of silks, cloths and woollens intended for Spanish America.[35] The Portuguese bought these articles of the Flemish, English, and French, loaded them at Lisbon and Oporto, ran their vessels to Brazil and up the La Plata as far as navigation permitted, and then transported the goods overland through Paraguay and Tucuman to Potosi and even to Lima. The Spanish merchants of Peru kept factors in Brazil as well as in Spain, and as Portuguese imposts were not so excessive as those levied at Cadiz and Seville, the Portuguese could undersell their Spanish rivals. The frequent possession of Assientos by the Portuguese and Dutch in the first half of the seventeenth century also facilitated this contraband, for when carrying negroes from Africa to Hispaniola, Cuba and the towns on the Main, they profited by their opportunities to sell merchandise also, and generally without the least obstacle.

Other nations in the seventeenth century were not slow to follow the same course; and two circumstances contributed to make that course easy. One was the great length of coast line on both the Atlantic and Pacific slopes over which a surveillance had to be exercised, making it difficult to catch the interlopers. The other was the venal connivance of the governors of the ports, who often tolerated and even encouraged the traffic on the plea that the colonists demanded it.[36] The subterfuges adopted by the interlopers were very simple. When a vessel wished to enter a Spanish port to trade, the captain, pretending that provisions had run low, or that the ship suffered from a leak or a broken mast, sent a polite note to the governor accompanied by a considerable gift. He generally obtained permission to enter, unload, and put the ship into a seaworthy condition. All the formalities were minutely observed. The unloaded goods were shut up in a storehouse, and the doors sealed. But there was always found another door unsealed, and by this they abstracted the goods during the night, and substituted coin or bars of gold and silver. When the vessel was repaired to the captain's satisfaction, it was reloaded and sailed away.

There was also, especially on the shores of the Caribbean Sea, a less elaborate commerce called "sloop-trade," for it was usually managed by sloops which hovered near some secluded spot on the coast, often at the mouth of a river, and informed the inhabitants of their presence in the neighbourhood by firing a shot from a cannon. Sometimes a large ship filled with merchandise was stationed in a bay close at hand, and by means of these smaller craft made its trade with the colonists. The latter, generally in disguise, came off in canoes by night. The interlopers, however, were always on guard against such dangerous visitors, and never admitted more than a few at a time; for when the Spaniards found themselves stronger than the crew, and a favourable opportunity presented itself, they rarely failed to attempt the vessel.

Thus the Spaniards of the seventeenth century, by persisting, both at home and in their colonies, in an economic policy which was fatally inconsistent with their powers and resources, saw their commerce gradually extinguished by the ships of the foreign interloper, and their tropical possessions fall a prey to marauding bands of half-piratical buccaneers. Although struggling under tremendous initial disabilities in Europe, they had attempted, upon the slender pleas of prior discovery and papal investiture, to reserve half the world to themselves. Without a marine, without maritime traditions, they sought to hold a colonial empire greater than any the world had yet seen, and comparable only with the empire of Great Britain three centuries later. By discouraging industry in Spain, and yet enforcing in the colonies an absolute commercial dependence on the home-country, by combining in their rule of distant America a solicitous paternalism with a restriction of initiative altogether disastrous in its consequences, the Spaniards succeeded in reducing their colonies to political impotence. And when, to make their grip the more firm, they evolved, as a method of outwitting the foreigner of his spoils, the system of great fleets and single ports of call, they found the very means they had contrived for their own safety to be the instrument of commercial disaster.

II. The Freebooters of the Sixteenth Century

It was the French chronologist, Scaliger, who in the sixteenth century asserted, "nulli melius piraticam exercent quam Angli"; and although he had no need to cross the Channel to find men proficient in this primitive calling, the remark applies to the England of his time with a force which we to-day scarcely realise. Certainly the inveterate hostility with which the Englishman learned to regard the Spaniard in the latter half of the sixteenth and throughout the seventeenth centuries found its most remarkable expression in the exploits of the Elizabethan "sea-dogs" and of the buccaneers of a later period. The religious differences and political jealousies which grew out of the turmoil of the Reformation, and the moral anarchy incident to the dissolution of ancient religious institutions, were the motive causes for an outburst of piratical activity comparable only with the professional piracy of the Barbary States.

Even as far back as the thirteenth century, indeed, lawless sea-rovers, mostly Bretons and Flemings, had infested the English Channel and the seas about Great Britain. In the sixteenth this mode of livelihood became the refuge for numerous young Englishmen, Catholic and Protestant, who, fleeing from the persecutions of Edward VI. and of Mary, sought refuge in French ports or in the recesses of the Irish coast, and became the leaders of wild roving bands living chiefly upon plunder. Among them during these persecutions were found many men belonging to the best families in England, and although with the accession of Elizabeth most of the leaders returned to the service of the State, the pirate crews remained at their old trade. The contagion spread, especially in the western counties, and great numbers of fishermen who found their old employment profitless were recruited into this new calling.[37] At the beginning of Elizabeth's reign we find these Anglo-Irish pirates venturing farther south, plundering treasure galleons off the coast of Spain, and cutting vessels out of the very ports of the Spanish king. Such outrages of course provoked reprisals, and the pirates, if caught, were sent to the galleys, rotted in the dungeons of the Inquisition, or, least of all, were burnt in the plaza at Valladolid. These cruelties only added fuel to a deadly hatred which was kindling between the two nations, a hatred which it took one hundred and fifty years to quench.

The most venturesome of these sea-rovers, however, were soon attracted to a larger and more distant sphere of activity. Spain, as we have seen, was then endeavouring to reserve to herself in the western hemisphere an entire new world; and this at a time when the great northern maritime powers, France, England and Holland, were in the full tide of economic development, restless with new thoughts, hopes and ambitions, and keenly jealous of new commercial and industrial outlets. The famous Bull of Alexander VI. had provoked Francis I. to express a desire "to see the clause in Adam's will which entitled his brothers of Castile and Portugal to divide the New World between them," and very early the French corsairs had been encouraged to test the pretensions of the Spaniards by the time-honoured proofs of fire and steel. The English nation, however, in the first half of the sixteenth century, had not disputed with Spain her exclusive trade and dominion in those regions. The hardy mariners of the north were still indifferent to the wonders of a new continent awaiting their exploitation, and it was left to the Spaniards to unfold before the eyes of Europe the vast riches of America, and to found empires on the plateaus of Mexico and beyond the Andes. During the reign of Philip II. all this was changed. English privateers began to extend their operations westward, and to sap the very sources of Spanish wealth and power, while the wars which absorbed the attention of the Spaniards in Europe, from the revolt of the Low Countries to the Treaty of Westphalia, left the field clear for these ubiquitous sea-rovers. The maritime powers, although obliged by the theory of colonial exclusion to pretend to acquiesce in the Spaniard's claim to tropical America, secretly protected and supported their mariners who coursed those western seas. France and England were now jealous and fearful of Spanish predominance in Europe, and kept eyes obstinately fixed on the inexhaustible streams of gold and silver by means of which Spain was enabled to pay her armies and man her fleets. Queen Elizabeth, while she publicly excused or disavowed to Philip II. the outrages committed by Hawkins and Drake, blaming the turbulence of the times and promising to do her utmost to suppress the disorders, was secretly one of the principal shareholders in their enterprises.

The policy of the marauders was simple. The treasure which oiled the machinery of Spanish policy came from the Indies where it was accumulated; hence there were only two means of obtaining possession of it: —bold raids on the ill-protected American continent, and the capture of vessels *en route*.[38] The counter policy of the Spaniards was also two-fold: —on the one hand, the establishment of commerce by means of annual fleets protected by a powerful convoy; on the other, the removal of the centres of population from the coasts to the interior of the country far from danger of attack.[39] The Spaniards in America, however, proved to be no match for the bold, intrepid mariners who disputed their supremacy. The descendants of the *Conquistadores* had deteriorated sadly from the type of their forbears. Softened by tropical heats and a crude, uncultured luxury, they seem to have lost initiative and power of resistance. The disastrous commercial system of monopoly and centralization forced them to vegetate; while the policy of confining political office to native-born Spaniards denied any outlet to creole talent and energy. Moreover, the productive power and administrative abilities of the native-born Spaniards themselves were gradually being paralyzed and reduced to impotence under the crushing obligation of preserving and defending so unwieldy an empire and of managing such disproportionate riches, a task for which they had neither the aptitude nor the means.[40] Privateering in the West Indies may indeed be regarded as a challenge to the Spaniards of America, sunk in lethargy and living upon the credit of past glory and achievement, a challenge to prove their right to retain their dominion and extend their civilization and culture over half the world.[41]

There were other motives which lay behind these piratical aggressions of the French and English in Spanish America. The Spaniards, ever since the days of the Dominican monk and bishop, Las Casas, had been reprobated as the heartless oppressors and murderers of the native Indians. The original owners of the soil had been dispossessed and reduced to slavery. In the West Indies, the great islands, Cuba and Hispaniola, were rendered desolate for want of inhabitants. Two great empires, Mexico and Peru, had been subdued by treachery, their kings murdered, and their people made to suffer a living death in the mines of Potosi and New Spain. Such was the Protestant Englishman's conception, in the sixteenth century, of the results of Spanish colonial policy. To avenge the blood of these innocent victims, and teach the true religion to the survivors, was to glorify the Church militant and strike a blow at Antichrist. Spain, moreover, in the eyes of the Puritans, was the lieutenant of Rome, the Scarlet Woman of the Apocalypse, who harried and burnt their Protestant brethren whenever she could lay hands upon them. That she was eager to repeat her ill-starred attempt of 1588 and introduce into the British Isles the accursed Inquisition was patent to everyone. Protestant England, therefore, filled with the enthusiasm and intolerance of a new faith, made no bones of despoiling the Spaniards, especially as the service of God was likely to be repaid with plunder.

A pamphlet written by Dalby Thomas in 1690 expresses with tolerable accuracy the attitude of the average Englishman toward Spain during the previous century. He says: —"We will make a short reflection on the unaccountable negligence, or rather stupidity, of this nation, during the reigns of Henry VII., Henry VIII., Edward VI. and Queen Mary, who could contentedly sit still and see the Spanish rifle, plunder and bring home undisturbed, all the wealth of that golden world; and to suffer them with forts and castles to shut up the doors and entrances unto all the rich provinces of America, having not the least title or pretence of right beyond any other nation; except that of being by accident the first discoverer of some parts of it; where the unprecedented cruelties, exorbitances and barbarities, their own histories witness, they practised on a poor, naked and innocent people, which inhabited the islands, as well as upon those truly civilized and mighty empires of Peru and Mexico, called to all mankind for succour and relief against their outrageous avarice and horrid massacres....(We) slept on until the ambitious Spaniard, by that inexhaustible spring of treasure, had corrupted most of the courts and senates of Europe, and had set on fire, by civil broils and discords, all our neighbour nations, or had subdued them to his yoke; contriving too to make us wear his chains and bear a share in the triumph of universal monarchy, not only projected but near accomplished, when Queen Elizabeth came to the crown ...and to the divided interests of Philip II. and Queen Elizabeth, in personal more than National concerns, we do owe that start of hers in letting loose upon him, and encouraging those daring adventurers, Drake, Hawkins, Rawleigh, the Lord Clifford and many other braves that age produced, who, by their privateering and bold undertaking (like those the buccaneers practise) now opened the way to our discoveries, and succeeding settlements in America."[42]

On the 19th of November 1527, some Spaniards in a caravel loading cassava at the Isle of Mona, between Hispaniola and Porto Rico, sighted a strange vessel of about 250 tons well-armed with cannon, and believing it to be a ship from Spain sent a boat to make inquiries. The new-comers at the same time were seen to launch a pinnace carrying some twenty-five men, all armed with corselets and bows. As the two boats approached the Spaniards inquired the nationality of the strangers and were told that they were English. The story given by the English master was that his ship and another had been fitted out by the King of England and had sailed from London to discover the land of the Great Khan; that they had been separated in a great storm; that this ship afterwards ran into a sea of ice, and unable to get through, turned south, touched at Bacallaos (Newfoundland), where the pilot was killed by Indians, and sailing 400 leagues along the coast of "terra nueva" had found her way to this island of Porto Rico. The Englishmen offered to show their commission written in Latin and Romance, which the Spanish captain could not read; and after sojourning at the island for two days, they inquired for the route to Hispaniola and sailed away. On the evening of 25th November this same vessel appeared before the port of San Domingo, the capital of Hispaniola, where the master with ten or twelve sailors went ashore in a boat to ask leave to enter and trade. This they obtained, for the *alguazil mayor* and two pilots were sent back with them to bring the ship into port. But early next morning, when they approached the shore, the Spanish *alcaide*, Francisco de Tapia, commanded a gun to be fired at the ship from the castle; whereupon the English, seeing the reception accorded them, sailed back to Porto Rico, there obtained some provisions in exchange for pewter and cloth, and departed for Europe, "where it is believed that they never arrived, for nothing is known of them." The *alcaide*, says Herrera, was imprisoned by the *oidores*, because he did not, instead of driving the ship away, allow her to enter the port, whence she could not have departed without the permission of the city and the fort.[43]

This is the earliest record we possess of the appearance of an English ship in the waters of Spanish America. Others, however, soon followed. In 1530 William Hawkins, father of the famous John Hawkins, ventured in "a tall and goodly ship ...called the 'Polo of Plymouth,'" down to the coast of Guinea, trafficked with the natives for gold-dust and ivory, and then crossed the ocean to Brazil, "where he behaved himself so wisely with those savage people" that one of the kings of the country took ship with him to England and was presented to Henry VIII. at Whitehall.[44] The real occasion, however, for the appearance of foreign ships in Spanish-American waters was the new occupation of carrying negroes from the African coast to the Spanish colonies to be sold as slaves. The rapid depopulation of the Indies, and the really serious concern of the Spanish crown for the preservation of the indigenes, had compelled the Spanish government to permit the introduction of negro slaves from an early period. At first restricted to Christian slaves carried from Spain, after 1510 licences to take over a certain number, subject of course to governmental imposts, were given to private individuals; and in August 1518, owing to the incessant clamour of the colonists for more negroes, Laurent de Gouvenot, Governor of Bresa and one of the foreign favourites of Charles V., obtained the first regular contract to carry 4000 slaves directly from Africa to the West Indies.[45] With slight modifications the contract system became permanent, and with it, as a natural consequence, came contraband trade. Cargoes of negroes were frequently "run" from Africa by Spaniards and Portuguese, and as early as 1506 an order was issued to expel all contraband slaves from Hispaniola.[46] The supply never equalled the demand, however, and this explains why John Hawkins found it so profitable to carry ship-loads of blacks across from the Guinea coast, and why Spanish colonists could not resist the temptation to buy them, notwithstanding the stringent laws against trading with foreigners.

The first voyage of John Hawkins was made in 1562-63. In conjunction with Thomas Hampton he fitted out three vessels and sailed for Sierra Leone. There he collected, "partly by the sword and partly by other means," some 300 negroes, and with this valuable human freight crossed the Atlantic to San Domingo in Hispaniola. Uncertain as to his reception, Hawkins on his arrival pretended that he had been driven in by foul weather, and was in need of provisions, but without ready money to pay for them. He therefore requested permission to sell "certain slaves he had with him." The opportunity was eagerly welcomed by the planters, and the governor, not thinking it necessary to construe his orders from home too stringently, allowed two-thirds of the cargo to be sold. As neither Hawkins nor the Spanish colonists anticipated any serious displeasure on the part of Philip II., the remaining 100 slaves were left as a deposit with the Council of the island. Hawkins invested the proceeds in a return cargo of hides, half of which he sent in Spanish vessels to Spain under the care of his partner, while he returned with the rest to England. The Spanish Government, however, was not going to sanction for a moment the intrusion of the English into the Indies. On Hampton's arrival at Cadiz his cargo was confiscated and he himself narrowly escaped the Inquisition. The slaves left in San Domingo were forfeited, and Hawkins, although he "cursed, threatened and implored," could not obtain a farthing for his lost hides and negroes. The only result of his demands was the dispatch of a peremptory order to the West Indies that no English vessel should be allowed under any pretext to trade there.[47]

The second of the great Elizabethan sea-captains to beard the Spanish lion was Hawkins' friend and pupil, Francis Drake. In 1567 he accompanied Hawkins on his third expedition. With six ships, one of which was lent by the Queen herself, they sailed from Plymouth in October, picked up about 450 slaves on the Guinea coast, sighted Dominica in the West Indies in March, and coasted along the mainland of South America past Margarita and Cape de la Vela, carrying on a "tolerable good trade." Rio de la Hacha they stormed with 200 men, losing only two in the encounter; but they were scattered by a tempest near Cartagena and driven into the Gulf of Mexico, where, on 16th September, they entered the narrow port of S. Juan d'Ulloa or Vera Cruz. The next day the fleet of New Spain, consisting of thirteen large ships, appeared outside, and after an exchange of pledges of peace and amity with the English intruders, entered on the 20th. On the morning of the 24th, however, a fierce encounter was begun, and Hawkins and Drake, stubbornly defending themselves against tremendous odds, were glad to escape with two shattered vessels and the loss of £100,000 treasure. After a voyage of terrible suffering, Drake, in the "Judith," succeeded in reaching England on 20th January 1569, and Hawkins followed five days later.[48] Within a few years, however, Drake was away again, this time alone and with the sole, unblushing purpose of robbing the Dons. With only two ships and seventy-three men he prowled about the waters of the West Indies for almost a year, capturing and rifling Spanish vessels, plundering towns on the Main and intercepting convoys of treasure across the Isthmus of Darien. In 1577 he sailed on the voyage which carried him round the world, a feat for which he was knighted, promoted to the rank of admiral, and visited by the Queen on board his ship, the "Golden Hind." While Drake was being feted in London as the hero of the hour, Philip of Spain from his cell in the Escorial must have execrated these English sea-rovers whose visits brought ruin to his colonies and menaced the safety of his treasure galleons.

In the autumn of 1585 Drake was again in command of a formidable armament intended against the West Indies. Supported by 2000 troops under General Carleill, and by Martin Frobisher and Francis Knollys in the fleet, he took and plundered San Domingo, and after occupying Cartagena for six weeks ransomed the city for 110,000 ducats. This fearless old Elizabethan sailed from Plymouth on his last voyage in August 1595. Though under the joint command of Drake and Hawkins, the expedition seemed doomed to disaster throughout its course. One vessel, the "Francis," fell into the hands of the Spaniards. While the fleet was passing through the Virgin Isles, Hawkins fell ill and died. A desperate attack was made on S. Juan de Porto Rico, but the English, after losing forty or fifty men, were compelled to retire. Drake then proceeded to the Main, where in turn he captured and plundered Rancherias, Rio de la Hacha, Santa Marta and Nombre de Dios. With 750 soldiers he made a bold attempt to cross the isthmus to the city of Panama, but turned back after the loss of eighty or ninety of his followers. A few days later, on 15th January 1596, he too fell ill, died on the 28th, and was buried in a leaden coffin off the coast of Darien.[49]

Hawkins and Drake, however, were by no means the only English privateers of that century in American waters. Names like Oxenham, Grenville, Raleigh and Clifford, and others of lesser fame, such as Winter, Knollys and Barker, helped to swell the roll of these Elizabethan sea-rovers. To many a gallant sailor the Caribbean Sea was a happy hunting-ground where he might indulge at his pleasure any propensities to lawless adventure. If in 1588 he had helped to scatter the Invincible Armada, he now pillaged treasure ships on the coasts of the Spanish Main; if he had been with Drake to flout his Catholic Majesty at Cadiz, he now closed with the Spaniards within their distant cities beyond the seas. Thus he lined his own pockets with Spanish doubloons, and incidentally curbed Philip's power of invading England. Nor must we think these mariners the same as the lawless buccaneers of a later period. The men of this generation were of a sterner and more fanatical mould, men who for their wildest acts often claimed the sanction of religious convictions. Whether they carried off the heathen from Africa, or plundered the fleets of Romish Spain, they were but entering upon "the heritage of the saints." Judged by the standards of our own century they were pirates and freebooters, but in the eyes of their fellow-countrymen their attacks upon the Spaniards seemed fair and honourable.

The last of the great privateering voyages for which Drake had set the example was the armament which Lord George Clifford, Earl of Cumberland, sent against Porto Rico in 1598. The ill-starred expeditions of Raleigh to Guiana in 1595 and again in 1617 belong rather to the history of exploration and colonization. Clifford, "courtier, gambler and buccaneer," having run through a great part of his very considerable fortune, had seized the opportunity offered him by the plunder of the Spanish colonies to re-coup himself; and during a period of twelve years, from 1586 to 1598, almost every year fitted out, and often himself commanded, an expedition against the Spaniards. In his last and most ambitious effort, in 1598, he equipped twenty vessels entirely at his own cost, sailed from Plymouth in March, and on 6th June laid siege to the city of San Juan, which he proposed to clear of Spaniards and establish as an English stronghold. Although the place was captured, the expedition proved a fiasco. A violent sickness broke out among the troops, and as Clifford had already sailed away with some of the ships to Flores to lie in wait for the treasure fleet, Sir Thomas Berkeley, who was left in command in Porto Rico, abandoned the island and returned to rejoin the Earl.[50]

The English in the sixteenth century, however, had no monopoly of this piratical game. The French did something in their own way, and the Dutch were not far behind. Indeed, the French may claim to have set the example for the Elizabethan freebooters, for in the first half of the sixteenth century privateers flocked to the Spanish Indies from Dieppe, Brest and the towns of the Basque coast. The gleam of the golden lingots of Peru, and the pale lights of the emeralds from the mountains of New Granada, exercised a hypnotic influence not only on ordinary seamen but on merchants and on seigneurs with depleted fortunes. Names like Jean Terrier, Jacques Sore and François le Clerc, the latter popularly called "Pie de Palo," or "wooden-leg," by the Spaniards, were as detestable in Spanish ears as those of the great English captains. Even before 1500 French corsairs hovered about Cape St Vincent and among the Azores and the Canaries; and their prowess and audacity were so feared that Columbus, on returning from his third voyage in 1498, declared that he had sailed for the island of Madeira by a new route to avoid meeting a French fleet which was awaiting him near St Vincent.[51] With the establishment of the system of armed convoys, however, and the presence of Spanish fleets on the coast of Europe, the corsairs suffered some painful reverses which impelled them to transfer their operations to American waters. Thereafter Spanish records are full of references to attacks by Frenchmen on Havana, St. Jago de Cuba, San Domingo and towns on the mainland of South and Central America; full of appeals, too, from the colonies to the neglectful authorities in Spain, urging them to send artillery, cruisers and munitions of war for their defence.[52]

A letter dated 8th April 1537, written by Gonzalo de Guzman to the Empress, furnishes us with some interesting details of the exploits of an anonymous French corsair in that year. In November 1536 this Frenchman had seized in the port of Chagre, on the Isthmus of Darien, a Spanish vessel laden with horses from San Domingo, had cast the cargo into the sea, put the crew on shore and sailed away with his prize. A month or two later he appeared off the coast of Havana and dropped anchor in a small bay a few leagues from the city. As there were then five Spanish ships lying in the harbour, the inhabitants compelled the captains to attempt the seizure of the pirate, promising to pay for the ships if they were lost. Three vessels of 200 tons each sailed out to the attack, and for several days they fired at the French corsair, which, being a patache of light draught, had run up the bay beyond their reach. Finally one morning the Frenchmen were seen pressing with both sail and oar to escape from the port. A Spanish vessel cut her cables to follow in pursuit, but encountering a heavy sea and contrary winds was abandoned by her crew, who made for shore in boats. The other two Spanish ships were deserted in similar fashion, whereupon the French, observing this new turn of affairs, re-entered the bay and easily recovered the three drifting vessels. Two of the prizes they burnt, and arming the third sailed away to cruise in the Florida straits, in the route of ships returning from the West Indies to Spain.[53]

The corsairs, however, were not always so uniformly successful. A band of eighty, who attempted to plunder the town of St. Jago de Cuba, were repulsed with some loss by a certain Diego Perez of Seville, captain of an armed merchant ship then in the harbour, who later petitioned for the grant of a coat-of-arms in recognition of his services.[54] In October 1544 six French vessels attacked the town of Santa Maria de los Remedios, near Cape de la Vela, but failed to take it in face of the stubborn resistance of the inhabitants. Yet the latter a few months earlier had been unable to preserve their homes from pillage, and had been obliged to flee to La Granjeria de las Perlas on the Rio de la Hacha.[55] There is small wonder, indeed, that the defenders were so rarely victorious. The Spanish towns were ill-provided with forts and guns, and often entirely without ammunition or any regular soldiers. The distance between the settlements as a rule was great, and the inhabitants, as soon as informed of the presence of the enemy, knowing that they had no means of resistance and little hope of succour, left their homes to the mercy of the freebooters and fled to the hills and woods with their families and most precious belongings. Thus when, in October 1554, another band of three hundred French privateers swooped down upon the unfortunate town of St. Jago de Cuba, they were able to hold it for thirty days, and plundered it to the value of 80,000 pieces of eight.[56] The following year, however, witnessed an even more remarkable action. In July 1555 the celebrated captain, Jacques Sore, landed two hundred men from a caravel a half-league from the city of Havana, and before daybreak marched on the town and forced the surrender of the castle. The Spanish governor had time to retire to the country, where he gathered a small force of Spaniards and negroes, and returned to surprise the French by night. Fifteen or sixteen of the latter were killed, and Sore, who himself was wounded, in a rage gave orders for the massacre of all the prisoners. He burned the cathedral and the hospital, pillaged the houses and razed most of the city to the ground. After transferring all the artillery to his vessel, he made several forays into the country, burned a few plantations, and finally sailed away in the beginning of August. No record remains of the amount of the booty, but it must have been enormous. To fill the cup of bitterness for the poor inhabitants, on 4th October there appeared on the coast another French ship, which had learned of Sore's visit and of the helpless state of the Spaniards. Several hundred men disembarked, sacked a few plantations neglected by their predecessors, tore down or burned the houses which the Spaniards had begun to rebuild, and seized a caravel loaded with leather which had recently entered the harbour.[57] It is true that during these years there was almost constant war in Europe between the Emperor and France; yet this does not entirely explain the activity of the French privateers in Spanish America, for we find them busy there in the years when peace reigned at home. Once unleash the sea-dogs and it was extremely difficult to bring them again under restraint.

With the seventeenth century began a new era in the history of the West Indies. If in the sixteenth the English, French and Dutch came to tropical America as piratical intruders into seas and countries which belonged to others, in the following century they came as permanent colonisers and settlers. The Spaniards, who had explored the whole ring of the West Indian islands before 1500, from the beginning neglected the lesser for the larger Antilles-Cuba, Hispaniola, Porto Rico and Jamaica-and for those islands like Trinidad, which lie close to the mainland. And when in 1519 Cortez sailed from Cuba for the conquest of Mexico, and twelve years later Pizarro entered Peru, the emigrants who left Spain to seek their fortunes in the New World flocked to the vast territories which the *Conquistadores* and their lieutenants had subdued on the Continent. It was consequently to the smaller islands which compose the Leeward and Windward groups that the English, French and Dutch first resorted as colonists. Small, and therefore "easy to settle, easy to depopulate and to re-people, attractive not only on account of their own wealth, but also as a starting-point for the vast and rich continent off which they lie," these islands became the pawns in a game of diplomacy and colonization which continued for 150 years.

In the seventeenth century, moreover, the Spanish monarchy was declining rapidly both in power and prestige, and its empire, though still formidable, no longer overshadowed the other nations of Europe as in the days of Charles V. and Philip II. France, with the Bourbons on the throne, was entering upon an era of rapid expansion at home and abroad, while the Dutch, by the truce of 1609, virtually obtained the freedom for which they had struggled so long. In England Queen Elizabeth had died in 1603, and her Stuart successor exchanged her policy of dalliance, of balance between France and Spain, for one of peace and conciliation. The aristocratic free-booters who had enriched themselves by harassing the Spanish Indies were succeeded by a less romantic but more business-like generation, which devoted itself to trade and planting. Abortive attempts at colonization had been made in the sixteenth century. The Dutch, who were trading in the West Indies as early as 1542, by 1580 seem to have gained some foothold in Guiana;[58] and the French Huguenots, under the patronage of the Admiral de Coligny, made three unsuccessful efforts to form settlements on the American continent, one in Brazil in 1555, another near Port Royal in South Carolina in 1562, and two years later a third on the St. John's River in Florida. The only English effort in the sixteenth century was the vain attempt of Sir Walter Raleigh between 1585 and 1590 to plant a colony on Roanoke Island, on the coast of what is now North Carolina. It was not till 1607 that the first permanent English settlement in America was made at Jamestown in Virginia. Between 1609 and 1619 numerous stations were established by English, Dutch and French in Guiana between the mouth of the Orinoco and that of the Amazon. In 1621 the Dutch West India Company was incorporated, and a few years later proposals for a similar company were broached in England. Among the West Indian Islands, St. Kitts received its first English settlers in 1623; and two years later the island was formally divided with the French, thus becoming the earliest nucleus of English and French colonization in those regions. Barbadoes was colonized in 1624-25. In 1628 English settlers from St. Kitts spread to Nevis and Barbuda, and within another four years to Antigua and Montserrat; while as early as 1625 English and Dutch took joint possession of Santa Cruz. The founders of the French settlement on St. Kitts induced Richelieu to incorporate a French West India Company with the title, "The Company of the Isles of America," and under its auspices Guadeloupe, Martinique and other islands of the Windward group were colonized in 1635 and succeeding years. Meanwhile between 1632 and 1634 the Dutch had established trading stations on St. Eustatius in the north, and on Tobago and Curaçao in the south near the Spanish mainland.

While these centres of trade and population were being formed in the very heart of the Spanish seas, the privateers were not altogether idle. To the treaty of Vervins between France and Spain in 1598 had been added a secret restrictive article whereby it was agreed that the peace should not hold good south of the Tropic of Cancer and west of the meridian of the Azores. Beyond these two lines (called "les lignes de l'enclos des Amitiés") French and Spanish ships might attack each other and take fair prize as in open war. The ministers of Henry IV. communicated this restriction verbally to the merchants of the ports, and soon private men-of-war from Dieppe, Havre and St. Malo flocked to the western seas.[59] Ships loaded with contraband goods no longer sailed for the Indies unless armed ready to engage all comers, and many ship-captains renounced trade altogether for the more profitable and exciting occupation of privateering. In the early years of the seventeenth century, moreover, Dutch fleets harassed the coasts of Chile and Peru,[60] while in Brazil[61] and the West Indies a second "Pie de Palo," this time the Dutch admiral, Piet Heyn, was proving a scourge to the Spaniards. Heyn was employed by the Dutch West India Company, which from the year 1623 onwards, carried the Spanish war into the transmarine possessions of Spain and Portugal. With a fleet composed of twenty-six ships and 3300 men, of which he was vice-admiral, he greatly distinguished himself at the capture of Bahia, the seat of Portuguese power in Brazil. Similar expeditions were sent out annually, and brought back the rich spoils of the South American colonies. Within two years the extraordinary number of eighty ships, with 1500 cannon and over 9000 sailors and soldiers, were despatched to American seas, and although Bahia was soon retaken, the Dutch for a time occupied Pernambuco, as well as San Juan de Porto Rico in the West Indies.[62] In 1628 Piet Heyn was in command of a squadron designed to intercept the plate fleet which sailed every year from Vera Cruz to Spain. With thirty-one ships, 700 cannon and nearly 3000 men he cruised along the northern coast of Cuba, and on 8th September fell in with his quarry near Cape San Antonio. The Spaniards made a running fight along the coast until they reached the Matanzas River near Havana, into which they turned with the object of running the great-bellied galleons aground and escaping with what treasure they could. The Dutch followed, however, and most of the rich cargo was diverted into the coffers of the Dutch West India Company. The gold, silver, indigo, sugar and logwood were sold in the Netherlands for fifteen million guilders, and the company was enabled to distribute to its shareholders the unprecedented dividend of 50 per cent. It was an exploit which two generations of English mariners had attempted in vain, and the unfortunate Spanish general, Don Juan de Benavides, on his return to Spain was imprisoned for his defeat and later beheaded.[63]

In 1639 we find the Spanish Council of War for the Indies conferring with the King on measures to be taken against English piratical ships in the Caribbean;[64] and in 1642 Captain William Jackson, provided with an ample commission from the Earl of Warwick[65] and duplicates under the Great Seal, made a raid in which he emulated the exploits of Sir Francis Drake and his contemporaries. Starting out with three ships and about 1100 men, mostly picked up in St. Kitts and Barbadoes, he cruised along the Main from Caracas to Honduras and plundered the towns of Maracaibo and Truxillo. On 25th March 1643 he dropped anchor in what is now Kingston Harbour in Jamaica, landed about 500 men, and after some sharp fighting and the loss of forty of his followers, entered the town of St. Jago de la Vega, which he ransomed for 200 beeves, 10,000 lbs. of cassava bread and 7000 pieces of eight. Many of the English were so captivated by the beauty and fertility of the island that twenty-three deserted in one night to the Spaniards.[66]

The first two Stuart Kings, like the great Queen who preceded them, and in spite of the presence of a powerful Spanish faction at the English Court, looked upon the Indies with envious eyes, as a source of perennial wealth to whichever nation could secure them. James I., to be sure, was a man of peace, and soon after his accession patched up a treaty with the Spaniards; but he had no intention of giving up any English claims, however shadowy they might be, to America. Cornwallis, the new ambassador at Madrid, from a vantage ground where he could easily see the financial and administrative confusion into which Spain, in spite of her colonial wealth, had fallen, was most dissatisfied with the treaty. In a letter to Cranborne, dated 2nd July 1605, he suggested that England never lost so great an opportunity of winning honour and wealth as by relinquishing the war with Spain, and that Philip and his kingdom "were reduced to such a state as they could not in all likelihood have endured for the space of two years more."[67] This opinion we find repeated in his letters in the following years, with covert hints that an attack upon the Indies might after all be the most profitable and politic thing to do. When, in October 1607, Zuniga, the Spanish ambassador in London, complained to James of the establishment of the new colony in Virginia, James replied that Virginia was land discovered by the English and therefore not within the jurisdiction of Philip; and a week later Salisbury, while confiding to Zuniga that he thought the English might not justly go to Virginia, still refused to prohibit their going or command their return, for it would be an acknowledgment, he said, that the King of Spain was lord of all the Indies.[68] In 1609, in the truce concluded between Spain and the Netherlands, one of the stipulations provided that for nine years the Dutch were to be free to trade in all places in the East and West Indies except those in actual possession of the Spaniards on the date of cessation of hostilities; and thereafter the English and French governments endeavoured with all the more persistence to obtain a similar privilege. Attorney-General Heath, in 1625, presented a memorial to the Crown on the advantages derived by the Spaniards and Dutch in the West Indies, maintaining that it was neither safe nor profitable for them to be absolute lords of those regions; and he suggested that his Majesty openly interpose or permit it to be done underhand.[69] In September 1637 proposals were renewed in England for a West India Company as the only method of obtaining a share in the wealth of America. It was suggested that some convenient port be seized as a safe retreat from which to plunder Spanish trade on land and sea, and that the officers of the company be empowered to conquer and occupy any part of the West Indies, build ships, levy soldiers and munitions of war, and make reprisals.[70] The temper of Englishmen at this time was again illustrated in 1640 when the Spanish ambassador, Alonzo de Cardenas, protested to Charles I. against certain ships which the Earls of Warwick and Marlborough were sending to the West Indies with the intention, Cardenas declared, of committing hostilities against the Spaniards. The Earl of Warwick, it seems, pretended to have received great injuries from the latter and threatened to recoup his losses at their expense. He procured from the king a broad commission which gave him the right to trade in the West Indies, and to "offend" such as opposed him. Under shelter of this commission the Earl of Marlborough was now going to sea with three or four armed ships, and Cardenas prayed the king to restrain him until he gave security not to commit any acts of violence against the Spanish nation. The petition was referred to a committee of the Lords, who concluded that as the peace had never been strictly observed by either nation in the Indies they would not demand any security of the Earl. "Whether the Spaniards will think this reasonable or not," concludes Secretary Windebank in his letter to Sir Arthur Hopton, "is no great matter."[71]

During this century and a half between 1500 and 1650, the Spaniards were by no means passive or indifferent to the attacks made upon their authority and prestige in the New World. The hostility of the mariners from the north they repaid with interest, and woe to the foreign interloper or privateer who fell into their clutches. When Henry II. of France in 1557 issued an order that Spanish prisoners be condemned to the galleys, the Spanish government retaliated by commanding its sea-captains to mete out the same treatment to their French captives, except that captains, masters and officers taken in the navigation of the Indies were to be hung or cast into the sea.[72] In December 1600 the governor of Cumana had suggested to the King, as a means of keeping Dutch and English ships from the salt mines of Araya, the ingenious scheme of poisoning the salt. This advice, it seems, was not followed, but a few years later, in 1605, a Spanish fleet of fourteen galleons sent from Lisbon surprised and burnt nineteen Dutch vessels found loading salt at Araya, and murdered most of the prisoners.[73] In December 1604 the Venetian ambassador in London wrote of "news that the Spanish in the West Indies captured two English vessels, cut off the hands, feet, noses and ears of the crews and smeared them with honey and tied them to trees to be tortured by flies and other insects. The Spanish here plead," he continued, "that they were pirates, not merchants, and that they did not know of the peace. But the barbarity makes people here cry out."[74] On 22nd June 1606, Edmondes, the English Ambassador at Brussels, in a letter to Cornwallis, speaks of a London ship which was sent to trade in Virginia, and putting into a river in Florida to obtain water, was surprised there by Spanish vessels from Havana, the men ill-treated and the cargo confiscated.[75] And it was but shortly after that Captain Chaloner's ship on its way to Virginia was seized by the Spaniards in the West Indies, and the crew sent to languish in the dungeons of Seville or condemned to the galleys.

By attacks upon some of the English settlements, too, the Spaniards gave their threats a more effective form. Frequent raids were made upon the English and Dutch plantations in Guiana;[76] and on 8th-18th September 1629 a Spanish fleet of over thirty sail, commanded by Don Federico de Toledo, nearly annihilated the joint French and English colony on St. Kitts. Nine English ships were captured and the settlements burnt. The French inhabitants temporarily evacuated the island and sailed for Antigua; but of the English some 550 were carried to Cartagena and Havana, whence they were shipped to England, and all the rest fled to the mountains and woods.[77] Within three months' time, however, after the departure of the Spaniards, the scattered settlers had returned and re-established the colony. Providence Island and its neighbour, Henrietta, being situated near the Mosquito Coast, were peculiarly exposed to Spanish attack;[78] while near the north shore of Hispaniola the island of Tortuga, which was colonized by the same English company, suffered repeatedly from the assaults of its hostile neighbours. In July 1635 a Spanish fleet from the Main assailed the island of Providence, but unable to land among the rocks, was after five days beaten off "considerably torn" by the shot from the fort.[79] On the strength of these injuries received and of others anticipated, the Providence Company obtained from the king the liberty "to right themselves" by making reprisals, and during the next six years kept numerous vessels preying upon Spanish commerce in those waters. King Philip was therefore all the more intent upon destroying the plantation.[80] He bided his time, however, until the early summer of 1641, when the general of the galleons, Don Francisco Diaz Pimienta, with twelve sail and 2000 men, fell upon the colony, razed the forts and carried off all the English, about 770 in number, together with forty cannon and half a million of plunder.[81] It was just ten years later that a force of 800 men from Porto Rico invaded Santa Cruz, whence the Dutch had been expelled by the English in 1646, killed the English governor and more than 100 settlers, seized two ships in the harbour and burnt and pillaged most of the plantations. The rest of the inhabitants escaped to the woods, and after the departure of the Spaniards deserted the colony for St. Kitts and other islands.[82]

Chapter II
The Beginnings of the Buccaneers

In the second half of the sixteenth and the early part of the seventeenth centuries, strangers who visited the great Spanish islands of Hispaniola, Jamaica or Porto Rico, usually remarked the extraordinary number of wild cattle and boars found roaming upon them. These herds were in every case sprung from domestic animals originally brought from Spain. For as the aborigines in the Greater Antilles decreased in numbers under the heavy yoke of their conquerors, and as the Spaniards themselves turned their backs upon the Antilles for the richer allurements of the continent, less and less land was left under cultivation; and cattle, hogs, horses and even dogs ran wild, increased at a rapid rate, and soon filled the broad savannas and deep woods which covered the greater part of these islands. The northern shore of Hispaniola the Spaniards had never settled, and thither, probably from an early period, interloping ships were accustomed to resort when in want of victuals. With a long range of uninhabited coast, good anchorage and abundance of provisions, this northern shore could not fail to induce some to remain. In time we find there scattered groups of hunters, mostly French and English, who gained a rude livelihood by killing wild cattle for their skins, and curing the flesh to supply the needs of passing vessels. The origin of these men we do not know. They may have been deserters from ships, crews of wrecked vessels, or even chance marooners. In any case the charm of their half-savage, independent mode of life must soon have attracted others, and a fairly regular traffic sprang up between them and the ubiquitous Dutch traders, whom they supplied with hides, tallow and cured meat in return for the few crude necessities and luxuries they required. Their numbers were recruited in 1629 by colonists from St. Kitts who had fled before Don Federico de Toledo. Making common lot with the hunters, the refugees found sustenance so easy and the natural bounty of the island so rich and varied, that many remained and settled.

To the north-west of Hispaniola lies a small, rocky island about eight leagues in length and two in breadth, separated by a narrow channel from its larger neighbour. From the shore of Hispaniola the island appears in form like a monster sea-turtle floating upon the waves, and hence was named by the Spaniards "Tortuga." So mountainous and inaccessible on the northern side as to be called the Côte-de-Fer, and with only one harbour upon the south, it offered a convenient refuge to the French and English hunters should the Spaniards become troublesome. These hunters probably ventured across to Tortuga before 1630, for there are indications that a Spanish expedition was sent against the island from Hispaniola in 1630 or 1631, and a division of the spoil made in the city of San Domingo after its return.[83] It was then, apparently, that the Spaniards left upon Tortuga an officer and twenty-eight men, the small garrison which, says Charlevoix, was found there when the hunters returned. The Spanish soldiers were already tired of their exile upon this lonely, inhospitable rock, and evacuated with the same satisfaction with which the French and English resumed their occupancy. From the testimony of some documents in the English colonial archives we may gather that the English from the first were in predominance in the new colony, and exercised almost sole authority. In the minutes of the Providence Company, under date of 19th May 1631, we find that a committee was "appointed to treat with the agents for a colony of about 150 persons, settled upon Tortuga";[84] and a few weeks later that "the planters upon the island of Tortuga desired the company to take them under their protection, and to be at the charge of their fortification, in consideration of a twentieth part of the commodities raised there yearly."[85] At the same time the Earl of Holland, governor of the company, and his associates petitioned the king for an enlargement of their grant "only of 3 or 4 degrees of northerly latitude, to avoid all doubts as to whether one of the islands (Tortuga) was contained in their former grant."[86] Although there were several islands named Tortuga in the region of the West Indies, all the evidence points to the identity of the island concerned in this petition with the Tortuga near the north coast of Hispaniola.[87]

The Providence Company accepted the offer of the settlers upon Tortuga, and sent a ship to reinforce the little colony with six pieces of ordnance, a supply of ammunition and provisions, and a number of apprentices or *engagés*. A Captain Hilton was appointed governor, with Captain Christopher Wormeley to succeed him in case of the governor's death or absence, and the name of the island was changed from Tortuga to Association.[88] Although consisting for the most part of high land covered with tall cedar woods, the island contained in the south and west broad savannas which soon attracted planters as well as cattle-hunters. Some of the inhabitants of St. Kitts, wearied of the dissensions between the French and English there, and allured by reports of quiet and plenty in Tortuga, deserted St. Kitts for the new colony. The settlement, however, was probably always very poor and struggling, for in January 1634 the Providence Company received advice that Captain Hilton intended to desert the island and draw most of the inhabitants after him; and a declaration was sent out from England to the planters, assuring them special privileges of trade and domicile, and dissuading them from "changing certain ways of profit already discovered for uncertain hopes suggested by fancy or persuasion."[89] The question of remaining or departing, indeed, was soon decided for the colonists without their volition, for in December 1634 a Spanish force from Hispaniola invaded the island and drove out all the English and French they found there. It seems that an Irishman named "Don Juan Morf" (John

Murphy?),[90] who had been "sargento-mayor" in Tortuga, became discontented with the *régime* there and fled to Cartagena. The Spanish governor of Cartagena sent him to Don Gabriel de Gaves, President of the Audiencia in San Domingo, thinking that with the information the renegade was able to supply the Spaniards of Hispaniola might drive out the foreigners. The President of San Domingo, however, died three months later without bestirring himself, and it was left to his successor to carry out the project. With the information given by Murphy, added to that obtained from prisoners, he sent a force of 250 foot under command of Rui Fernandez de Fuemayor to take the island.[91] At this time, according to the Spaniards' account, there were in Tortuga 600 men bearing arms, besides slaves, women and children. The harbour was commanded by a platform of six cannon. The Spaniards approached the island just before dawn, but through the ignorance of the pilot the whole armadilla was cast upon some reefs near the shore. Rui Fernandez with about thirty of his men succeeded in reaching land in canoes, seized the fort without any difficulty, and although his followers were so few managed to disperse a body of the enemy who were approaching, with the English governor at their head, to recover it. In the mêlée the governor was one of the first to be killed-stabbed, say the Spaniards, by the Irishman, who took active part in the expedition and fought by the side of Rui Fernandez. Meanwhile some of the inhabitants, thinking that they could not hold the island, had regained the fort, spiked the guns and transferred the stores to several ships in the harbour, which sailed away leaving only two dismantled boats and a patache to fall into the hands of the Spaniards. Rui Fernandez, reinforced by some 200 of his men who had succeeded in escaping from the stranded armadilla, now turned his attention to the settlement. He found his way barred by another body of several hundred English, but dispersed them too, and took seventy prisoners. The houses were then sacked and the tobacco plantations burned by the soldiers, and the Spaniards returned to San Domingo with four captured banners, the six pieces of artillery and 180 muskets.[92]

The Spanish occupation apparently did not last very long, for in the following April the Providence Company appointed Captain Nicholas Riskinner to be governor of Tortuga in place of Wormeley, and in February 1636 it learned that Riskinner was in possession of the island.[93] Two planters just returned from the colony, moreover, informed the company that there were then some 80 English in the settlement, besides 150 negroes. It is evident that the colonists were mostly cattle-hunters, for they assured the company that they could supply Tortuga with 200 beasts a month from Hispaniola, and would deliver calves there at twenty shillings apiece.[94] Yet at a later meeting of the Adventurers on 20th January 1637, a project for sending more men and ammunition to the island was suddenly dropped "upon intelligence that the inhabitants had quitted it and removed to Hispaniola."[95] For three years thereafter the Providence records are silent concerning Tortuga. A few Frenchmen must have remained on the island, however, for Charlevoix informs us that in 1638 the general of the galleons swooped down upon the colony, put to the sword all who failed to escape to the hills and woods, and again destroyed all the habitations.[96] Persuaded that the hunters would not expose themselves to a repetition of such treatment, the Spaniards neglected to leave a garrison, and a few scattered Frenchmen gradually filtered back to their ruined homes. It was about this time, it seems, that the President of San Domingo formed a body of 500 armed lancers in an effort to drive the intruders from the larger island of Hispaniola. These lancers, half of whom were always kept in the field, were divided into companies of fifty each, whence they were called by the French, "cinquantaines." Ranging the woods and savannas this Spanish constabulary attacked isolated hunters wherever they found them, and they formed an important element in the constant warfare between the French and Spanish colonists throughout the rest of the century.[97]

Meanwhile an English adventurer, some time after the Spanish descent of 1638, gathered a body of 300 of his compatriots in the island of Nevis near St. Kitts, and sailing for Tortuga dispossessed the few Frenchmen living there of the island. According to French accounts he was received amicably by the inhabitants and lived with them for four months, when he turned upon his hosts, disarmed them and marooned them upon the opposite shore of Hispaniola.

A few made their way to St. Kitts and complained to M. de Poincy, the governor-general of the French islands, who seized the opportunity to establish a French governor in Tortuga. Living at that time in St. Kitts was a Huguenot gentleman named Levasseur, who had been a companion-in-arms of d'Esnambuc when the latter settled St. Kitts in 1625, and after a short visit to France had returned and made his fortune in trade. He was a man of courage and command as well as a skilful engineer, and soon rose high in the councils of de Poincy. Being a Calvinist, however, he had drawn upon the governor the reproaches of the authorities at home; and de Poincy proposed to get rid of his presence, now become inconvenient, by sending him to subdue Tortuga. Levasseur received his commission from de Poincy in May 1640, assembled forty or fifty followers, all Calvinists, and sailed in a barque to Hispaniola. He established himself at Port Margot, about five leagues from Tortuga, and entered into friendly relations with his English neighbours. He was but biding his time, however, and on the last day of August 1640, on the plea that the English had ill-used some of his followers and had seized a vessel sent by de Poincy to obtain provisions, he made a sudden descent upon the island with only 49 men and captured the governor. The inhabitants retired to Hispaniola, but a few days later returned and besieged Levasseur for ten days. Finding that they could not dislodge him, they sailed away with all their people to the island of Providence.[98]

Levasseur, fearing perhaps another descent of the Spaniards, lost no time in putting the settlement in a state of defence. Although the port of Tortuga was little more than a roadstead, it offered a good anchorage on a bottom of fine sand, the approaches to which were easily defended by a hill or promontory overlooking the harbour. The top of this hill, situated 500 or 600 paces from the shore, was a level platform, and upon it rose a steep rock some 30 feet high. Nine or ten paces from the base of the rock gushed forth a perennial fountain of fresh water. The new governor quickly made the most of these natural advantages. The platform he shaped into terraces, with means for accommodating several hundred men. On the top of the rock he built a house for himself, as well as a magazine, and mounted a battery of two guns. The only access to the rock was by a narrow approach, up half of which steps were cut in the stone, the rest of the ascent being by means of an iron ladder which could easily be raised and lowered.[99] This little fortress, in which the governor could repose with a feeling of entire security, he euphuistically called his "dove-cote." The dove-cote was not finished any too soon, for the Spaniards of San Domingo in 1643 determined to destroy this rising power in their neighbourhood, and sent against Levasseur a force of 500 or 600 men. When they tried to land within a half gunshot of the shore, however, they were greeted with a discharge of artillery from the fort, which sank one of the vessels and forced the rest to retire. The Spaniards withdrew to a place two leagues to leeward, where they succeeded in disembarking, but fell into an ambush laid by Levasseur, lost, according to the French accounts, between 100 and 200 men, and fled to their ships and back to Hispaniola. With this victory the reputation of Levasseur spread far and wide throughout the islands, and for ten years the Spaniards made no further attempt to dislodge the French settlement.[100]

Planters, hunters and corsairs now came in greater numbers to Tortuga. The hunters, using the smaller island merely as a headquarters for supplies and a retreat in time of danger, penetrated more boldly than ever into the interior of Hispaniola, plundering the Spanish plantations in their path, and establishing settlements on the north shore at Port Margot and Port de Paix. Corsairs, after cruising and robbing along the Spanish coasts, retired to Tortuga to refit and find a market for their spoils. Plantations of tobacco and sugar were cultivated, and although the soil never yielded such rich returns as upon the other islands, Dutch and French trading ships frequently resorted there for these commodities, and especially for the skins prepared by the hunters, bringing in exchange brandy, guns, powder and cloth. Indeed, under the active, positive administration of Levasseur, Tortuga enjoyed a degree of prosperity which almost rivalled that of the French settlements in the Leeward Islands.

The term "buccaneer," though usually applied to the corsairs who in the seventeenth century ravaged the Spanish possessions in the West Indies and the South Seas, should really be restricted to these cattle-hunters of west and north-west Hispaniola. The flesh of the wild-cattle was cured by the hunters after a fashion learnt from the Caribbee Indians. The meat was cut into long strips, laid upon a grate or hurdle constructed of green sticks, and dried over a slow wood fire fed with bones and the trimmings of the hide of the animal. By this means an excellent flavour was imparted to the meat and a fine red colour. The place where the flesh was smoked was called by the Indians a "boucan," and the same term, from the poverty of an undeveloped language, was applied to the frame or grating on which the flesh was dried. In course of time the dried meat became known as "viande boucannée," and the hunters themselves as "boucaniers" or "buccaneers." When later circumstances led the hunters to combine their trade in flesh and hides with that of piracy, the name gradually lost its original significance and acquired, in the English language at least, its modern and better-known meaning of corsair or freebooter. The French adventurers, however, seem always to have restricted the word "boucanier" to its proper signification, that of a hunter and curer of meat; and when they developed into corsairs, by a curious contrast they adopted an English name and called themselves "filibustiers," which is merely the French sailor's way of pronouncing the English word "freebooter."[101]

The buccaneers or West Indian corsairs owed their origin as well as their name to the cattle and hog-hunters of Hispaniola and Tortuga. Doubtless many of the wilder, more restless spirits in the smaller islands of the Windward and Leeward groups found their way into the ranks of this piratical fraternity, or were willing at least to lend a hand in an occasional foray against their Spanish neighbours. We know that Jackson, in 1642, had no difficulty in gathering 700 or 800 men from Barbadoes and St. Kitts for his ill-starred dash upon the Spanish Main. And when the French in later years made their periodical descents upon the Dutch stations on Tobago, Curaçao and St. Eustatius, they always found in their island colonies of Martinique and Guadeloupe buccaneers enough and more, eager to fill their ships. It seems to be generally agreed, however, among the Jesuit historians of the West Indies-and upon these writers we are almost entirely dependent for our knowledge of the origins of buccaneering-that the corsairs had their source and nucleus in the hunters who infested the coasts of Hispaniola. Between the hunter and the pirate at first no impassable line was drawn. The same person combined in himself the occupations of cow-killing and cruising, varying the monotony of the one by occasionally trying his hand at the other. In either case he lived at constant enmity with the Spaniards. With the passing of time the sea attracted more and more away from their former pursuits. Even the planters who were beginning to filter into the new settlements found the attractions of coursing against the Spaniards to be irresistible. Great extremes of fortune, such as those to which the buccaneers were subject, have always exercised an attraction over minds of an adventurous stamp. It was the same allurement which drew the "forty-niners" to California, and in 1897 the gold-seekers to the Canadian Klondyke. If the suffering endured was often great, the prize to be gained was worth it. Fortune, if fickle one day, might the next bring incredible bounty, and the buccaneers who sweltered in a tropical sea, with starvation staring them in the face, dreamed of rolling in the oriental wealth of a Spanish argosy. Especially to the cattle-hunter must this temptation have been great, for his mode of life was the very rudest. He roamed the woods by day with his dog and apprentices, and at night slept in the open air or in a rude shed hastily constructed of leaves and skins, which served as a house, and which he called after the Indian name, "ajoupa" or "barbacoa." His dress was of the simplest-coarse cloth trousers, and a shirt which hung loosely over them, both pieces so black and saturated with the blood and grease of slain animals that they looked as if they had been tarred ("de toile gaudronnée").[102] A belt of undressed bull's hide bound the shirt, and supported on one side three or four large knives, on the other a pouch for powder and shot. A cap with a short pointed brim extending over the eyes, rude shoes of cowhide or pigskin made all of one piece bound over the foot, and a short, large-bore musket, completed the hunter's grotesque outfit. Often he carried wound about his waist a sack of netting into which he crawled at night to keep off the pestiferous mosquitoes. With creditable regularity he and his apprentices arose early in the morning and started on foot for the hunt, eating no food until they had killed and skinned as many wild cattle or swine as there were persons in the company. After having skinned the last animal, the master-hunter broke its softest bones and made a meal for himself and his followers on the marrow. Then each took up a hide and returned to the boucan, where they dined on the flesh they had killed.[103] In this fashion the hunter lived for the space of six months or a year. Then he made a division of the skins and dried meat, and repaired to Tortuga or one of the French settlements on the coast of Hispaniola to recoup his stock of ammunition and spend the rest of his gains in a wild carouse of drunkenness and debauchery. His money gone, he returned again to the hunt. The cow-killers, as they had neither wife nor children, commonly associated in pairs with the right of inheriting from each other, a custom which was called "matelotage." These private associations, however, did not prevent the property of all from being in a measure common. Their mode of settling quarrels was the most primitive-the duel. In other things they governed themselves by a certain "coutumier," a medley of bizarre laws which they had originated among themselves. At any attempt to bring them under civilised rules, the reply always was, "telle étoit la coutume de la côte"; and that definitely closed the matter. They based their rights thus to live upon the fact, they said, of having passed the Tropic, where, borrowing from the sailor's well-known superstition, they pretended to have drowned all their former obligations.[104] Even their family names they discarded, and the saying was in those days that one knew a man in the Isles only when he was married. From a life of this sort, cruising against Spanish ships, if not an unmixed good, was at least always a desirable recreation. Every Spanish prize brought into Tortuga, moreover, was an incitement to fresh adventure against the common foe. The "gens de la côte," as they called themselves, ordinarily associated a score or more together, and having taken or built themselves a canoe, put to sea with intent to seize a Spanish barque or some other coasting vessel. With silent paddles, under cover of darkness, they approached the unsuspecting prey, killed the frightened sailors or drove them overboard, and carried the prize to Tortuga. There the raiders either dispersed to their former occupations, or gathered a larger crew of congenial spirits and sailed away for bigger game.

All the Jesuit historians of the West Indies, Dutertre, Labat and Charlevoix, have left us accounts of the manners and customs of the buccaneers. The Dutch physician, Exquemelin, who lived with the buccaneers for several years, from 1668 to 1674, and wrote a picturesque narrative from materials at his disposal, has also been a source for the ideas of most later writers on the subject. It may not be out of place to quote his description of the men whose deeds he recorded.

"Before the Pirates go out to sea," he writes, "they give notice to every one who goes upon the voyage of the day on which they ought precisely to embark, intimating also to them their obligation of bringing each man in particular so many pounds of powder and bullets as they think necessary for that expedition. Being all come on board, they join together in council, concerning what place they ought first to go wherein to get provisions-especially of flesh, seeing they scarce eat anything else. And of this the most common sort among them is pork. The next food is tortoises, which they are accustomed to salt a little. Sometimes they resolve to rob such or such hog-yards, wherein the Spaniards often have a thousand heads of swine together. They come to these places in the dark of night, and having beset the keeper's lodge, they force him to rise, and give them as many heads as they desire, threatening withal to kill him in case he disobeys their command or makes any noise. Yea, these menaces are oftentimes put in execution, without giving any quarter to the miserable swine-keepers, or any other person that endeavours to hinder their robberies.

"Having got provisions of flesh sufficient for their voyage, they return to their ship. Here their allowance, twice a day to every one, is as much as he can eat, without either weight or measure. Neither does the steward of the vessel give any greater proportion of flesh or anything else to the captain than to the meanest mariner. The ship being well victualled, they call another council, to deliberate towards what place they shall go, to seek their desperate fortunes. In this council, likewise, they agree upon certain Articles, which are put in writing, by way of bond or obligation, which everyone is bound to observe, and all of them, or the chief, set their hands to it. Herein they specify, and set down very distinctly, what sums of money each particular person ought to have for that voyage, the fund of all the payments being the common stock of what is gotten by the whole expedition; for otherwise it is the same law, among these people, as with other Pirates, 'No prey, no pay.' In the first place, therefore, they mention how much the Captain ought to have for his ship. Next the salary of the carpenter, or shipwright, who careened, mended and rigged the vessel. This commonly amounts to 100 or 150 pieces of eight, being, according to the agreement, more or less. Afterwards for provisions and victualling they draw out of the same common stock about 200 pieces of eight. Also a competent salary for the surgeon and his chest of medicaments, which is usually rated at 200 or 250 pieces of eight. Lastly they stipulate in writing what recompense or reward each one ought to have, that is either wounded or maimed in his body, suffering the loss of any limb, by that voyage. Thus they order for the loss of a right arm 600 pieces of eight, or six slaves; for the loss of a left arm 500 pieces of eight, or five slaves; for a right leg 500 pieces of eight, or five slaves; for the left leg 400 pieces of eight, or four slaves; for an eye 100 pieces of eight or one slave; for a finger of the hand the same reward as for the eye. All which sums of money, as I have said before, are taken out of the capital sum or common stock of what is got by their piracy. For a very exact and equal dividend is made of the remainder among them all. Yet herein they have also regard to qualities and places. Thus the Captain, or chief Commander, is allotted five or six portions to what the ordinary seamen have; the Master's Mate only two; and other Officers proportionate to their employment. After whom they draw equal parts from the highest even to the lowest mariner, the boys not being omitted. For even these draw half a share, by reason that, when they happen to take a better vessel than their own, it is the duty of the boys to set fire to the ship or boat wherein they are, and then retire to the prize which they have taken.

"They observe among themselves very good orders. For in the prizes they take it is severely prohibited to everyone to usurp anything in particular to themselves. Hence all they take is equally divided, according to what has been said before. Yea, they make a solemn oath to each other not to abscond or conceal the least thing they find amongst the prey. If afterwards anyone is found unfaithful, who has contravened the said oath, immediately he is separated and turned out of the society. Among themselves they are very civil and charitable to each other. Insomuch that if any wants what another has, with great liberality they give it one to another. As soon as these pirates have taken any prize of ship or boat, the first thing they endeavour is to set on shore the prisoners, detaining only some few for their own help and service, to whom also they give their liberty after the space of two or three years. They put in very frequently for refreshment at one island or another; but more especially into those which lie on the southern side of the Isle of Cuba. Here they careen their vessels, and in the meanwhile some of them go to hunt, others to cruise upon the seas in canoes, seeking their fortune. Many times they take the poor fishermen of tortoises, and carrying them to their habitations they make them work so long as the pirates are pleased."

The articles which fixed the conditions under which the buccaneers sailed were commonly called the "chasse-partie."[105] In the earlier days of buccaneering, before the period of great leaders like Mansfield, Morgan and Grammont, the captain was usually chosen from among their own number. Although faithfully obeyed he was removable at will, and had scarcely more prerogative than the ordinary sailor. After 1655 the buccaneers generally sailed under commissions from the governors of Jamaica or Tortuga, and then they always set aside one tenth of the profits for the governor. But when their prizes were unauthorised they often withdrew to some secluded coast to make a partition of the booty, and on their return to port eased the governor's conscience with politic gifts; and as the governor generally had little control over these difficult people he found himself all the more obliged to dissimulate. Although the buccaneers were called by the Spaniards "ladrones" and "demonios," names which they richly deserved, they often gave part of their spoil to churches in the ports which they frequented, especially if among the booty they found any ecclesiastical ornaments or the stuffs for making them-articles which not infrequently formed an important part of the cargo of Spanish treasure ships. In March 1694 the Jesuit writer, Labat, took part in a Mass at Martinique which was performed for some French buccaneers in pursuance of a vow made when they were taking two English vessels near Barbadoes. The French vessel and its two prizes were anchored near the church, and fired salutes of all their cannon at the beginning of the Mass, at the Elevation of the Host, at the Benediction, and again at the end of the Te Deum sung after the Mass.[106] Labat, who, although a priest, is particularly lenient towards the crimes of the buccaneers, and who we suspect must have been the recipient of numerous "favours" from them out of their store of booty, relates a curious tale of the buccaneer, Captain Daniel, a tale which has often been used by other writers, but which may bear repetition. Daniel, in need of provisions, anchored one night off one of the "Saintes," small islands near Dominica, and landing without opposition, took possession of the house of the curé and of some other inhabitants of the neighbourhood. He carried the curé and his people on board his ship without offering them the least violence, and told them that he merely wished to buy some wine, brandy and fowls. While these were being gathered, Daniel requested the curé to celebrate Mass, which the poor priest dared not refuse. So the necessary sacred vessels were sent for and an altar improvised on the deck for the service, which they chanted to the best of their ability. As at Martinique, the Mass was begun by a discharge of artillery, and after the Exaudiat and prayer for the King was closed by a loud "Vive le Roi!" from the throats of the buccaneers. A single incident, however, somewhat disturbed the devotions. One of the buccaneers, remaining in an indecent attitude during the Elevation, was rebuked by the captain, and instead of heeding the correction, replied with an impertinence and a fearful oath. Quick as a flash Daniel whipped out his pistol and shot the buccaneer through the head, adjuring God that he would do as much to the first who failed in his respect to the Holy Sacrifice. The shot was fired close by the priest, who, as we can readily imagine, was considerably agitated. "Do not be troubled, my father," said Daniel; "he is a rascal lacking in his duty and I have punished him to teach him better." A very efficacious means, remarks Labat, of preventing his falling into another like mistake. After the Mass the body of the dead man was thrown into the sea, and the curé was recompensed for his pains by some goods out of their stock and the present of a negro slave.[107]

The buccaneers preferred to sail in barques, vessels of one mast and rigged with triangular sails. This type of boat, they found, could be more easily manœuvred, was faster and sailed closer to the wind. The boats were built of cedar, and the best were reputed to come from Bermuda. They carried very few guns, generally from six to twelve or fourteen, the corsairs believing that four muskets did more execution than one cannon.[108] The buccaneers sometimes used brigantines, vessels with two masts, the fore or mizzenmast being square-rigged with two sails and the mainmast rigged like that of a barque. The corsair at Martinique of whom Labat speaks was captain of a corvette, a boat like a brigantine, except that all the sails were square-rigged. At the beginning of a voyage the freebooters were generally so crowded in their small vessels that they suffered much from lack of room. Moreover, they had little protection from sun and rain, and with but a small stock of provisions often faced starvation. It was this as much as anything which frequently inspired them to attack without reflection any possible prize, great or small, and to make themselves masters of it or perish in the attempt. Their first object was to come to close quarters; and although a single broadside would have sunk their small craft, they manœuvred so skilfully as to keep their bow always presented to the enemy, while their musketeers cleared the enemy's decks until the time when the captain judged it proper to board. The buccaneers rarely attacked Spanish ships on the outward voyage from Europe to America, for such ships were loaded with wines, cloths, grains and other commodities for which they had little use, and which they could less readily turn into available wealth. Outgoing vessels also carried large crews and a considerable number of passengers. It was the homeward-bound ships, rather, which attracted their avarice, for in such vessels the crews were smaller and the cargo consisted of precious metals, dye-woods and jewels, articles which the freebooters could easily dispose of to the merchants and tavern-keepers of the ports they frequented.

The Gulf of Honduras and the Mosquito Coast, dotted with numerous small islands and protecting reefs, was a favourite retreat for the buccaneers. As the clumsy Spanish war-vessels of the period found it ticklish work threading these tortuous channels, where a sudden adverse wind usually meant disaster, the buccaneers there felt secure from interference; and in the creeks, lagoons and river-mouths densely shrouded by tropical foliage, they were able to careen and refit their vessels, divide their booty, and enjoy a respite from their sea-forays. Thence, too, they preyed upon the Spanish ships which sailed from the coast of Cartagena to Porto Bello, Nicaragua, Mexico, and the larger Antilles, and were a constant menace to the great treasure galleons of the Terra-Firma fleet. The English settlement on the island of Providence, lying as it did off the Nicaragua coast and in the very track of Spanish commerce in those regions, was, until captured in 1641, a source of great fear to Spanish mariners; and when in 1642 some English occupied the island of Roatan, near Truxillo, the governor of Cuba and the Presidents of the Audiencias at Gautemala and San Domingo jointly equipped an expedition of four vessels under D. Francisco de Villalba y Toledo, which drove out the intruders.[109] Closer to the buccaneering headquarters in Tortuga (and later in Jamaica) were the straits separating the great West Indian islands: —the Yucatan Channel at the western end of Cuba, the passage between Cuba and Hispaniola in the east, and the Mona Passage between Hispaniola and Porto Rico. In these regions the corsairs waited to pick up stray Spanish merchantmen, and watched for the coming of the galleons or the Flota.[110] When the buccaneers returned from their cruises they generally squandered in a few days, in the taverns of the towns which they frequented, the wealth which had cost them such peril and labour. Some of these outlaws, says Exquemelin, would spend 2000 or 3000 pieces of eight[111] in one night, not leaving themselves a good shirt to wear on their backs in the morning. "My own master," he continues, "would buy, on like occasions, a whole pipe of wine, and placing it in the street would force every one that passed by to drink with him; threatening also to pistol them in case they would not do it. At other times he would do the same with barrels of ale or beer. And, very often, with both in his hands, he would throw these liquors about the streets, and wet the clothes of such as walked by, without regarding whether he spoiled their apparel or not, were they men or women." The taverns and ale-houses always welcomed the arrival of these dissolute corsairs; and although they extended long credits, they also at times sold as indentured servants those who had run too deeply into debt, as happened in Jamaica to this same patron or master of whom Exquemelin wrote.

Until 1640 buccaneering in the West Indies was more or less accidental, occasional, in character. In the second half of the century, however, the numbers of the freebooters greatly increased, and men entirely deserted their former occupations for the excitement and big profits of the "course." There were several reasons for this increase in the popularity of buccaneering. The English adventurers in Hispaniola had lost their profession of hunting very early, for with the coming of Levasseur the French had gradually elbowed them out of the island, and compelled them either to retire to the Lesser Antilles or to prey upon their Spanish neighbours. But the French themselves were within the next twenty years driven to the same expedient. The Spanish colonists on Hispaniola, unable to keep the French from the island, at last foolishly resolved, according to Charlevoix's account, to remove the principal attraction by destroying all the wild cattle. If the trade with French vessels and the barter of hides for brandy could be arrested, the hunters would be driven from the woods by starvation. This policy, together with the wasteful methods pursued by the hunters, caused a rapid decrease in the number of cattle. The Spaniards, however, did not dream of the consequences of their action. Many of the French, forced to seek another occupation, naturally fell into the way of buccaneering. The hunters of cattle became hunters of Spaniards, and the sea became the savanna on which they sought their game. Exquemelin tells us that when he arrived at the island there were scarcely three hundred engaged in hunting, and even these found their livelihood precarious. It was from this time forward to the end of the century that the buccaneers played so important a rôle on the stage of West Indian history.

Another source of recruits for the freebooters were the indentured servants or *engagés*. We hear a great deal of the barbarity with which West Indian planters and hunters in the seventeenth century treated their servants, and we may well believe that many of the latter, finding their situation unendurable, ran away from their plantations or ajoupas to join the crew of a chance corsair hovering in the neighbourhood. The hunters' life, as we have seen, was not one of revelry and ease. On the one side were all the insidious dangers lurking in a wild, tropical forest; on the other, the relentless hostility of the Spaniards. The environment of the hunters made them rough and cruel, and for many an *engagé* his three years of servitude must have been a veritable purgatory. The servants of the planters were in no better position. Decoyed from Norman and Breton towns and villages by the loud-sounding promises of sea-captains and West Indian agents, they came to seek an El Dorado, and often found only despair and death. The want of sufficient negroes led men to resort to any artifice in order to obtain assistance in cultivating the sugar-cane and tobacco. The apprentices sent from Europe were generally bound out in the French Antilles for eighteen months or three years, among the English for seven years. They were often resold in the interim, and sometimes served ten or twelve years before they regained their freedom. They were veritable convicts, often more ill-treated than the slaves with whom they worked side by side, for their lives, after the expiration of their term of service, were of no consequence to their masters. Many of these apprentices, of good birth and tender education, were unable to endure the debilitating climate and hard labour, let alone the cruelty of their employers. Exquemelin, himself originally an *engagé*, gives a most piteous description of their sufferings. He was sold to the Lieutenant-Governor of Tortuga, who treated him with great severity and refused to take less than 300 pieces of eight for his freedom. Falling ill through vexation and despair, he passed into the hands of a surgeon, who proved kind to him and finally gave him his liberty for 100 pieces of eight, to be paid after his first buccaneering voyage.[112]

We left Levasseur governor in Tortuga after the abortive Spanish attack of 1643. Finding his personal ascendancy so complete over the rude natures about him, Levasseur, like many a greater man in similar circumstances, lost his sense of the rights of others. His character changed, he became suspicious and intolerant, and the settlers complained bitterly of his cruelty and overbearing temper. Having come as the leader of a band of Huguenots, he forbade the Roman Catholics to hold services on the island, burnt their chapel and turned out their priest. He placed heavy imposts on trade, and soon amassed a considerable fortune.[113] In his eyrie upon the rock fortress, he is said to have kept for his enemies a cage of iron, in which the prisoner could neither stand nor lie down, and which Levasseur, with grim humour, called his "little hell." A dungeon in his castle he termed in like fashion his "purgatory." All these stories, however, are reported by the Jesuits, his natural foes, and must be taken with a grain of salt. De Poincy, who himself ruled with despotic authority and was guilty of similar cruelties, would have turned a deaf ear to the denunciations against his lieutenant, had not his jealousy been aroused by the suspicion that Levasseur intended to declare himself an independent prince.[114] So the governor-general, already in bad odour at court for having given Levasseur means of establishing a little Geneva in Tortuga, began to disavow him to the authorities at home. He also sent his nephew, M. de Lonvilliers, to Tortuga, on the pretext of complimenting Levasseur on his victory over the Spaniards, but really to endeavour to entice him back to St. Kitts. Levasseur, subtle and penetrating, skilfully avoided the trap, and Lonvilliers returned to St. Kitts alone.

Charlevoix relates an amusing instance of the governor's stubborn resistance to de Poincy's authority. A silver statue of the Virgin, captured by some buccaneer from a Spanish ship, had been appropriated by Levasseur, and de Poincy, desiring to decorate his chapel with it, wrote to him demanding the statue, and observing that a Protestant had no use for such an object. Levasseur, however, replied that the Protestants had a great adoration for silver virgins, and that Catholics being "trop spirituels pour tenir à la matière," he was sending him, instead, a madonna of painted wood.

After a tenure of power for twelve years, Levasseur came to the end of his tether. While de Poincy was resolving upon an expedition to oust him from authority, two adventurers named

Martin and Thibault, whom Levasseur had adopted as his heirs, and with whom, it is said, he had quarrelled over a mistress, shot him as he was descending from the fort to the shore, and completed the murder by a poniard's thrust. They then seized the government without any opposition from the inhabitants.[115] Meanwhile there had arrived at St. Kitts the Chevalier de Fontenay, a soldier of fortune who had distinguished himself against the Turks and was attracted by the gleam of Spanish gold. He it was whom de Poincy chose as the man to succeed Levasseur. The opportunity for action was eagerly accepted by de Fontenay, but the project was kept secret, for if Levasseur had got wind of it all the forces in St. Kitts could not have dislodged him. Volunteers were raised on the pretext of a privateering expedition to the coasts of Cartagena, and to complete the deception de Fontenay actually sailed for the Main and captured several prizes. The rendezvous was on the coast of Hispaniola, where de Fontenay was eventually joined by de Poincy's nephew, M. de Treval, with another frigate and materials for a siege. Learning of the murder of Levasseur, the invaders at once sailed for Tortuga and landed several hundred men at the spot where the Spaniards had formerly been repulsed. The two assassins, finding the inhabitants indisposed to support them, capitulated to de Fontenay on receiving pardon for their crime and the peaceful possession of their property. Catholicism was restored, commerce was patronized and buccaneers encouraged to use the port. Two stone bastions were raised on the platform and more guns were mounted.[116] De Fontenay himself was the first to bear the official title of "Governor for the King of Tortuga and the Coast of S. Domingo."

The new governor was not fated to enjoy his success for any length of time. The President of S. Domingo, Don Juan Francisco de Montemayor, with orders from the King of Spain, was preparing for another effort to get rid of his troublesome neighbour, and in November 1653 sent an expedition of five vessels and 400 infantry against the French, under command of Don Gabriel Roxas de Valle-Figueroa. The ships were separated by a storm, two ran aground and a third was lost, so that only the "Capitana" and "Almirante" reached Tortuga on 10th January. Being greeted with a rough fire from the platform and fort as they approached the harbour, they dropped anchor a league to leeward and landed with little opposition. After nine days of fighting and siege of the fort, de Fontenay capitulated with the honours of war.[117] According to the French account, the Spaniards, lashing their cannon to rough frames of wood, dragged a battery of eight or ten guns to the top of some hills commanding the fort, and began a furious bombardment. Several sorties of the besieged to capture the battery were unsuccessful. The inhabitants began to tire of fighting, and de Fontenay, discovering some secret negotiations with the enemy, was compelled to sue for terms. With incredible exertions, two half-scuttled ships in the harbour were fitted up and provisioned within three days, and upon them the French sailed for Port Margot.[118] The Spaniards claimed that the booty would have been considerable but for some Dutch trading-ships in the harbour which conveyed all the valuables from the island. They burned the settlements, however, carried away with them some guns, munitions of war and slaves, and this time taking the precaution to leave behind a garrison of 150 men, sailed for Hispaniola. Fearing that the French might join forces with the buccaneers and attack their small squadron on the way back, they retained de Fontenay's brother as a hostage until they reached the city of San Domingo. De Fontenay, indeed, after his brother's release, did determine to try and recover the island. Only 130 of his men stood by him, the rest deserting to join the buccaneers in western Hispaniola. While he was careening his ship at Port Margot, however, a Dutch trader arrived with commodities for Tortuga, and learning of the disaster, offered him aid with men and supplies. A descent was made upon the smaller island, and the Spaniards were besieged for twenty days, but after several encounters they compelled the French to withdraw. De Fontenay, with only thirty companions, sailed for Europe, was wrecked among the Azores, and eventually reached France, only to die a short time afterwards.

A Correct Map of Jamaica, From the Royal Magazine, 1760.

Chapter III
The Conquest of Jamaica

The capture of Jamaica by the expedition sent out by Cromwell in 1655 was the blundering beginning of a new era in West Indian history. It was the first permanent annexation by another European power of an integral part of Spanish America. Before 1655 the island had already been twice visited by English forces. The first occasion was in January 1597, when Sir Anthony Shirley, with little opposition, took and plundered St. Jago de la Vega. The second was in 1643, when William Jackson repeated the same exploit with 500 men from the Windward Islands. Cromwell's expedition, consisting of 2500 men and a considerable fleet, set sail from England in December 1654, with the secret object of "gaining an interest" in that part of the West Indies in possession of the Spaniards. Admiral Penn commanded the fleet, and General Venables the land forces.[119] The expedition reached Barbadoes at the end of January, where some 4000 additional troops were raised, besides about 1200 from Nevis, St. Kitts, and neighbouring islands. The commanders having resolved to direct their first attempt against Hispaniola, on 13th April a landing was effected at a point to the west of San Domingo, and the army, suffering terribly from a tropical sun and lack of water, marched thirty miles through woods and savannahs to attack the city. The English received two shameful defeats from a handful of Spaniards on 17th and 25th April, and General Venables, complaining loudly of the cowardice of his men and of Admiral Penn's failure to co-operate with him, finally gave up the attempt and sailed for Jamaica. On 11th May, in the splendid harbour on which Kingston now stands, the English fleet dropped anchor. Three small forts on the western side were battered by the guns from the ships, and as soon as the troops began to land the garrisons evacuated their posts. St. Jago, six miles inland, was occupied next day. The terms offered by Venables to the Spaniards (the same as those exacted from the English settlers on Providence Island in 1641 —emigration within ten days on pain of death, and forfeiture of all their property) were accepted on the 17th; but the Spaniards were soon discovered to have entered into negotiations merely to gain time and retire with their families and goods to the woods and mountains, whence they continued their resistance. Meanwhile the army, wretchedly equipped with provisions and other necessities, was decimated by sickness. On the 19th two long-expected store-ships arrived, but the supplies brought by them were limited, and an appeal for assistance was sent to New England. Admiral Penn, disgusted with the fiasco in Hispaniola and on bad terms with Venables, sailed for England with part of his fleet on 25th June; and Venables, so ill that his life was despaired of, and also anxious to clear himself of the responsibility for the initial failure of the expedition, followed in the "Marston Moor" nine days later. On 20th September both commanders appeared before the Council of State to answer the charge of having deserted their posts, and together they shared the disgrace of a month in the Tower.[120]

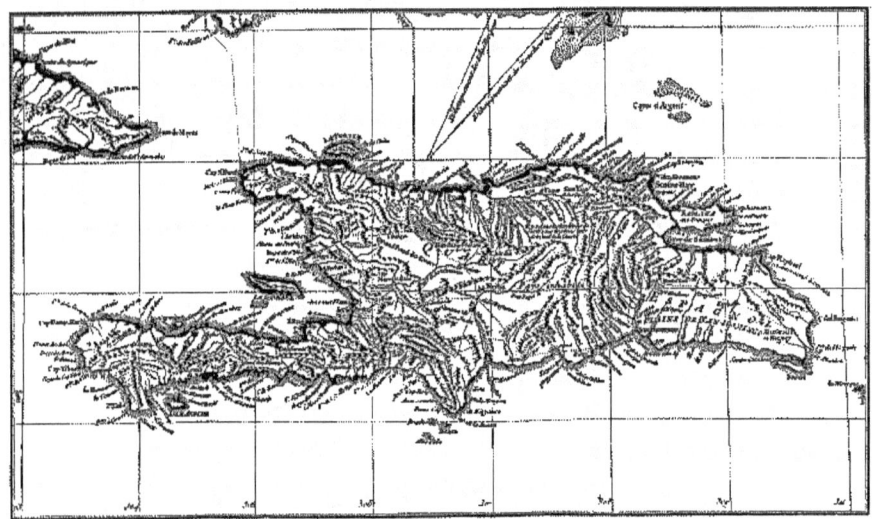

Map of San Domingo, From Charlevoix' Histoire de S. Domingue.

The army of General Venables was composed of very inferior and undisciplined troops, mostly the rejected of English regiments or the offscourings of the West Indian colonies; yet the chief reasons for the miscarriage before San Domingo were the failure of Venables to command the confidence of his officers and men, his inexcusable errors in the management of the attack, and the lack of cordial co-operation between him and the Admiral. The difficulties with which he had to struggle were, of course, very great. On the other hand, he seems to have been deficient both in strength of character and in military capacity; and his ill-health made still more difficult a task for which he was fundamentally incompetent. The comparative failure of this, Cromwell's pet enterprise, was a bitter blow to the Protector. For a whole day he shut himself up in his room, brooding over the disaster for which he, more than any other, was responsible. He had aimed not merely to plant one more colony in America, but to make himself master of such parts of the West Indian islands and Spanish Main as would enable him to dominate the route of the Spanish-American treasure fleets. To this end Jamaica contributed few advantages beyond those possessed by Barbadoes and St. Kitts, and it was too early for him to realize that island for island Jamaica was much more suitable than Hispaniola as the seat of an English colony.[121]

Religious and economic motives form the key to Cromwell's foreign policy, and it is difficult to discover which, the religious or the economic, was uppermost in his mind when he planned this expedition. He inherited from the Puritans of Elizabeth's time the traditional religious hatred of Spain as the bulwark of Rome, and in his mind as in theirs the overthrow of the Spaniards in the West Indies was a blow at antichrist and an extension of the true religion. The religious ends of the expedition were fully impressed upon Venables and his successors in Jamaica.[122] Second only, however, to Oliver's desire to protect "the people of God," was his ambition to extend England's empire beyond the seas. He desired the unquestioned supremacy of England over the other nations of Europe, and that supremacy, as he probably foresaw, was to be commercial and colonial. Since the discovery of America the world's commerce had enormously increased, and its control brought with it national power. America had become the treasure-house of Europe. If England was to be set at the head of the world's commerce and navigation, she must break through Spain's monopoly of the Indies and gain a control in Spanish America. San Domingo was to be but a preliminary step, after which the rest of the Spanish dominions in the New World would be gradually absorbed.[123]

The immediate excuse for the attack on Hispaniola and Jamaica was the Spaniards' practice of seizing English ships and ill-treating English crews merely because they were found in some part of the Caribbean Sea, and even though bound for a plantation actually in possession of English colonists. It was the old question of effective occupation *versus* papal donation, and both Cromwell and Venables convinced themselves that Spanish assaults in the past on English ships and colonies supplied a sufficient *casus belli*.[124] There was no justification, however, for a secret attack upon Spain. She had been the first to recognize the young republic, and was willing and even anxious to league herself with England. There had been actual negotiations for an alliance, and Cromwell's offers, though rejected, had never been really withdrawn. Without a declaration of war or formal notice of any sort, a fleet was fitted out and sent in utmost secrecy to fall unawares upon the colonies of a friendly nation. The whole aspect of the exploit was Elizabethan. It was inspired by Drake and Raleigh, a reversion to the Elizabethan gold-hunt. It was the first of the great buccaneering expeditions.[125]

Cromwell was doubtless influenced, too, by the representations of Thomas Gage. Gage was an Englishman who had joined the Dominicans and had been sent by his Order out to Spanish America. In 1641 he returned to England, announced his conversion to Protestantism, took the side of Parliament and became a minister. His experiences in the West Indies and Mexico he published in 1648 under the name of "The English-American, or a New Survey of the West Indies," a most entertaining book, which aimed to arouse Englishmen against Romish "idolatries," to show how valuable the Spanish-American provinces might be to England in trade and bullion and how easily they might be seized. In the summer of 1654, moreover, Gage had laid before the Protector a memorial in which he recapitulated the conclusions of his book, assuring Cromwell that the Spanish colonies were sparsely peopled and that the few whites were unwarlike and scantily provided with arms and ammunition. He asserted that the conquest of Hispaniola and Cuba would be a matter of no difficulty, and that even Central America was too weak to oppose a long resistance.[126] All this was true, and had Cromwell but sent a respectable force under an efficient leader the result would have been different. The exploits of the buccaneers a few years later proved it.

It was fortunate, considering the distracted state of affairs in Jamaica in 1655-56, that the Spaniards were in no condition to attempt to regain the island. Cuba, the nearest Spanish territory to Jamaica, was being ravaged by the most terrible pestilence known there in years, and the inhabitants, alarmed for their own safety, instead of trying to dispossess the English, were busy providing for the defence of their own coasts.[127] In 1657, however, some troops under command of the old Spanish governor of Jamaica, D. Christopher Sasi Arnoldo, crossed from St. Jago de Cuba and entrenched themselves on the northern shore as the advance post of a greater force expected from the mainland. Papers of instructions relating to the enterprise were intercepted by Colonel Doyley, then acting-governor of Jamaica; and he with 500 picked men embarked for the north side, attacked the Spaniards in their entrenchments and utterly routed them.[128] The next year about 1000 men, the long-expected corps of regular Spanish infantry, landed and erected a fort at Rio Nuevo. Doyley, displaying the same energy, set out again on 11th June with 750 men, landed under fire on the 22nd, and next day captured the fort in a brilliant attack in which about 300 Spaniards were killed and 100 more, with many officers and flags, captured. The English lost about sixty in killed and wounded.[129] After the failure of a similar, though weaker, attempt in 1660, the Spaniards despaired of regaining Jamaica, and most of those still upon the island embraced the first opportunity to retire to Cuba and other Spanish settlements.

As colonists the troops in Jamaica proved to be very discouraging material, and the army was soon in a wretched state. The officers and soldiers plundered and mutinied instead of working and planting. Their wastefulness led to scarcity of food, and scarcity of food brought disease and death.[130] They wished to force the Protector to recall them, or to employ them in assaulting the opulent Spanish towns on the Main, an occupation far more lucrative than that of planting corn and provisions for sustenance. Cromwell, however, set himself to develop and strengthen his new colony. He issued a proclamation encouraging trade and settlement in the island by exempting the inhabitants from taxes, and the Council voted that 1000 young men and an equal number of girls be shipped over from Ireland. The Scotch government was instructed to apprehend and transport idlers and vagabonds, and commissioners were sent into New England and to the Windward and Leeward Islands to try and attract settlers.[131] Bermudians, Jews, Quakers from Barbadoes and criminals from Newgate, helped to swell the population of the new colony, and in 1658 the island is said to have contained 4500 whites, besides 1500 or more negro slaves.[132]

To dominate the Spanish trade routes was one of the principal objects of English policy in the West Indies. This purpose is reflected in all of Cromwell's instructions to the leaders of the Jamaican design, and it appears again in his instructions of 10th October 1655 to Major-General Fortescue and Vice-Admiral Goodson. Fortescue was given power and authority to land men upon territory claimed by the Spaniards, to take their forts, castles and places of strength, and to pursue, kill and destroy all who opposed him. The Vice-Admiral was to assist him with his sea-forces, and to use his best endeavours to seize all ships belonging to the King of Spain or his subjects in America.[133] The soldiers, as has been said, were more eager to fight the Spaniards than to plant, and opportunities were soon given them to try their hand. Admiral Penn had left twelve ships under Goodson's charge, and of these, six were at sea picking up a few scattered Spanish prizes which helped to pay for the victuals supplied out of New England.[134] Goodson, however, was after larger prey, no less than the galleons or a Spanish town upon the mainland. He did not know where the galleons were, but at the end of July he seems to have been lying with eight vessels before Cartagena and Porto Bello, and on 22nd November he sent Captain Blake with nine ships to the same coast to intercept all vessels going thither from Spain or elsewhere. The fleet was broken up by foul weather, however, and part returned on 14th December to refit, leaving a few small frigates to lie in wait for some merchantmen reported to be in that region.[135] The first town on the Main to feel the presence of this new power in the Indies was Santa Marta, close to Cartagena on the shores of what is now the U.S. of Columbia. In the latter part of October, just a month before the departure of Blake, Goodson sailed with a fleet of eight vessels to ravage the Spanish coasts. According to one account his original design had been against Rio de la Hacha near the pearl fisheries, "but having missed his aim" he sailed for Santa Marta. He landed 400 sailors and soldiers under the protection of his guns, took and demolished the two forts which barred his way, and entered the town. Finding that the inhabitants had already fled with as much of their belongings as they could carry, he pursued them some twelve miles up into the country; and on his return plundered and burnt their houses, embarked with thirty pieces of cannon and other booty, and sailed for Jamaica.[136] It was a gallant performance with a handful of men, but the profits were much less than had been expected. It had been agreed that the seamen and soldiers should receive half the spoil, but on counting the proceeds it was found that their share amounted to no more than £400, to balance which the State took the thirty pieces of ordnance and some powder, shot, hides, salt and Indian corn.[137] Sedgwick wrote to Thurloe that "reckoning all got there on the State's share, it did not pay for the powder and shot spent in that service."[138] Sedgwick was one of the civil commissioners appointed for the government of Jamaica. A brave, pious soldier with a long experience and honourable military record in the Massachusetts colony, he did not approve of this type of warfare against the Spaniards. "This kind of marooning cruising West India trade of plundering and burning towns," he writes, "though it hath been long practised in these parts, yet is not honourable for a princely navy, neither was it, I think, the work designed, though perhaps it may be tolerated at present." If Cromwell was to accomplish his original purpose of blocking up the Spanish treasure route, he wrote again, permanent foothold must be gained in some important Spanish fortress, either Cartagena or Havana, places strongly garrisoned, however, and requiring for their reduction a considerable army and fleet, such as Jamaica did not then possess. But to waste and burn towns of inferior rank without retaining them merely dragged on the war indefinitely and effected little advantage or profit to anybody.[139] Captain Nuberry visited Santa Marta several weeks after Goodson's descent, and, going on shore, found that about a hundred people had made bold to return and rebuild their devastated homes. Upon sight of the English the poor people again fled incontinently to the woods, and Nuberry and his men destroyed their houses a second time.[140]

On 5th April 1656 Goodson, with ten of his best ships, set sail again and steered eastward along the coast of Hispaniola as far as Alta Vela, hoping to meet with some Spanish ships reported in that region. Encountering none, he stood for the Main, and landed on 4th May with about 450 men at Rio de la Hacha. The story of the exploit is merely a repetition of what happened at Santa Marta. The people had sight of the English fleet six hours before it could drop anchor, and fled from the town to the hills and surrounding woods. Only twelve men were left behind to hold the fort, which the English stormed and took within half an hour. Four large brass cannon were carried to the ships and the fort partly demolished. The Spaniards pretended to parley for the ransom of their town, but when after a day's delay they gave no sign of complying with the admiral's demands, he burned the place on 8th May and sailed away.[141] Goodson called again at Santa Marta on the 11th to get water, and on the 14th stood before Cartagena to view the harbour. Leaving three vessels to ply there, he returned to Jamaica, bringing back with him only two small prizes, one laden with wine, the other with cocoa.

The seamen of the fleet, however, were restless and eager for further enterprises of this nature, and Goodson by the middle of June had fourteen of his vessels lying off the Cuban coast near Cape S. Antonio in wait for the galleons or the Flota, both of which fleets were then expected at Havana. His ambition to repeat the achievement of Piet Heyn was fated never to be realised. The fleet of Terra-Firma, he soon learned, had sailed into Havana on 15th May, and on 13th June, three days before his arrival on that coast, had departed for Spain.[142] Meanwhile, one of his own vessels, the "Arms of Holland," was blown up, with the loss of all on board but three men and the captain, and two other ships were disabled. Five of the fleet returned to England on 23rd August, and with the rest Goodson remained on the Cuban coast until the end of the month, watching in vain for the fleet from Vera Cruz which never sailed.[143]

Colonel Edward Doyley, the officer who so promptly defeated the attempts of the Spaniards in 1657-58 to re-conquer Jamaica, was now governor of the island. He had sailed with the expedition to the West Indies as lieutenant-colonel in the regiment of General Venables, and on the death of Major-General Fortescue in November 1655 had been chosen by Cromwell's commissioners in Jamaica as commander-in-chief of the land forces. In May 1656 he was superseded by Robert Sedgwick, but the latter died within a few days, and Doyley petitioned the Protector to appoint him to the post. William Brayne, however, arrived from England in December 1656 to take chief command; and when he, like his two predecessors, was stricken down by disease nine months later, the place devolved permanently upon Doyley. Doyley was a very efficient governor, and although he has been accused of showing little regard or respect for planting and trade, the charge appears to be unjust.[144] He firmly maintained order among men disheartened and averse to settlement, and at the end of his service delivered up the colony a comparatively well-ordered and thriving community. He was confirmed in his post by Charles II. at the Restoration, but superseded by Lord Windsor in August 1661. Doyley's claim to distinction rests mainly upon his vigorous policy against the Spaniards, not only in defending Jamaica, but by encouraging privateers and carrying the war into the enemies' quarters. In July 1658, on learning from some prisoners that the galleons were in Porto Bello awaiting the plate from Panama, Doyley embarked 300 men on a fleet of five vessels and sent it to lie in an obscure bay between that port and Cartagena to intercept the Spanish ships. On 20th October the galleons were espied, twenty-nine vessels in all, fifteen galleons and fourteen stout merchantmen. Unfortunately, all the English vessels except the "Hector" and the "Marston Moor" were at that moment absent to obtain fresh water. Those two alone could do nothing, but passing helplessly through the Spaniards, hung on their rear and tried without success to scatter them. The English fleet later attacked and burnt the town of Tolu on the Main, capturing two Spanish ships in the road; and afterwards paid another visit to the unfortunate Santa Marta, where they remained three days, marching several miles into the country and burning and destroying everything in their path.[145]

On 23rd April 1659, however, there returned to Port Royal another expedition whose success realised the wildest dreams of avarice. Three frigates under command of Captain Christopher Myngs,[146] with 300 soldiers on board, had been sent by Doyley to harry the South American coast. They first entered and destroyed Cumana, and then ranging along the coast westward, landed again at Puerto Cabello and at Coro. At the latter town they followed the inhabitants into the woods, where besides other plunder they came upon twenty-two chests of royal treasure intended for the King of Spain, each chest containing 400 pounds of silver.[147] Embarking this money and other spoil in the shape of plate, jewels and cocoa, they returned to Port Royal with the richest prize that ever entered Jamaica. The whole pillage was estimated at between £200,000 and £300,000.[148] The abundance of new wealth introduced into Jamaica did much to raise the spirits of the colonists, and set the island well upon the road to more prosperous times. The sequel to this brilliant exploit, however, was in some ways unfortunate. Disputes were engendered between the officers of the expedition and the governor and other authorities on shore over the disposal of the booty, and in the early part of June 1659 Captain Myngs was sent home in the "Marston Moor," suspended for disobeying orders and plundering the hold of one of the prizes to the value of 12,000 pieces of eight. Myngs was an active, intrepid commander, but apparently avaricious and impatient of control. He seems to have endeavoured to divert most of the prize money into the pockets of his officers and men, by disposing of the booty on his own initiative before giving a strict account of it to the governor or steward-general of the island. Doyley writes that there was a constant market aboard the "Marston Moor," and that Myngs and his officers, alleging it to be customary to break and plunder the holds, permitted the twenty-two chests of the King of Spain's silver to be divided among the men without any provision whatever for the claims of the State.[149] There was also some friction over the disposal of six Dutch prizes which Doyley had picked up for illegal trading at Barbadoes on his way out from England. These, too, had been plundered before they reached Jamaica, and when Myngs found that there was no power in the colony to try and condemn ships taken by virtue of the Navigation Laws, it only added fuel to his dissatisfaction. When Myngs reached England he lodged counter-complaints against Governor Doyley, Burough, the steward-general, and Vice-Admiral Goodson, alleging that they received more than their share of the prize money; and a war of mutual recrimination followed.[150] Amid the distractions of the Restoration, however, little seems ever to have been made of the matter in England. The insubordination of officers in 1659-60 was a constant source of difficulty and impediment to the governor in his efforts to establish peace and order in the colony. In England nobody was sure where the powers of government actually resided. As Burough wrote from Jamaica on 19th January 1660, "We are here just like you at home; when we heard of the Lord-Protector's death we proclaimed his son, and when we heard of his being turned out we proclaimed a Parliament and now own a Committee of safety."[151] The effect of this uncertainty was bound to be prejudicial in Jamaica, a new colony filled with adventurers, for it loosened the reins of authority and encouraged lawless spirits to set the governor at defiance.

On 8th May 1660 Charles II. was proclaimed King of England, and entered London on 29th May. The war which Cromwell had begun with Spain was essentially a war of the Common-wealth. The Spanish court was therefore on friendly terms with the exiled prince, and when he returned into possession of his kingdom a cessation of hostilities with Spain naturally followed.

Charles wrote a note to Don Luis de Haro on 2nd June 1660, proposing an armistice in Europe and America which was to lead to a permanent peace and a re-establishment of commercial relations between the two kingdoms.[152] At the same time Sir Henry Bennett, the English resident in Madrid, made similar proposals to the Spanish king. A favourable answer was received in July, and the cessation of arms, including a revival of the treaty of 1630 was proclaimed on 10th-20th September 1660. Preliminary negotiations for a new treaty were entered upon at Madrid, but the marriage of Charles to Catherine of Braganza in 1662, and the consequent alliance with Portugal, with whom Spain was then at war, put a damper upon all such designs. The armistice with Spain was not published in Jamaica until 5th February of the following year. On 4th February Colonel Doyley received from the governor of St. Jago de Cuba a letter enclosing an order from Sir Henry Bennett for the cessation of arms, and this order Doyley immediately made public.[153] About thirty English prisoners were also returned by the Spaniards with the letter. Doyley was confirmed in his command of Jamaica by Charles II., but his commission was not issued till 8th February 1661.[154] He was very desirous, however, of returning to England to look after his private affairs, and on 2nd August another commission was issued to Lord Windsor, appointing him as Doyley's successor.[155] Just a year later, in August 1662, Windsor arrived at Port Royal, fortified with instructions "to endeavour to obtain and preserve a good correspondence and free commerce with the plantations belonging to the King of Spain," even resorting to force if necessary.[156]

The question of English trade with the Spanish colonies in the Indies had first come to the surface in the negotiations for the treaty of 1604, after the long wars between Elizabeth and Philip II. The endeavour of the Spaniards to obtain an explicit prohibition of commerce was met by the English demand for entire freedom. The Spaniards protested that it had never been granted in former treaties or to other nations, or even without restriction to Spanish subjects, and clamoured for at least a private article on the subject; but the English commissioners steadfastly refused, and offered to forbid trade only with ports actually under Spanish authority. Finally a compromise was reached in the words "in quibus ante bellum fuit commercium, juxta et secundum usum et observantiam."[157] This article was renewed in Cottington's Treaty of 1630. The Spaniards themselves, indeed, in 1630, were willing to concede a free navigation in the American seas, and even offered to recognise the English colony of Virginia if Charles I. would admit articles prohibiting trade and navigation in certain harbours and bays. Cottington, however, was too far-sighted, and wrote to Lord Dorchester: "For my own part, I shall ever be far from advising His Majesty to think of such restrictions, for certainly a little more time will open the navigation to those parts so long as there are no negative capitulations or articles to hinder it."[158] The monopolistic pretensions of the Spanish government were evidently relaxing, for in 1634 the Conde de Humanes confided to the English agent, Taylor, that there had been talk in the Council of the Indies of admitting the English to a share in the freight of ships sent to the West Indies, and even of granting them a limited permission to go to those regions on their own account. And in 1637 the Conde de Linhares, recently appointed governor of Brazil, told the English ambassador, Lord Aston, that he was very anxious that English ships should do the carrying between Lisbon and Brazilian ports.

The settlement of the Windward and Leeward Islands and the conquest of Jamaica had given a new impetus to contraband trade. The commercial nations were setting up shop, as it were, at the very doors of the Spanish Indies. The French and English Antilles, condemned by the Navigation Laws to confine themselves to agriculture and a passive trade with the home country, had no recourse but to traffic with their Spanish neighbours. Factors of the Assiento established at Cartagena, Porto Bello and Vera Cruz every year supplied European merchants with detailed news of the nature and quantity of the goods which might be imported with advantage; while the buccaneers, by dominating the whole Caribbean Sea, hindered frequent communication between Spain and her colonies. It is not surprising, therefore, that the commerce of Seville, which had hitherto held its own, decreased with surprising rapidity, that the sailings of the galleons and the Flota were separated by several years, and that the fairs of Porto Bello and

Vera Cruz were almost deserted. To put an effective restraint, moreover, upon this contraband trade was impossible on either side. The West Indian dependencies were situated far from the centre of authority, while the home governments generally had their hands too full of other matters to adequately control their subjects in America. The Spanish viceroys, meanwhile, and the governors in the West Indian Islands, connived at a practice which lined their own pockets with the gold of bribery, and at the same time contributed to the public interest and prosperity of their respective colonies. It was this illicit commerce with Spanish America which Charles II., by negotiation at Madrid and by instructions to his governors in the West Indies, tried to get within his own control. At the Spanish court, Fanshaw, Sandwich and Godolphin in turn were instructed to sue for a free trade with the Colonies. The Assiento of negroes was at this time held by two Genoese named Grillo and Lomelin, and with them the English ambassadors several times entered into negotiation for the privilege of supplying blacks from the English islands. By the treaty of 1670 the English colonies in America were for the first time formally recognised by the Spanish Crown. Freedom of commerce, however, was as far as ever from realisation, and after this date Charles seems to have given up hope of ever obtaining it through diplomatic channels.

The peace of 1660 between England and Spain was supposed to extend to both sides of the "Line." The Council in Jamaica, however, were of the opinion that it applied only to Europe,[159] and from the tenor of Lord Windsor's instructions it may be inferred that the English Court at that time meant to interpret it with the same limitations. Windsor, indeed, was not only instructed to force the Spanish colonies to a free trade, but was empowered to call upon the governor of Barbadoes for aid "in case of any considerable attempt by the Spaniards against Jamaica."[160] The efforts of the Governor, however, to come to a good correspondence with the Spanish colonies were fruitless. In the minutes of the Council of Jamaica of 20th August 1662, we read: "Resolved that the letters from the Governors of Porto Rico and San Domingo are an absolute denial of trade, and that according to His Majesty's instructions to Lord Windsor a trade by force or otherwise be endeavoured;"[161] and under 12th September we find another resolution "that men be enlisted for a design by sea with the 'Centurion' and other vessels."[162] This "design" was an expedition to capture and destroy St. Jago de Cuba, the Spanish port nearest to Jamaican shores. An attack upon St. Jago had been projected by Goodson as far back as 1655. "The Admiral," wrote Major Sedgwick to Thurloe just after his arrival in Jamaica, "was intended before our coming in to have taken some few soldiers and gone over to St. Jago de Cuba, a town upon Cuba, but our coming hindered him without whom we could not well tell how to do anything."[163] In January 1656 the plan was definitely abandoned, because the colony could not spare a sufficient number of soldiers for the enterprise.[164] It was to St. Jago that the Spaniards, driven from Jamaica, mostly betook themselves, and from St. Jago as a starting-point had come the expedition of 1658 to reconquer the island. The instructions of Lord Windsor afforded a convenient opportunity to avenge past attacks and secure Jamaica from molestation in that quarter for the future. The command of the expedition was entrusted to Myngs, who in 1662 was again in the Indies on the frigate "Centurion." Myngs sailed from Port Royal on 21st September with eleven ships and 1300 men,[165] but, kept back by unfavourable winds, did not sight the castle of St. Jago until 5th October. Although he had intended to force the entrance of the harbour, he was prevented by the prevailing land breeze; so he disembarked his men to windward, on a rocky coast, where the path up the bluffs was so narrow that but one man could march at a time. Night had fallen before all were landed, and "the way (was) soe difficult and the night soe dark that they were forced to make stands and fires, and their guides with brands in their hands, to beat the path."[166] At daybreak they reached a plantation by a river's side, some six miles from the place of landing and three from St. Jago. There they refreshed themselves, and advancing upon the town surprised the enemy, who knew of the late landing and the badness of the way and did not expect them so soon. They found 200 Spaniards at the entrance to the town, drawn up under their governor, Don Pedro de Moralis, and supported by Don Christopher de Sasi Arnoldo, the former Spanish governor of Jamaica, with a reserve of 500 more. The Spaniards fled before the first charge of the Jamaicans, and the place was easily mastered.

The next day parties were despatched into the country to pursue the enemy, and orders sent to the fleet to attack the forts at the mouth of the harbour. This was successfully done, the Spaniards deserting the great castle after firing but two muskets. Between scouring the country for hidden riches, most of which had been carried far inland beyond their reach, and dismantling and demolishing the forts, the English forces occupied their time until October 19th. Thirty-four guns were found in the fortifications and 1000 barrels of powder. Some of the guns were carried to the ships and the rest flung over the precipice into the sea; while the powder was used to blow up the castle and the neighbouring country houses.[167] The expedition returned to Jamaica on 22nd October.[168] Only six men had been killed by the Spaniards, twenty more being lost by other "accidents." Of these twenty some must have been captured by the enemy, for when Sir Richard Fanshaw was appointed ambassador to Spain in January 1664, he was instructed among other things to negotiate for an exchange of prisoners taken in the Indies. In July we find him treating for the release of Captain Myngs' men from the prisons of Seville and Cadiz,[169] and on 7th November an order to this effect was obtained from the King of Spain.[170]

The instructions of Lord Windsor gave him leave, as soon as he had settled the government in Jamaica, to appoint a deputy and return to England to confer with the King on colonial affairs. Windsor sailed for England on 28th October, and on the same day Sir Charles Lyttleton's commission as deputy-governor was read in the Jamaican Council.[171] During his short sojourn of three months the Governor had made considerable progress toward establishing an ordered constitution in the island. He disbanded the old army, and reorganised the military under a stricter discipline and better officers. He systematised legal procedure and the rules for the conveyance of property. He erected an Admiralty Court at Port Royal, and above all, probably in pursuance of the recommendation of Colonel Doyley,[172] had called in all the privateering commissions issued by previous governors, and tried to submit the captains to orderly rules by giving them new commissions, with instructions to bring their Spanish prizes to Jamaica for judicature.[173]

The departure of Windsor did not put a stop to the efforts of the Jamaicans to "force a trade" with the Spanish plantations, and we find the Council, on 11th December 1662, passing a motion that to this end an attempt should be made to leeward on the coasts of Cuba, Honduras and the Gulf of Campeache. On 9th and 10th January between 1500 and 1600 soldiers, many of them doubtless buccaneers, were embarked on a fleet of twelve ships and sailed two days later under command of the redoubtable Myngs. About ninety leagues this side of Campeache the fleet ran into a great storm, in which one of the vessels foundered and three others were separated from their fellows. The English reached the coast of Campeache, however, in the early morning of Friday, 9th February, and landing a league and a half from the town, marched without being seen along an Indian path with "such speed and good fortune" that by ten o'clock in the morning they already masters of the city and of all the forts save one, the Castle of Santa Cruz. At the second fort Myngs was wounded by a gun in three places. The town itself, Myngs reported, might have been defended like a fortress, for the houses were contiguous and strongly built of stone with flat roofs.[174] The forts were partly demolished, a portion of the town was destroyed by fire, and the fourteen sail lying in the harbour were seized by the invaders. Altogether the booty must have been considerable. The Spanish licentiate, Maldonado de Aldana, placed it at 150,000 pieces of eight,[175] and the general damage to the city in the destruction of houses and munitions by the enemy, and in the expenditure of treasure for purposes of defence, at half a million more. Myngs and his fleet sailed away on 23rd February, but the "Centurion" did not reach Port Royal until 13th April, and the rest of the fleet followed a few days later. The number of casualties on each side was surprisingly small. The invaders lost only thirty men killed, and the Spaniards between fifty and sixty, but among the latter were the two alcaldes and many other officers and prominent citizens of the town.[176]

To satisfactorily explain at Madrid these two presumptuous assaults upon Spanish territory in America was an embarrassing problem for the English Government, especially as Myngs' men imprisoned at Seville and Cadiz were said to have produced commissions to justify their actions.[177] The Spanish king instructed his resident in London to demand whether Charles accepted responsibility for the attack upon St. Jago, and the proceedings of English cases in the Spanish courts arising from the depredations of Galician corsairs were indefinitely suspended.[178] When, however, there followed upon this, in May 1663, the news of the sack and burning of Campeache, it stirred up the greatest excitement in Madrid.[179] Orders and, what was rarer in Spain, money were immediately sent to Cadiz to the Duke of Albuquerque to hasten the work on the royal Armada for despatch to the Indies; and efforts were made to resuscitate the defunct Armada de Barlovento, a small fleet which had formerly been used to catch interlopers and protect the coasts of Terra-Firma. In one way the capture of Campeache had touched Spain in her most vulnerable spot. The Mexican Flota, which was scheduled to sail from Havana in June 1663, refused to stir from its retreat at Vera Cruz until the galleons from Porto Bello came to convoy it. The arrival of the American treasure in Spain was thus delayed for two months, and the bankrupt government put to sore straits for money.

The activity of the Spaniards, however, was merely a blind to hide their own impotence, and their clamours were eventually satisfied by the King of England's writing to Deputy-Governor Lyttleton a letter forbidding all such undertakings for the future. The text of the letter is as follows: "Understanding with what jealousy and offence the Spaniards look upon our island of Jamaica, and how disposed they are to make some attempt upon it, and knowing how disabled it will remain in its own defence if encouragement be given to such undertakings as have lately been set on foot, and are yet pursued, and which divert the inhabitants from that industry which alone can render the island considerable, the king signifies his dislike of all such undertakings, and commands that no such be pursued for the future, but that they unitedly apply themselves to the improvement of the plantation and keeping the force in proper condition."[180] The original draft of the letter was much milder in tone, and betrays the real attitude of Charles II. toward these half-piratical enterprises: "His Majesty has heard of the success of the undertaking upon Cuba, in which he cannot choose but please himself in the vigour and resolution wherein it was performed … but because His Majesty cannot foresee any utility likely to arise thereby … he has thought fit hereby to command him to give no encouragement to such undertakings unless they may be performed by the frigates or men-of-war attending that place without any addition from the soldiers or inhabitants."[181] Other letters were subsequently sent to Jamaica, which made it clear that the war of the privateers was not intended to be called off by the king's instructions; and Sir Charles Lyttleton, therefore, did not recall their commissions. Nevertheless, in the early part of 1664, the assembly in Jamaica passed an act prohibiting public levies of men upon foreign designs, and forbidding any person to leave the island on any such design without first obtaining leave from the governor, council and assembly.[182]

When the instructions of the authorities at home were so ambiguous, and the incentives to corsairing so alluring, it was natural that this game of baiting the Spaniards should suffer little interruption. English freebooters who had formerly made Hispaniola and Tortuga their headquarters now resorted to Jamaica, where they found a cordial welcome and a better market for their plunder. Thus in June 1663 a certain Captain Barnard sailed from Port Royal to the Orinoco, took and plundered the town of Santo Tomas and returned in the following March.[183] On 19th October another privateer named Captain Cooper brought into Port Royal two Spanish prizes, the larger of which, the "Maria" of Seville, was a royal azogue and carried 1000 quintals of quicksilver for the King of Spain's mines in Mexico, besides oil, wine and olives.[184] Cooper in his fight with the smaller vessel so disabled his own ship that he was forced to abandon it and enter the prize; and it was while cruising off Hispaniola in this prize that he fell in with the "Maria," and captured her after a four hours' combat. There were seventy prisoners, among them a number of friars going to Campeache and Vera Cruz. Some of the prize goods were carried to England, and Don Patricio Moledi, the Spanish resident in London, importuned the English government for its restoration.[185] Sir Charles Lyttleton had sailed for England on 2nd May 1664, leaving the government of Jamaica in the hands of the Council with Colonel Thomas Lynch as president;[186] and on his arrival in England he made formal answer to the complaints of Moledi. His excuse was that Captain Cooper's commission had been derived not from the deputy-governor himself but from Lord Windsor; and that the deputy-governor had never received any order from the king for recalling commissions, or for the cessation of hostilities against the Spaniards.[187] Lyttleton and the English government were evidently attempting the rather difficult circus feat of riding two mounts at the same time. The instructions from England, as Lyttleton himself acknowledged in his letter of 15th October 1663, distinctly forbade further hostilities against the Spanish plantations; on the other hand, there were no specific orders that privateers should be recalled. Lyttleton was from first to last in sympathy with the freebooters, and probably believed with many others of his time that "the Spaniard is most pliable when best beaten." In August 1664 he presented to the Lord Chancellor his reasons for advocating a continuance of the privateers in Jamaica. They are sufficiently interesting to merit a *résumé* of the principal points advanced. 1st. Privateering maintained a great number of seamen by whom the island was protected without the immediate necessity of a naval force. 2nd. If privateering were forbidden, the king would lose many men who, in case of a war in the West Indies, would be of incalculable service, being acquainted, as they were, with the coasts, shoals, currents, winds, etc., of the Spanish dominions. 3rd. Without the privateers, the Jamaicans would have no intelligence of Spanish designs against them, or of the size or neighbourhood of their fleets, or of the strength of their resources. 4th. If prize-goods were no longer brought into Port Royal, few merchants would resort to Jamaica and prices would become excessively high. 5th. To reduce the privateers would require a large number of frigates at considerable trouble and expense; English seamen, moreover, generally had the privateering spirit and would be more ready to join with them than oppose them, as previous experience had shown. Finally, the privateers, if denied the freedom of Jamaican ports, would not take to planting, but would resort to the islands of other nations, and perhaps prey upon English commerce.[188]

Chapter IV
Tortuga — 1655-1664

When the Chevalier de Fontenay was driven from Tortuga in January 1654, the Spaniards left a small garrison to occupy the fort and prevent further settlements of French and English buccaneers. These troops possessed the island for about eighteen months, but on the approach of the expedition under Penn and Venables were ordered by the Conde de Penalva, President of S. Domingo, to demolish the fort, bury the artillery and other arms, and retire to his aid in Hispaniola.[189] Some six months later an Englishman, Elias Watts,[190] with his family and ten or twelve others, came from Jamaica in a shallop, re-settled the island, and raised a battery of four guns upon the ruins of the larger fort previously erected by the French. Watts received a commission for the island from General Brayne, who was then governor of Jamaica, and in a short time gathered about him a colony of about 150, both English and French. Among these new-comers was a "poor distressed gentleman" by the name of James Arundell, formerly a colonel in the Royalist army and now banished from England, who eventually married Watts' daughter and became the head of the colony.

It was while Watts was governor of Tortuga, if we are to believe the Jesuit, Dutertre, that the buccaneers determined to avenge the treachery of the Spaniards to a French vessel in that neighbourhood by plundering the city of St. Jago in Hispaniola. According to this historian, who from the style of the narrative seems to be reporting the words of an eye-witness, the buccaneers, including doubtless both hunters and corsairs, formed a party of 400 men under the leadership of four captains and obtained a commission for the enterprise from the English governor, who was very likely looking forward to a share of the booty. Compelling the captain of a frigate which had just arrived from Nantes to lend his ship, they embarked in it and in two or three other boats found on the coast for Puerta de Plata, where they landed on Palm Sunday of 1659.[191] St. Jago, which lay in a pleasant, fertile plain some fifteen or twenty leagues in the interior of Hispaniola, they approached through the woods on the night of Holy Wednesday, entered before daybreak, and surprised the governor in his bed. The buccaneers told him to prepare to die, whereupon he fell on his knees and prayed to such effect that they finally offered him his life for a ransom of 60,000 pieces of eight. They pillaged for twenty-four hours, taking even the bells, ornaments and sacred vessels of the churches, and after refreshing themselves with food and drink, retreated with their plunder and prisoners, including the governor and chief inhabitants. Meanwhile the alarm had been given for ten or twelve leagues round about. Men came in from all directions, and rallying with the inhabitants of the town till they amounted to about 1000 men, marched through the woods by a by-route, got ahead of the buccaneers and attacked them from ambush. The English and French stood their ground in spite of inferior numbers, for they were all good marksmen and every shot told. As the Spaniards persisted, however, they finally threatened to stab the governor and all the other prisoners, whereupon the Spaniards took counsel and retired to their homes. The invaders lost only ten killed and five or six wounded. They tarried on the coast several days waiting for the rest of the promised ransom, but as it failed to arrive they liberated the prisoners and returned to Tortuga, each adventurer receiving 300 crowns as his share of the pillage.[192]

In the latter part of 1659 a French gentleman, Jérémie Deschamps, seigneur du Rausset, who had been one of the first inhabitants of Tortuga under Levasseur and de Fontenay, repaired to England and had sufficient influence there to obtain an order from the Council of State to Colonel Doyley to give him a commission as governor of Tortuga, with such instructions as Doyley might think requisite.[193] This same du Rausset, it seems, had received a French commission from Louis XIV. as early as November 1656.[194] At any rate, he came to Jamaica in 1660 and obtained his commission from Doyley on condition that he held Tortuga in the English interest.[195] Watts, it seems, had meanwhile learnt that he was to be superseded by a Frenchman, whereupon he embarked with his family and all his goods and sought refuge in New England. About two months later, according to one story, Doyley heard that Deschamps had given a commission to a privateer and committed insolences for which Doyley feared to be called to account. He sent to remonstrate with him, but Deschamps answered that he possessed a French commission and that he had better interest with the powers in England than had the governor of Jamaica. As there were more French than English on the island, Deschamps then proclaimed the King of France and set up the French colours.[196] Doyley as yet had received no authority from the newly-restored king, Charles II., and hesitated to use any force; but he did give permission to Arundell, Watts' son-in-law, to surprise Deschamps and carry him to Jamaica for trial. Deschamps was absent at the time at Santa Cruz, but Arundell, relying upon the friendship and esteem which the inhabitants had felt for his father-in-law, surprised the governor's nephew and deputy, the Sieur de la Place, and possessed himself of the island. By some mischance or neglect, however, he was disarmed by the French and sent back to Jamaica.[197] This was not the end of his misfortunes. On the way to Jamaica he and his company were surprised by Spaniards in the bay of Matanzas in Cuba, and carried to Puerto Principe. There, after a month's imprisonment, Arundell and Barth. Cock, his shipmaster, were taken out by negroes into the bush and murdered, and their heads brought into the town.[198] Deschamps later returned to France because of ill-health, leaving la Place to govern the island in his stead, and when the property of the French Antilles was vested in the new French West India Company in 1664 he was arrested and sent to the Bastille. The cause of his arrest is obscure, but it seems that he had been in correspondence with the English government, to whom he had offered to restore Tortuga on condition of being reimbursed with £6000 sterling. A few days in the Bastille made him think better of his resolution. He ceded his rights to the company for 15,000 livres, and was released from confinement in November.[199]

The fiasco of Arundell's attempt was not the only effort of the English to recover the island. In answer to a memorial presented by Lord Windsor before his departure for Jamaica, an Order in Council was delivered to him in February 1662, empowering him to use his utmost endeavours to reduce Tortuga and its governor to obedience.[200] The matter was taken up by the Jamaican Council in September, shortly after Windsor's arrival;[201] and on 16th December an order was issued by deputy-governor Lyttleton to Captain Robert Munden of the "Charles" frigate for the transportation of Colonel Samuel Barry and Captain Langford to Tortuga, where Munden was to receive orders for reducing the island.[202] The design miscarried again, however, probably because of ill-blood between Barry and Munden. Clement de Plenneville, who accompanied Barry, writes that "the expedition failed through treachery";[203] and Beeston says in his Journal that Barry, approaching Tortuga on 30th January, found the French armed and ready to oppose him, whereupon he ordered Captain Munden to fire. Munden however refused, sailed away to Corydon in Hispaniola, where he put Barry and his men on shore, and then "went away about his merchandize."[204] Barry made his way in a sloop to Jamaica where he arrived on 1st March. Langford, however, was sent to Petit-Goave, an island about the size of Tortuga in the *cul-de-sac* at the western end of Hispaniola, where he was chosen governor by the inhabitants and raised the first English standard. Petit-Goave had been frequented by buccaneers since 1659, and after d'Ogeron succeeded du Rausset as governor for the French in those regions, it became with Tortuga one of their chief resorts. In the latter part of 1664 we find Langford in England petitioning the king for a commission as governor of Tortuga and the coast of Hispaniola, and for two ships to go and seize the smaller island.[205] Such a design, however, with the direct sanction and aid of the English government, might have endangered a rupture with France. Charles preferred to leave such irregular warfare to his governor in Jamaica, whom he could support or disown as best suited the exigencies of the moment. Langford, moreover, seems not to have made a brilliant success of his short stay at Petit-Goave, and was probably distrusted by the authorities both in England and in the West Indies. When Modyford came as governor to Jamaica, the possibility of recovering Tortuga was still discussed, but no effort to effect it was ever made again.

Chapter V
Porto Bello and Panama

On 4th January 1664, the king wrote to Sir Thomas Modyford in Barbadoes that he had chosen him governor of Jamaica.[206] Modyford, who had lived as a planter in Barbadoes since 1650, had taken a prominent share in the struggles between Parliamentarians and Royalists in the little island. He was a member of the Council, and had been governor for a short time in 1660. His commission and instructions for Jamaica[207] were carried to the West Indies by Colonel Edward Morgan, who went as Modyford's deputy-governor and landed in Barbadoes on 21st April.[208] Modyford was instructed, among other things, to prohibit the granting of letters of marque, and particularly to encourage trade and maintain friendly relations with the Spanish dominions. Sir Richard Fanshaw had just been appointed to go to Spain and negotiate a treaty for wider commercial privileges in the Indies, and Charles saw that the daily complaints of violence and depredation done by Jamaican ships on the King of Spain's subjects were scarcely calculated to increase the good-will and compliance of the Spanish Court. Nor had the attempt in the Indies to force a trade upon the Spaniards been brilliantly successful. It was soon evident that another course of action was demanded. Sir Thomas Modyford seems at first to have been sincerely anxious to suppress privateering and conciliate his Spanish neighbours. On receiving his commission and instructions he immediately prepared letters to the President of San Domingo, expressing his fair intentions and requesting the co-operation of the Spaniards.[209] Modyford himself arrived in Jamaica on 1st June,[210] proclaimed an entire cessation of hostilities,[211] and on the 16th sent the "Swallow" ketch to Cartagena to acquaint the governor with what he had done.

On almost the same day letters were forwarded from England and from Ambassador Fanshaw in Madrid, strictly forbidding all violences in the future against the Spanish nation, and ordering Modyford to inflict condign punishment on every offender, and make entire restitution and satisfaction to the sufferers.[212]

The letters for San Domingo, which had been forwarded to Jamaica with Colonel Morgan and thence dispatched to Hispaniola before Modyford's arrival, received a favourable answer, but that was about as far as the matter ever got. The buccaneers, moreover, the principal grievance of the Spaniards, still remained at large. As Thomas Lynch wrote on 25th May, "It is not in the power of the governor to have or suffer a commerce, nor will any necessity or advantage bring private Spaniards to Jamaica, for we and they have used too many mutual barbarisms to have a sudden correspondence. When the king was restored, the Spaniards thought the manners of the English nation changed too, and adventured twenty or thirty vessels to Jamaica for blacks, but the surprises and irruptions by C. Myngs, for whom the governor of San Domingo has upbraided the commissioners, made the Spaniards redouble their malice, and nothing but an order from Spain can give us admittance or trade."[213] For a short time, however, a serious effort was made to recall the privateers. Several prizes which were brought into Port Royal were seized and returned to their owners, while the captors had their commissions taken from them. Such was the experience of one Captain Searles, who in August brought in two Spanish vessels, both of which were restored to the Spaniards, and Searles deprived of his rudder and sails as security against his making further depredations upon the Dons.[214] In November Captain Morris Williams sent a note to Governor Modyford, offering to come in with a rich prize of logwood, indigo and silver, if security were given that it should be condemned to him for the payment of his debts in Jamaica; and although the governor refused to give any promises the prize was brought in eight days later. The goods were seized and sold in the interest of the Spanish owner.[215] Nevertheless, the effects of the proclamation were not at all encouraging. In the first month only three privateers came in with their commissions, and Modyford wrote to Secretary Bennet on 30th June that he feared the only effect of the proclamation would be to drive them to the French in Tortuga. He therefore thought it prudent, he continued, to dispense somewhat with the strictness of his instructions, "doing by degrees and moderation what he had at first resolved to execute suddenly and severely."[216]

Tortuga was really the crux of the whole difficulty. Back in 1662 Colonel Doyley, in his report to the Lord Chancellor after his return to England, had suggested the reduction of Tortuga to English obedience as the only effective way of dealing with the buccaneers;[217] and Modyford in 1664 also realized the necessity of this preliminary step.[218] The conquest of Tortuga, however, was no longer the simple task it might have been four or five years earlier. The inhabitants of the island were now almost entirely French, and with their companions on the coast of Hispaniola had no intention of submitting to English dictation. The buccaneers, who had become numerous and independent and made Tortuga one of their principal retreats, would throw all their strength in the balance against an expedition the avowed object of whose coming was to make their profession impossible. The colony, moreover, received an incalculable accession of strength in the arrival of Bertrand d'Ogeron, the governor sent out in 1665 by the new French West India Company. D'Ogeron was one of the most remarkable figures in the West Indies in the second half of the seventeenth century. Of broad imagination and singular kindness of heart, with an indomitable will and a mind full of resource, he seems to have been an ideal man for the task, not only of reducing to some semblance of law and order a people who had never given obedience to any authority, but also of making palatable the *régime* and exclusive privileges of a private trading company. D'Ogeron first established himself at Port Margot on the coast of Hispaniola opposite Tortuga in the early part of 1665; and here the adventurers at once gave him to understand that they would never submit to any mere company, much less suffer an interruption of their trade with the Dutch, who had supplied them with necessities at a time when it was not even known in France that there were Frenchmen in that region. D'Ogeron pretended to subscribe to these conditions, passed over to Tortuga where he received the submission of la Place, and then to Petit-Goave and Leogane, in the *cul-de-sac* of Hispaniola. There he made his headquarters, adopted every means to attract planters and *engagés*, and firmly established his authority. He made advances from his own purse without interest to adventurers who wished to settle down to planting, bought two ships to facilitate trade between the colony and France, and even contrived to have several lots of fifty women each brought over from France to be sold and distributed as wives amongst the colonists. The settlements soon put on a new air of prosperity, and really owed their existence as a permanent French colony to the efforts of this new governor.[219] It was under the administration of d'Ogeron that l'Olonnais,[220] Michel le Basque, and most of the French buccaneers flourished, whose exploits are celebrated in Exquemelin's history.

The conquest of Tortuga was not the only measure necessary for the effectual suppression of the buccaneers. Five or six swift cruisers were also required to pursue and bring to bay those corsairs who refused to come in with their commissions.[221] Since the Restoration the West Indies had been entirely denuded of English men-of-war; while the buccaneers, with the tacit consent or encouragement of Doyley, had at the same time increased both in numbers and boldness. Letters written from Jamaica in 1664 placed the number scattered abroad in privateering at from 1500 to 2000, sailing in fourteen or fifteen ships.[222] They were desperate men, accustomed to living at sea, with no trade but burning and plundering, and unlikely to take orders from any but stronger and faster frigates. Nor was this condition of affairs surprising when we consider that, in the seventeenth century, there flowed from Europe to the West Indies adventurers from every class of society; men doubtless often endowed with strong personalities, enterprising and intrepid; but often, too, of mediocre intelligence or little education, and usually without either money or scruples. They included many who had revolted from the narrow social laws of European countries, and were disinclined to live peaceably within the bounds of any organized society. Many, too, had belonged to rebellious political factions at home, men of the better classes who were banished or who emigrated in order to keep their heads upon their shoulders. In France the total exhaustion of public and private fortune at the end of the religious wars disposed many to seek to recoup themselves out of the immense colonial riches of the Spaniards; while the disorders of the Rebellion and the Commonwealth in England caused successive emigrations of Puritans and Loyalists to the newer England beyond the seas. At the close of the Thirty Years' War, too, a host of French and English adventurers, who had fattened upon Germany and her misfortunes, were left without a livelihood, and doubtless many resorted to emigration as the sole means of continuing their life of freedom and even of licence. Coming to the West Indies these men, so various in origin and character, hoped soon to acquire there the riches which they lost or coveted at home; and their expectations deceived, they often broke in a formal and absolute manner the bonds which attached them to their fellow humanity. Jamaica especially suffered in this respect, for it had been colonized in the first instance by a discontented, refractory soldiery, and it was being recruited largely by transported criminals and vagabonds. In contrast with the policy of Spain, who placed the most careful restrictions upon the class of emigrants sent to her American possessions, England from the very beginning used her colonies, and especially the West Indian islands, as a dumping-ground for her refuse population. Within a short time a regular trade sprang up for furnishing the colonies with servile labour from the prisons of the mother country. Scots captured at the battles of Dunbar and Worcester,[223] English, French, Irish and Dutch pirates lying in the gaols of Dorchester and Plymouth,[224] if "not thought fit to be tried for their lives," were shipped to Barbadoes, Jamaica, and the other Antilles. In August 1656 the Council of State issued an order for the apprehension of all lewd and dangerous persons, rogues, vagrants and other idlers who had no way of livelihood and refused to work, to be transported by contractors to the English plantations in America;[225] and in June 1661 the Council for Foreign Plantations appointed a committee to consider the same matter.[226] Complaints were often made that children and apprentices were "seduced or spirited away" from their parents and masters and concealed upon ships sailing for the colonies; and an office of registry was established to prevent this abuse.[227] In 1664 Charles granted a licence for five years to Sir James Modyford, brother of Sir Thomas, to take all felons convicted in the circuits and at the Old Bailey who were afterwards reprieved for transportation to foreign plantations, and to transmit them to the governor of Jamaica;[228] and this practice was continued throughout the whole of the buccaneering period.

Privateering opened a channel by which these disorderly spirits, impatient of the sober and laborious life of the planter, found an employment agreeable to their tastes. An example had been set by the plundering expeditions sent out by Fortescue, Brayne and Doyley, and when these naval excursions ceased, the sailors and others who had taken part in them fell to robbing on their private account. Sir Charles Lyttleton, we have seen, zealously defended and encouraged the freebooters; and Long, the historian of Jamaica, justified their existence on the ground that many traders were attracted to the island by the plunder with which Port Royal was so abundantly stocked, and that the prosperity of the colony was founded upon the great demand for provisions for the outfit of the privateers. These effects, however, were but temporary and superficial, and did not counterbalance the manifest evils of the practice, especially the discouragement to planting, and the element of turbulence and unrest ever present in the island. Under such conditions Governor Modyford found it necessary to temporise with the marauders, and perhaps he did so the more readily because he felt that they were still needed for the security of the colony. A war between England and the States-General then seemed imminent, and the governor considered that unless he allowed the buccaneers to dispose of their booty when they came in to Port Royal, they might, in event of hostilities breaking out, go to the Dutch at Curaçao and other islands, and prey upon Jamaican commerce. On the other hand, if, by adopting a conciliatory attitude, he retained their allegiance, they would offer the handiest and most effective instrument for driving the Dutch themselves out of the Indies.[229] He privately told one captain, who brought in a Spanish prize, that he only stopped the Admiralty proceedings to "give a good relish to the Spaniard"; and that although the captor should have satisfaction, the governor could not guarantee him his ship. So Sir Thomas persuaded some merchants to buy the prize-goods and contributed one quarter of the money himself, with the understanding that he should receive nothing if the Spaniards came to claim their property.[230] A letter from Secretary Bennet, on 12th November 1664, confirmed the governor in this course;[231] and on 2nd February 1665, three weeks before the declaration of war against Holland, a warrant was issued to the Duke of York, High Admiral of England, to grant, through the colonial governors and vice-admirals, commissions of reprisal upon the ships and goods of the Dutch.[232] Modyford at once took advantage of this liberty. Some fourteen pirates, who in the beginning of February had been tried and condemned to death, were pardoned; and public declaration was made that commissions would be granted against the Hollanders. Before nightfall two commissions had been taken out, and all the rovers were making applications and planning how to seize Curaçao.[233] Modyford drew up an elaborate design[234] for rooting out at one and the same time the Dutch settlements and the French buccaneers, and on 20th April he wrote that Lieutenant-Colonel Morgan had sailed with ten ships and some 500 men, chiefly "reformed prisoners," resolute fellows, and well armed with fusees and pistols.[235] Their plan was to fall upon the Dutch fleet trading at St. Kitts, capture St. Eustatius, Saba, and perhaps Curaçao, and on the homeward voyage visit the French settlements on Hispaniola and Tortuga. "All this is prepared," he wrote, "by the honest privateer, at the old rate of no purchase no pay, and it will cost the king nothing considerable, some powder and mortar-pieces." On the same day, 20th April, Admiral de Ruyter, who had arrived in the Indies with a fleet of fourteen sail, attacked the forts and shipping at Barbadoes, but suffered considerable damage and retired after a few hours. At Montserrat and Nevis, however, he was more successful and captured sixteen merchant ships, after which he sailed for Virginia and New York.[236]

The buccaneers enrolled in Colonel Morgan's expedition proved to be troublesome allies. Before their departure from Jamaica most of them mutinied, and refused to sail until promised by Morgan that the plunder should be equally divided.[237] On 17th July, however, the expedition made its rendezvous at Montserrat, and on the 23rd arrived before St. Eustatius. Two vessels had been lost sight of, a third, with the ironical name of the "Olive Branch," had sailed for Virginia, and many stragglers had been left behind at Montserrat, so that Morgan could muster only 326 men for the assault. There was only one landing-place on the island, with a narrow path accommodating but two men at a time leading to an eminence which was crowned with a fort and 450 Dutchmen. Morgan landed his division first, and Colonel Carey followed. The enemy, it seems, gave them but one small volley and then retreated to the fort. The governor sent forward three men to parley, and on receiving a summons to surrender, delivered up the fort with eleven large guns and considerable ammunition. "It is supposed they were drunk or mad," was the comment made upon the rather disgraceful defence.[238] During the action Colonel Morgan, who was an old man and very corpulent, was overcome by the hard marching and extraordinary heat, and died. Colonel Carey, who succeeded him in command, was anxious to proceed at once to the capture of the Dutch forts on Saba, St. Martins and Tortola; but the buccaneers refused to stir until the booty got at St. Eustatius was divided—nor were the officers and men able to agree on the manner of sharing. The plunder, besides guns and ammunition, included about 900 slaves, negro and Indian, with a large quantity of live stock and cotton. Meanwhile a party of seventy had crossed over to the island of Saba, only four leagues distant, and secured its surrender on the same terms as St. Eustatius. As the men had now become very mutinous, and on a muster numbered scarcely 250, the officers decided that they could not reasonably proceed any further and sailed for Jamaica, leaving a small garrison on each of the islands. Most of the Dutch, about 250 in number, were sent to St. Martins, but a few others, with some threescore English, Irish and Scotch, took the oath of allegiance and remained.[239]

Encouraged by a letter from the king,[240] Governor Modyford continued his exertions against the Dutch. In January (?) 1666 two buccaneer captains, Searles and Stedman, with two small ships and only eighty men took the island of Tobago, near Trinidad, and destroyed everything they could not carry away. Lord Willoughby, governor of Barbadoes, had also fitted out an expedition to take the island, but the Jamaicans were three or four days before him. The latter were busy with their work of pillage, when Willoughby arrived and demanded the island in the name of the king; and the buccaneers condescended to leave the fort and the governor's house standing only on condition that Willoughby gave them liberty to sell their plunder in Barbadoes.[241] Modyford, meanwhile, greatly disappointed by the miscarriage of the design against Curaçao, called in the aid of the "old privateer," Captain Edward Mansfield, and in the autumn of 1665, with the hope of sending another armament against the island, appointed a rendezvous for the buccaneers in Bluefields Bay.[242]

In January 1666 war against England was openly declared by France in support of her Dutch allies, and in the following month Charles II. sent letters to his governors in the West Indies and the North American colonies, apprising them of the war and urging them to attack their French neighbours.[243] The news of the outbreak of hostilities did not reach Jamaica until 2nd July, but already in December of the previous year warning had been sent out to the West Indies of the coming rupture.[244] Governor Modyford, therefore, seeing the French very much increased in Hispaniola, concluded that it was high time to entice the buccaneers from French service and bind them to himself by issuing commissions against the Spaniards. The French still permitted the freebooters to dispose of Spanish prizes in their ports, but the better market afforded by Jamaica was always a sufficient consideration to attract not only the English buccaneers, but the Dutch and French as well. Moreover, the difficulties of the situation, which Modyford had repeatedly enlarged upon in his letters, seem to have been appreciated by the authorities in England, for in the spring of 1665, following upon Secretary Bennet's letter of 12th November and shortly after the outbreak of the Dutch war, the Duke of Albemarle had written to Modyford in the name of the king, giving him permission to use his own discretion in granting commissions against the Dons.[245] Modyford was convinced that all the circumstances were favourable to such a course of action, and on 22nd February assembled the Council. A resolution was passed that it was to the interest of the island to grant letters of marque against the Spaniards,[246] and a proclamation to this effect was published by the governor at Port Royal and Tortuga. In the following August Modyford sent home to Bennet, now become Lord Arlington, an elaborate defence of his actions. "Your Lordship very well knows," wrote Modyford, "how great an aversion I had for the privateers while at Barbadoes, but after I had put His Majesty's orders for restitution in strict execution, I found my error in the decay of the forts and wealth of this place, and also the affections of this people to His Majesty's service; yet I continued discountenancing and punishing those kind of people till your Lordship's of the 12th November 1664 arrived, commanding a gentle usage of them; still we went to decay, which I represented to the Lord General faithfully the 6th of March following, who upon serious consideration with His Majesty and the Lord Chancellor, by letter of 1st June 1665, gave me latitude to grant or not commissions against the Spaniard, as I found it for the advantage of His Majesty's service and the good of this island. I was glad of this power, yet resolved not to use it unless necessity drove me to it; and that too when I saw how poor the fleets returning from Statia were, so that vessels were broken up and the men disposed of for the coast of Cuba to get a livelihood and so be wholly alienated from us. Many stayed at the Windward Isles, having not enough to pay their engagements, and at Tortuga and among the French buccaneers; still I forebore to make use of my power, hoping their hardships and great hazards would in time reclaim them from that course of life. But about the beginning of March last I found that the guards of Port Royal, which under Colonel Morgan were 600, had fallen to 138, so I assembled the Council to advise how to strengthen that most important place with some of the inland forces; but they all agreed that the only way to fill Port Royal with men was to grant commissions against the Spaniards, which they were very pressing in … and looking on our weak condition, the chief merchants gone from Port Royal, no credit given to privateers for victualling, etc., and rumours of war with the French often repeated, I issued a declaration of my intentions to grant commissions against the Spaniards. Your Lordship cannot imagine what an universal change there was on the faces of men and things, ships repairing, great resort of workmen and labourers to Port Royal, many returning, many debtors released out of prison, and the ships from the Curaçao voyage, not daring to come in for fear of creditors, brought in and fitted out again, so that the regimental forces at Port Royal are near 400. Had it not been for that seasonable action, I could not have kept my place against the French buccaneers, who would have ruined all the seaside plantations at least, whereas I now draw from them mainly, and lately David Marteen, the best man of Tortuga, that has two frigates at sea, has promised to bring in both."[247]

In so far as the buccaneers affected the mutual relations of England and Spain, it after all could make little difference whether commissions were issued in Jamaica or not, for the plundering and burning continued, and the harassed Spanish-Americans, only too prone to call the rogues English of whatever origin they might really be, continued to curse and hate the English nation and make cruel reprisals whenever possible. Moreover, every expedition into Spanish territory, finding the Spaniards very weak and very rich, gave new incentive to such endeavour. While Modyford had been standing now on one foot, now on the other, uncertain whether to repulse the buccaneers or not, secretly anxious to welcome them, but fearing the authorities at home, the corsairs themselves had entirely ignored him. The privateers whom Modyford had invited to rendezvous in Bluefield's Bay in November 1665 had chosen Captain Mansfield as their admiral, and in the middle of January sailed from the south cays of Cuba for Curaçao. In the meantime, however, because they had been refused provisions which, according to Modyford's account, they sought to buy from the Spaniards in Cuba, they had marched forty-two miles into the island, and on the strength of Portuguese commissions which they held against the Spaniards, had plundered and burnt the town of Sancti Spiritus, routed a body of 200 horse, carried some prisoners to the coast, and for their ransom extorted 300 head of cattle.[248] The rich and easy profits to be got by plundering the Spaniards were almost too much for the loyalty of the men, and Modyford, hearing of many defections from their ranks, had despatched Captain Beeston on 10th November to divert them, if possible, from Sancti Spiritus, and confirm them in their designs against Curaçao.[249] The officers of the expedition, indeed, sent to the governor a letter expressing their zeal for the enterprise; but the men still held off, and the fleet, in consequence, eventually broke up. Two vessels departed for Tortuga, and four others, joined by two French rovers, sailed under Mansfield to attempt the recapture of Providence Island, which, since 1641, had been garrisoned by the Spaniards and used as a penal settlement.[250] Being resolved, as Mansfield afterwards told the governor of Jamaica, never to see Modyford's face until he had done some service to the king, he sailed for Providence with about 200 men,[251] and approaching the island in the night by an unusual passage among the reefs, landed early in the morning, and surprised and captured the Spanish commander. The garrison of about 200 yielded up the fort on the promise that they would be carried to the mainland. Twenty-seven pieces of ordnance were taken, many of which, it is said, bore the arms of Queen Elizabeth engraved upon them. Mansfield left thirty-five men under command of a Captain Hattsell to hold the island, and sailed with his prisoners for Central America. After cruising along the shores of the mainland, he ascended the San Juan River and entered and sacked Granada, the capital of Nicaragua. From Granada the buccaneers turned south into Costa Rica, burning plantations, breaking the images in the churches, ham-stringing cows and mules, cutting down the fruit trees, and in general destroying everything they found. The Spanish governor had only thirty-six soldiers at his disposal and scarcely any firearms; but he gathered the inhabitants and some Indians, blocked the roads, laid ambuscades, and did all that his pitiful means permitted to hinder the progress of the invaders. The freebooters had designed to visit Cartago, the chief city of the province, and plunder it as they had plundered Granada. They penetrated only as far as Turrialva, however, whence weary and footsore from their struggle through the Cordillera, and harassed by the Spaniards, they retired through the province of Veragua in military order to their ships.[252] On 12th June the buccaneers, laden with booty, sailed into Port Royal. There was at that moment no declared war between England and Spain. Yet the governor, probably because he believed Mansfield to be justified, *ex post facto*, by the issue of commissions against the Spaniards in the previous February, did no more than mildly reprove him for acting without his orders; and "considering its good situation for favouring any design on the rich main," he accepted the tender of the island in behalf of the king. He despatched Major Samuel Smith, who had been one of Mansfield's party, with a few soldiers to reinforce the English garrison;[253] and on 10th November the Council in England set the stamp of their approval upon his actions by issuing a commission to his brother, Sir James Modyford, to be lieutenant-governor of the new acquisition.[254]

In August 1665, only two months before the departure of Mansfield from Jamaica, there had returned to Port Royal from a raid in the same region three privateer captains named Morris, Jackman and Morgan.[255] These men, with their followers, doubtless helped to swell the ranks of Mansfield's buccaneers, and it was probably their report of the wealth of Central America which induced Mansfield to emulate their performance. In the previous January these three captains, still pretending to sail under commissions from Lord Windsor, had ascended the river Tabasco, in the province of Campeache, with 107 men, and guided by Indians made a detour of 300 miles, according to their account, to Villa de Mosa,[256] which they took and plundered. When they returned to the mouth of the river, they found that their ships had been seized by Spaniards, who, on their approach, attacked them 300 strong. The Spaniards, softened by the heat and indolent life of the tropics, were no match for one-third their number of desperadoes, and the buccaneers beat them off without the loss of a man. The freebooters then fitted up two barques and four canoes, sailed to Rio Garta and stormed the place with only thirty men; crossed the Gulf of Honduras to the Island of Roatan to rest and obtain fresh water, and then captured and plundered the port of Truxillo. Down the Mosquito Coast they passed like a devouring flame, consuming all in their path. Anchoring in Monkey Bay, they ascended the San Juan River in canoes for a distance of 100 miles to Lake Nicaragua. The basin into which they entered they described as a veritable paradise, the air cool and wholesome, the shores of the lake full of green pastures and broad savannahs dotted with horses and cattle, and round about all a coronal of azure mountains. Hiding by day among the numerous islands and rowing all night, on the fifth night they landed near the city of Granada, just a year before Mansfield's visit to the place. The buccaneers marched unobserved to the central square of the city, overturned eighteen cannon mounted there, seized the magazine, and took and imprisoned in the cathedral 300 of the citizens. They plundered for sixteen hours, then released their prisoners, and taking the precaution to scuttle all the boats, made their way back to the sea coast. The town was large and pleasant, containing seven churches besides several colleges and monasteries, and most of the buildings were constructed of stone. About 1000 Indians, driven to rebellion by the cruelty and oppression of the Spaniards, accompanied the marauders and would have massacred the prisoners, especially the religious, had they not been told that the English had no intentions of retaining their conquest. The news of the exploit produced a lively impression in Jamaica, and the governor suggested Central America as the "properest place" for an attack from England on the Spanish Indies.[257]

Providence Island was now in the hands of an English garrison, and the Spaniards were not slow to realise that the possession of this outpost by the buccaneers might be but the first step to larger conquests on the mainland. The President of Panama, Don Juan Perez de Guzman, immediately took steps to recover the island. He transferred himself to Porto Bello, embargoed an English ship of thirty guns, the "Concord," lying at anchor there with licence to trade in negroes, manned it with 350 Spaniards under command of José Sánchez Jiménez, and sent it to Cartagena. The governor of Cartagena contributed several small vessels and a hundred or more men to the enterprise, and on 10th August 1666 the united Spanish fleet appeared off the shores of Providence. On the refusal of Major Smith to surrender, the Spaniards landed, and on 15th August, after a three days' siege, forced the handful of buccaneers, only sixty or seventy in number, to capitulate. Some of the English defenders later deposed before Governor Modyford that the Spaniards had agreed to let them depart in a barque for Jamaica. However this may be, when the English came to lay down their arms they were made prisoners by the Spaniards, carried to Porto Bello, and all except Sir Thomas Whetstone, Major Smith and Captain Stanley, the three English captains, submitted to the most inhuman cruelties. Thirty-three were chained to the ground in a dungeon 12 feet by 10. They were forced to work in the water from five in the morning till seven at night, and at such a rate that the Spaniards themselves confessed they made one of them do more work than any three negroes; yet when weak for want of victuals and sleep, they were knocked down and beaten with cudgels so that four or five died. "Having no clothes, their backs were blistered with the sun, their heads scorched, their necks, shoulders and hands raw with carrying stones and mortar, their feet chopped and their legs bruised and battered with the irons, and their corpses were noisome to one another." The three English captains were carried to Panama, and there cast into a dungeon and bound in irons for seventeen months.[258]

On 8th January 1664 Sir Richard Fanshaw, formerly ambassador to Portugal, had arrived in Madrid from England to negotiate a treaty of commerce with Spain, and if possible to patch up a peace between the Spanish and Portuguese crowns. He had renewed the old demand for a free commerce in the Indies; and the negotiations had dragged through the years of 1664 and 1665, hampered and crossed by the factions in the Spanish court, the hostile machinations of the Dutch resident in Madrid, and the constant rumours of cruelties and desolations by the freebooters in America.[259] The Spanish Government insisted that by sole virtue of the articles of 1630 there was peace on both sides of the "Line," and that the violences of the buccaneers in the West Indies, and even the presence of English colonists there, was a breach of the articles. In this fashion they endeavoured to reduce Fanshaw to the position of a suppliant for favours which they might only out of their grace and generosity concede. It was a favourite trick of Spanish diplomacy, which had been worked many times before. The English ambassador was, in consequence, compelled strenuously to deny the existence of any peace in America, although he realised how ambiguous his position had been rendered by the original orders of Charles II. to Modyford in 1664.[260] After the death of Philip IV. in 1665, negotiations were renewed with the encouragement of the Queen Regent, and on 17th December provisional articles were signed by Fanshaw and the Duke de Medina de los Torres and sent to England for ratification.[261]

Fanshaw died shortly after, and Lord Sandwich, his successor, finally succeeded in concluding a treaty on 23rd May 1667.[262] The provisions of the treaty extended to places "where hitherto trade and commerce hath been accustomed," and the only privileges obtained in America were those which had been granted to the Low Countries by the Treaty of Munster. On 21st July of the same year a general peace was concluded at Breda between England, Holland and France.

It was in the very midst of Lord Sandwich's negotiations that Modyford had, as Beeston expresses it in his Journal, declared war against the Spaniards by the re-issue of privateering commissions. He had done it all in his own name, however, so that the king might disavow him should the exigencies of diplomacy demand it.[263] Moreover, at this same time, in the middle of 1666, Albemarle was writing to Modyford that notwithstanding the negotiations, in which, as he said, the West Indies were not at all concerned, the governor might still employ the privateers as formerly, if it be for the benefit of English interests in the Indies.[264] The news of the general peace reached Jamaica late in 1667; yet Modyford did not change his policy. It is true that in February Secretary Lord Arlington had sent directions to restrain the buccaneers from further acts of violence against the Spaniards;[265] but Modyford drew his own conclusions from the contradictory orders received from England, and was conscious, perhaps, that he was only reflecting the general policy of the home government when he wrote to Arlington: —"Truly it must be very imprudent to run the hazard of this place, for obtaining a correspondence which could not but by orders from Madrid be had.... The Spaniards look on us as intruders and trespassers, wheresoever they find us in the Indies, and use us accordingly; and were it in their power, as it is fixed in their wills, would soon turn us out of all our plantations; and is it reasonable that we should quietly let them grow upon us until they are able to do it? It must be force alone that can cut in sunder that unneighbourly maxim of their government to deny all access to strangers."[266]

These words were very soon translated into action, for in June 1668 Henry Morgan, with a fleet of nine or ten ships and between 400 and 500 men, took and sacked Porto Bello, one of the strongest cities of Spanish America, and the emporium for most of the European trade of the South American continent. Henry Morgan was a nephew of the Colonel Edward Morgan who died in the assault of St. Eustatius. He is said to have been kidnapped at Bristol while he was a mere lad and sold as a servant in Barbadoes, whence, on the expiration of his time, he found his way to Jamaica. There he joined the buccaneers and soon rose to be captain of a ship. It was probably he who took part in the expedition with Morris and Jackman to Campeache and Central America. He afterwards joined the Curaçao armament of Mansfield and was with the latter when he seized the island of Providence. After Mansfield's disappearance Morgan seems to have taken his place as the foremost buccaneer leader in Jamaica, and during the next twenty years he was one of the most considerable men in the colony. He was but thirty-three years old when he led the expedition against Porto Bello.[267]

In the beginning of 1668 Sir Thomas Modyford, having had "frequent and strong advice" that the Spaniards were planning an invasion of Jamaica, had commissioned Henry Morgan to draw together the English privateers and take some Spanish prisoners in order to find out if these rumours were true. The buccaneers, according to Morgan's own report to the governor, were driven to the south cays of Cuba, where being in want of victuals and "like to starve," and meeting some Frenchmen in a similar plight, they put their men ashore to forage. They found all the cattle driven up into the country, however, and the inhabitants fled. So the freebooters marched twenty leagues to Puerto Principe on the north side of the island, and after a short encounter, in which the Spanish governor was killed, possessed themselves of the place. Nothing of value escaped the rapacity of the invaders, who resorted to the extremes of torture to draw from their prisoners confessions of hidden wealth. On the entreaty of the Spaniards they forebore to fire the town, and for a ransom of 1000 head of cattle released all the prisoners; but they compelled the Spaniards to salt the beef and carry it to the ships.[268] Morgan reported, with what degree of truth we have no means of judging, that seventy men had been impressed in Puerto Principe to go against Jamaica, and that a similar levy had been made throughout the island. Considerable forces, moreover, were expected from the mainland to rendezvous at Havana and St. Jago, with the final object of invading the English colony.

On returning to the ships from the sack of Puerto Principe, Morgan unfolded to his men his scheme of striking at the very heart of Spanish power in the Indies by capturing Porto Bello. The Frenchmen among his followers, it seems, wholly refused to join him in this larger design, full of danger as it was; so Morgan sailed away with only the English freebooters, some 400 in number, for the coasts of Darien. Exquemelin has left us a narrative of this exploit which is more circumstantial than any other we possess, and agrees so closely with what we know from other sources that we must accept the author's statement that he was an eye-witness. He relates the whole story, moreover, in so entertaining and picturesque a manner that he deserves quotation.

"Captain Morgan," he says, "who knew very well all the avenues of this city, as also all the neighbouring coasts, arrived in the dusk of the evening at the place called Puerto de Naos, distant ten leagues towards the west of Porto Bello.[269] Being come unto this place, they mounted the river in their ships, as far as another harbour called Puerto Pontin, where they came to anchor. Here they put themselves immediately into boats and canoes, leaving in the ships only a few men to keep them and conduct them the next day unto the port. About midnight they came to a certain place called Estera longa Lemos, where they all went on shore, and marched by land to the first posts of the city. They had in their company a certain Englishman, who had been formerly a prisoner in those parts, and who now served them for a guide. Unto him, and three or four more, they gave commission to take the sentry, if possible, or to kill him upon the place. But they laid hands on him and apprehended him with such cunning as he had no time to give warning with his musket, or make any other noise. Thus they brought him, with his hands bound, unto Captain Morgan, who asked him: 'How things went in the city, and what forces they had'; with many other circumstances, which he was desirous to know. After every question they made him a thousand menaces to kill him, in case he declared not the truth. Thus they began to advance towards the city, carrying always the said sentry bound before them. Having marched about one quarter of a league, they came to the castle that is nigh unto the city, which presently they closely surrounded, so that no person could get either in or out of the said fortress.

"Being thus posted under the walls of the castle, Captain Morgan commanded the sentry, whom they had taken prisoner, to speak to those that were within, charging them to surrender, and deliver themselves up to his discretion; otherwise they should be all cut in pieces, without giving quarter to any one. But they would hearken to none of these threats, beginning instantly to fire; which gave notice unto the city, and this was suddenly alarmed. Yet, notwithstanding, although the Governor and soldiers of the said castle made as great resistance as could be performed, they were constrained to surrender unto the Pirates. These no sooner had taken the castle, than they resolved to be as good as their words, in putting the Spaniards to the sword, thereby to strike a terror into the rest of the city. Hereupon, having shut up all the soldiers and officers as prisoners into one room, they instantly set fire to the powder (whereof they found great quantity), and blew up the whole castle into the air, with all the Spaniards that were within. This being done, they pursued the course of their victory, falling upon the city, which as yet was not in order to receive them. Many of the inhabitants cast their precious jewels and moneys into wells and cisterns or hid them in other places underground, to excuse, as much as were possible, their being totally robbed. One party of the Pirates being assigned to this purpose, ran immediately to the cloisters, and took as many religious men and women as they could find. The Governor of the city not being able to rally the citizens, through the huge confusion of the town, retired unto one of the castles remaining, and from thence began to fire incessantly at the Pirates. But these were not in the least negligent either to assault him or defend themselves with all the courage imaginable. Thus it was observed that, amidst the horror of the assault, they made very few shot in vain. For aiming with great dexterity at the mouths of the guns, the Spaniards were certain to lose one or two men every time they charged each gun anew.

"The assault of this castle where the Governor was continued very furious on both sides, from break of day until noon. Yea, about this time of the day the case was very dubious which party should conquer or be conquered. At last the Pirates, perceiving they had lost many men and as yet advanced but little towards the gaining either this or the other castles remaining, thought to make use of fireballs, which they threw with their hands, designing, if possible, to burn the doors of the castle. But going about to put this in execution, the Spaniards from the walls let fall great quantity of stones and earthen pots full of powder and other combustible matter, which forced them to desist from that attempt. Captain Morgan, seeing this generous defence made by the Spaniards, began to despair of the whole success of the enterprise. Hereupon many faint and calm meditations came into his mind; neither could he determine which way to turn himself in that straitness of affairs. Being involved in these thoughts, he was suddenly animated to continue the assault, by seeing the English colours put forth at one of the lesser castles, then entered by his men, of whom he presently after spied a troop that came to meet him proclaiming victory with loud shouts of joy. This instantly put him upon new resolutions of making new efforts to take the rest of the castles that stood out against him; especially seeing the chief citizens were fled unto them, and had conveyed thither great part of their riches, with all the plate belonging to the churches, and other things dedicated to divine service.

"To this effect, therefore, he ordered ten or twelve ladders to be made, in all possible haste, so broad that three or four men at once might ascend by them. These being finished, he commanded all the religious men and women whom he had taken prisoners to fix them against the walls of the castle. Thus much he had beforehand threatened the Governor to perform, in case he delivered not the castle. But his answer was: 'He would never surrender himself alive.' Captain Morgan was much persuaded that the Governor would not employ his utmost forces, seeing religious women and ecclesiastical persons exposed in the front of the soldiers to the greatest dangers. Thus the ladders, as I have said, were put into the hands of religious persons of both sexes; and these were forced, at the head of the companies, to raise and apply them to the walls. But Captain Morgan was deceived in his judgment of this design. For the Governor, who acted like a brave and courageous soldier, refused not, in performance of his duty, to use his utmost endeavours to destroy whosoever came near the walls. The religious men and women ceased not to cry unto him and beg of him by all the Saints of Heaven he would deliver the castle, and hereby spare both his and their own lives. But nothing could prevail with the obstinacy and fierceness that had possessed the Governor's mind. Thus many of the religious men and nuns were killed before they could fix the ladders. Which at last being done, though with great loss of the said religious people, the Pirates mounted them in great numbers, and with no less valour; having fireballs in their hands, and earthen pots full of powder. All which things, being now at the top of the walls, they kindled and cast in among the Spaniards.

"This effort of the Pirates was very great, insomuch as the Spaniards could no longer resist nor defend the castle, which was now entered. Hereupon they all threw down their arms, and craved quarter for their lives. Only the Governor of the city would admit or crave no mercy; but rather killed many of the Pirates with his own hands, and not a few of his own soldiers, because they did not stand to their arms. And although the Pirates asked him if he would have quarter, yet he constantly answered: 'By no means; I had rather die as a valiant soldier, than be hanged as a coward.' They endeavoured as much as they could to take him prisoner. But he defended himself so obstinately that they were forced to kill him; notwithstanding all the cries and tears of his own wife and daughter, who begged of him upon their knees he would demand quarter and save his life. When the Pirates had possessed themselves of the castle, which was about night, they enclosed therein all the prisoners they had taken, placing the women and men by themselves, with some guards upon them. All the wounded were put into a certain apartment by itself, to the intent their own complaints might be the cure of their diseases; for no other was afforded them.

"This being done, they fell to eating and drinking after their usual manner; that is to say, committing in both these things all manner of debauchery and excess....After such manner they delivered themselves up unto all sort of debauchery, that if there had been found only fifty courageous men, they might easily have re-taken the city, and killed all the Pirates. The next day, having plundered all they could find, they began to examine some of the prisoners (who had been persuaded by their companions to say they were the richest of the town), charging them severely to discover where they had hidden their riches and goods. But not being able to extort anything out of them, as they were not the right persons that possessed any wealth, they at last resolved to torture them. This they performed with such cruelty that many of them died upon the rack, or presently after. Soon after, the President of Panama had news brought him of the pillage and ruin of Porto Bello. This intelligence caused him to employ all his care and industry to raise forces, with design to pursue and cast out the Pirates from thence. But these cared little for what extraordinary means the President used, as having their ships nigh at hand, and being determined to set fire unto the city and retreat. They had now been at Porto Bello fifteen days, in which space of time they had lost many of their men, both by the unhealthiness of the country and the extravagant debaucheries they had committed.[270]

"Hereupon they prepared for a departure, carrying on board their ships all the pillage they had gotten. But, before all, they provided the fleet with sufficient victuals for the voyage. While these things were getting ready, Captain Morgan sent an injunction unto the prisoners, that they should pay him a ransom for the city, or else he would by fire consume it to ashes, and blow up all the castles into the air. Withal, he commanded them to send speedily two persons to seek and procure the sum he demanded, which amounted to one hundred thousand pieces of eight. Unto this effect, two men were sent to the President of Panama, who gave him an account of all these tragedies. The President, having now a body of men in readiness, set forth immediately towards Porto Bello, to encounter the Pirates before their retreat. But these people, hearing of his coming, instead of flying away, went out to meet him at a narrow passage through which of necessity he ought to pass. Here they placed an hundred men very well armed; the which, at the first encounter, put to flight a good party of those of Panama. This accident obliged the President to retire for that time, as not being yet in a posture of strength to proceed any farther. Presently after this rencounter he sent a message unto Captain Morgan to tell him: 'That in case he departed not suddenly with all his forces from Porto Bello, he ought to expect no quarter for himself nor his companions, when he should take them, as he hoped soon to do.' Captain Morgan, who feared not his threats knowing he had a secure retreat in his ships which were nigh at hand, made him answer: 'He would not deliver the castles, before he had received the contribution money he had demanded. Which in case it were not paid down, he would certainly burn the whole city, and then leave it, demolishing beforehand the castles and killing the prisoners.'

"The Governor of Panama perceived by this answer that no means would serve to mollify the hearts of the Pirates, nor reduce them to reason. Hereupon he determined to leave them; as also those of the city, whom he came to relieve, involved in the difficulties of making the best agreement they could with their enemies.[271] Thus, in a few days more, the miserable citizens gathered the contribution wherein they were fined, and brought the entire sum of one hundred thousand pieces of eight unto the Pirates, for a ransom of the cruel captivity they were fallen into. But the President of Panama, by these transactions, was brought into an extreme admiration, considering that four hundred men had been able to take such a great city, with so many strong castles; especially seeing they had no pieces of cannon, nor other great guns, wherewith to raise batteries against them. And what was more, knowing that the citizens of Porto Bello had always great repute of being good soldiers themselves, and who had never wanted courage in their own defence. This astonishment was so great, that it occasioned him, for to be satisfied therein, to send a messenger unto Captain Morgan, desiring him to send him some small pattern of those arms wherewith he had taken with such violence so great a city. Captain Morgan received this messenger very kindly, and treated him with great civility. Which being done, he gave him a pistol and a few small bullets of lead, to carry back unto the President, his Master, telling him withal: 'He desired him to accept that slender pattern of the arms wherewith he had taken

Porto Bello and keep them for a twelvemonth; after which time he promised to come to Panama and fetch them away.' The governor of Panama returned the present very soon unto Captain Morgan, giving him thanks for the favour of lending him such weapons as he needed not, and withal sent him a ring of gold, with this message: 'That he desired him not to give himself the labour of coming to Panama, as he had done to Porto Bello; for he did certify unto him, he should not speed so well here as he had done there.'

"After these transactions, Captain Morgan (having provided his fleet with all necessaries, and taken with him the best guns of the castles, nailing the rest which he could not carry away) set sail from Porto Bello with all his ships. With these he arrived in a few days unto the Island of Cuba, where he sought out a place wherein with all quiet and repose he might make the dividend of the spoil they had gotten. They found in ready money two hundred and fifty thousand pieces of eight, besides all other merchandises, as cloth, linen, silks and other goods. With this rich purchase they sailed again from thence unto their common place of rendezvous, Jamaica. Being arrived, they passed here some time in all sorts of vices and debauchery, according to their common manner of doing, spending with huge prodigality what others had gained with no small labour and toil."[272]

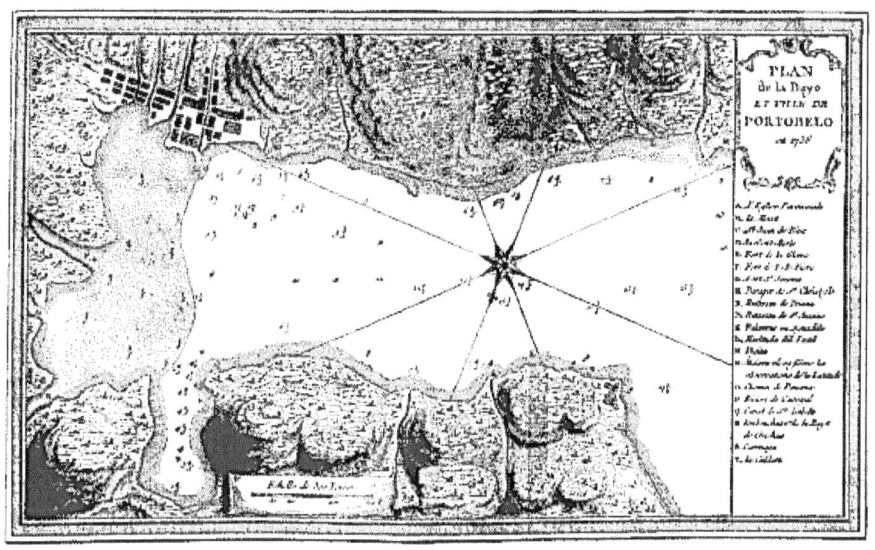

Plan of the Bay and Town of Portobelo, From Prevost d'Exiles' Voyages.

Morgan and his officers, on their return to Jamaica in the middle of August, made an official report which places their conduct in a peculiarly mild and charitable light,[273] and forms a sharp contrast to the account left us by Exquemelin. According to Morgan the town and castles were restored "in as good condition as they found them," and the people were so well treated that "several ladies of great quality and other prisoners" who were offered "their liberty to go to the President's camp, refused, saying they were now prisoners to a person of quality, who was more tender of their honours than they doubted to find in the president's camp, and so voluntarily continued with them till the surrender of the town and castles." This scarcely tallies with what we know of the manners of the freebooters, and Exquemelin's evidence is probably nearer the truth. When Morgan returned to Jamaica Modyford at first received him somewhat doubtfully, for Morgan's commission, as the Governor told him, was only against ships, and the Governor was not at all sure how the exploit would be taken in England. Morgan, however, had reported that at Porto Bello, as well as in Cuba, levies were being made for an attack upon Jamaica, and

Modyford laid great stress upon this point when he forwarded the buccaneer's narrative to the Duke of Albemarle.

The sack of Porto Bello was nothing less than an act of open war against Spain, and Modyford, now that he had taken the decisive step, was not satisfied with half measures. Before the end of October 1668 the whole fleet of privateers, ten sail and 800 men, had gone out again under Morgan to cruise on the coasts of Caracas, while Captain Dempster with several other vessels and 300 followers lay before Havana and along the shores of Campeache.[274] Modyford had written home repeatedly that if the king wished him to exercise any adequate control over the buccaneers, he must send from England two or three nimble fifth-rate frigates to command their obedience and protect the island from hostile attacks. Charles in reply to these letters sent out the "Oxford," a frigate of thirty-four guns, which arrived at Port Royal on 14th October. According to Beeston's Journal, it brought instructions countenancing the war, and empowering the governor to commission whatever persons he thought good to be partners with His Majesty in the plunder, "they finding victuals, wear and tear."[275] The frigate was immediately provisioned for a several months' cruise, and sent under command of Captain Edward Collier to join Morgan's fleet as a private ship-of-war. Morgan had appointed the Isle la Vache, or Cow Island, on the south side of Hispaniola, as the rendezvous for the privateers; and thither flocked great numbers, both English and French, for the name of Morgan was, by his exploit at Porto Bello, rendered famous in all the neighbouring islands. Here, too, arrived the "Oxford" in December. Among the French privateers were two men-of-war, one of which, the "Cour Volant" of La Rochelle, commanded by M. la Vivon, was seized by Captain Collier for having robbed an English vessel of provisions. A few days later, on 2nd January, a council of war was held aboard the "Oxford," where it was decided that the privateers, now numbering about 900 men, should attack Cartagena. While the captains were at dinner on the quarter-deck, however, the frigate blew up, and about 200 men, including five captains, were lost.[276] "I was eating my dinner with the rest," writes the surgeon, Richard Browne, "when the mainmasts blew out, and fell upon Captains Aylett, Bigford, and others, and knocked them on the head; I saved myself by getting astride the mizzenmast." It seems that out of the whole ship only Morgan and those who sat on his side of the table were saved. The accident was probably caused by the carelessness of a gunner. Captain Collier sailed in la Vivon's ship for Jamaica, where the French captain was convicted of piracy in the Admiralty Court, and reprieved by Governor Modyford, but his ship confiscated.[277]

Morgan, from the rendezvous at the Isle la Vache, had coasted along the southern shores of Hispaniola and made several inroads upon the island for the purpose of securing beef and other provisions. Some of his ships, meanwhile, had been separated from the body of the fleet, and at last he found himself with but eight vessels and 400 or 500 men, scarcely more than half his original company. With these small numbers he changed his resolution to attempt Cartagena, and set sail for Maracaibo, a town situated on the great lagoon of that name in Venezuela. This town had been pillaged in 1667, just before the peace of Aix-la-Chapelle, by 650 buccaneers led by two French captains, L'Olonnais and Michel le Basque, and had suffered all the horrors attendant upon such a visit. In March 1669 Morgan appeared at the entrance to the lake, forced the passage after a day's hot bombardment, dismantled the fort which commanded it, and entered Maracaibo, from which the inhabitants had fled before him. The buccaneers sacked the town, and scoured the woods in search of the Spaniards and their valuables. Men, women and children were brought in and cruelly tortured to make them confess where their treasures were hid. Morgan, at the end of three weeks, "having now got by degrees into his hands about 100 of the chief families," resolved to go to Gibraltar, near the head of the lake, as L'Olonnais had done before him. Here the scenes of inhuman cruelty, "the tortures, murders, robberies and such like insolences," were repeated for five weeks; after which the buccaneers, gathering up their rich booty, returned to Maracaibo, carrying with them four hostages for the ransom of the town and prisoners, which the inhabitants promised to send after them. At Maracaibo Morgan learnt that three large Spanish men-of-war were lying off the entrance of the lake, and that the fort, in the meantime, had been armed and manned and put into a posture of defence. In order to gain time he entered into negotiations with the Spanish admiral, Don Alonso del Campo y Espinosa, while the privateers carefully made ready a fireship disguised as a man-of-war. At dawn on 1st May 1669, according to Exquemelin, they approached the Spanish ships riding at anchor within the entry of the lake, and sending the fireship ahead of the rest, steered directly for them. The fireship fell foul of the "Almirante," a vessel of forty guns, grappled with her and set her in flames. The second Spanish ship, when the plight of the Admiral was discovered, was run aground and burnt by her own men. The third was captured by the buccaneers. As no quarter was given or taken, the loss of the Spaniards must have been considerable, although some of those on the Admiral, including Don Alonso, succeeded in reaching shore. From a pilot picked up by the buccaneers, Morgan learned that in the flagship was a great quantity of plate to the value of 40,000 pieces of eight. Of this he succeeded in recovering about half, much of it melted by the force of the heat. Morgan then returned to Maracaibo to refit his prize, and opening negotiations again with Don Alonso, he actually succeeded in obtaining 20,000 pieces of eight and 500 head of cattle as a ransom for the city. Permission to pass the fort, however, the Spaniard refused. So, having first made a division of the spoil,[278] Morgan resorted to an ingenious stratagem to effect his egress from the lake. He led the Spaniards to believe that he was landing his men for an attack on the fort from the land side; and while the Spaniards were moving their guns in that direction, Morgan in the night, by the light of the moon, let his ships drop gently down with the tide till they were abreast of the fort, and then suddenly spreading sail made good his escape. On 17th May the buccaneers returned to Port Royal.

These events in the West Indies filled the Spanish Court with impotent rage, and the Conde de Molina, ambassador in England, made repeated demands for the punishment of Modyford, and for the restitution of the plate and other captured goods which were beginning to flow into England from Jamaica. The English Council replied that the treaty of 1667 was not understood to include the Indies, and Charles II. sent him a long list of complaints of ill-usage to English ships at the hands of the Spaniards in America.[279] Orders seem to have been sent to Modyford, however, to stop hostilities, for in May 1669 Modyford again called in all commissions,[280] and Beeston writes in his Journal, under 14th June, that peace was publicly proclaimed with the Spaniards. In November, moreover, the governor told Albemarle that most of the buccaneers were turning to trade, hunting or planting, and that he hoped soon to reduce all to peaceful pursuits.[281] The Spanish Council of State, in the meantime, had determined upon a course of active reprisal. A commission from the queen-regent, dated 20th April 1669, commanded her governors in the Indies to make open war against the English;[282] and a fleet of six vessels, carrying from eighteen to forty-eight guns, was sent from Spain to cruise against the buccaneers. To this fleet belonged the three ships which tried to bottle up Morgan in Lake Maracaibo. Port Royal was filled with report and rumour of English ships captured and plundered, of cruelties to English prisoners in the dungeons of Cartagena, of commissions of war issued at Porto Bello and St. Jago de Cuba, and of intended reprisals upon the settlements in Jamaica. The privateers became restless and spoke darkly of revenge, while Modyford, his old supporter the Duke of Albemarle having just died, wrote home begging for orders which would give him liberty to retaliate.[283] The last straw fell in June 1670, when two Spanish men-of-war from St. Jago de Cuba, commanded by a Portuguese, Manuel Rivero Pardal, landed men on the north side of the island, burnt some houses and carried off a number of the inhabitants as prisoners.[284] On 2nd July the governor and council issued a commission to Henry Morgan, as commander-in-chief of all ships of war belonging to Jamaica, to get together the privateers for the defence of the island, to attack, seize and destroy all the enemy's vessels he could discover, and in case he found it feasible, "to land and attack St. Jago or any other place where … are stores for this war or a rendezvous for their forces." In the accompanying instructions he was bidden "to advise his fleet and soldiers that they were upon the old pleasing account of no purchase, no pay, and therefore that all which is got, shall be divided amongst them, according to the accustomed rules."[285]

Morgan sailed from Jamaica on 14th August 1670 with eleven vessels and 600 men for the Isle la Vache, the usual rendezvous, whence during the next three months squadrons were detailed to the coast of Cuba and the mainland of South America to collect provisions and intelligence. Sir William Godolphin was at that moment in Madrid concluding articles for the establishment of peace and friendship in America; and on 12th June Secretary Arlington wrote to Modyford that in view of these negotiations his Majesty commanded the privateers to forbear all hostilities on land against the Spaniards.[286] These orders reached Jamaica on 13th August, whereupon the governor recalled Morgan, who had sailed from the harbour the day before, and communicated them to him, "strictly charging him to observe the same and behave with all moderation possible in carrying on the war." The admiral replied that necessity would compel him to land in the Spaniards' country for wood, water and provisions, but unless he was assured that the enemy in their towns were making hostile preparations against the Jamaicans, he would not touch any of them.[287] On 6th September, however, Vice-Admiral Collier with six sail and 400 men was dispatched by Morgan to the Spanish Main. There on 4th November he seized, in the harbour of Santa Marta, two frigates laden with provisions for Maracaibo. Then coasting eastward to Rio de la Hacha, he attacked and captured the fort with its commander and all its garrison, sacked the city, held it to ransom for salt, maize, meat and other provisions, and after occupying it for almost a month returned on 28th October to the Isle la Vache.[288] One of the frigates captured at Santa Marta, "La Gallardina," had been with Pardal when he burnt the coast of Jamaica. Pardal's own ship of fourteen guns had been captured but a short time before by Captain John Morris at the east end of Cuba, and Pardal himself shot through the neck and killed.[289] He was called by the Jamaicans "the vapouring admiral of St. Jago," for in June he had nailed a piece of canvas to a tree on the Jamaican coast, with a curious challenge written both in English and Spanish: —

"I, Captain Manuel Rivero Pardal, to the chief of the squadron of privateers in Jamaica. I am he who this year have done that which follows. I went on shore at Caimanos, and burnt 20 houses, and fought with Captain Ary, and took from him a catch laden with provisions and a canoe. And I am he who took Captain Baines and did carry the prize to Cartagena, and now am arrived to this coast, and have burnt it. And I come to seek General Morgan, with 2 ships of 20 guns, and having seen this, I crave he would come out upon the coast and seek me, that he might see the valour of the Spaniards. And because I had no time I did not come to the mouth of Port Royal to speak by word of mouth in the name of my king, whom God preserve. Dated the 5th of July 1670."[290]

Meanwhile, in the middle of October, there sailed into Port Royal three privateers, Captains Prince, Harrison and Ludbury, who six weeks before had ascended the river San Juan in Nicaragua with 170 men and again plundered the unfortunate city of Granada. The town had rapidly decayed, however, under the repeated assaults of the buccaneers, and the plunderers secured only £20 or £30 per man. Modyford reproved the captains for acting without commissions, but "not deeming it prudent to press the matter too far in this juncture," commanded them to join Morgan at the Isle la Vache.[291] There Morgan was slowly mustering his strength. He negotiated with the French of Tortuga and Hispaniola who were then in revolt against the *régime* of the French Company; and he added to his forces seven ships and 400 men sent him by the indefatigable Governor of Jamaica. On 7th October, indeed, the venture was almost ruined by a violent storm which cast the whole fleet, except the Admiral's vessel, upon the shore. All of the ships but three, however, were eventually got off and repaired, and on 6th December Morgan was able to write to Modyford that he had 1800 buccaneers, including several hundred French, and thirty-six ships under his command.[292] Upon consideration of the reports brought from the Main by his own men, and the testimony of prisoners they had taken, Morgan decided that it was impossible to attempt what seems to have been his original design, a descent upon St. Jago de Cuba, without great loss of men and ships. On 2nd December, therefore, it was unanimously agreed by a general council of all the captains, thirty-seven in number, "that it stands most for the good of Jamaica and safety of us all to take Panama, the President thereof having granted several commissions against the English."[293] Six days later the fleet put to sea from Cape Tiburon, and on the morning of the 14th sighted Providence Island. The Spanish governor capitulated next day, on condition of being transported with his garrison to the mainland, and four of his soldiers who had formerly been banditti in the province of Darien agreed to become guides for the English.[294] After a delay of five days more, Lieutenant-Colonel Joseph Bradley, with between 400 and 500 men in three ships, was sent ahead by Morgan to the isthmus to seize the Castle of San Lorenzo, situated at the mouth of the Chagre river.

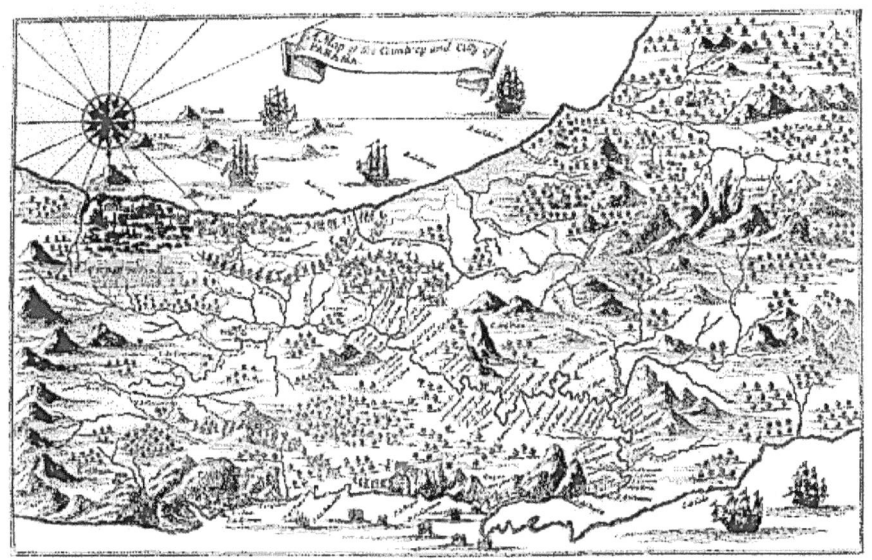

The Isthmus of Darien, From Exquelmelin's Bucaniers, 1684-5.

The President of Panama, meanwhile, on 15th December, had received a messenger from the governor of Cartagena with news of the coming of the English.[295] The president immediately dispatched reinforcements to the Castle of Chagre, which arrived fifteen days before the buccaneers and raised its strength to over 350 men. Two hundred men were sent to Porto Bello, and 500 more were stationed at Venta Cruz and in ambuscades along the Chagre river to oppose the advance of the English. The president himself rose from a bed of sickness to head a reserve of 800, but most of his men were raw recruits without a professional soldier amongst them. This militia in a few days became so panic-stricken that one-third deserted in a night, and the president was compelled to retire to Panama. There the Spaniards managed to load some of the treasure upon two or three ships lying in the roadstead; and the nuns and most of the citizens of importance also embarked with their wives, children and personal property.[296]

The fort or castle of San Lorenzo, which stood on a hill commanding the river Chagre, seems to have been built of double rows of wooden palisades, the space between being filled with earth; and it was protected by a ditch 12 feet deep and by several smaller batteries nearer the water's edge. Lieutenant-Colonel Bradley, who, according to Exquemelin, had been on these coasts before with Captain Mansfield, landed near the fort on the 27th of December. He and his men fought in the trenches from early afternoon till eight o'clock next morning, when they stormed and carried the place. The buccaneers suffered severely, losing about 150 in killed and wounded, including Bradley himself who died ten days later. Exquemelin gives a very vivid account of the action. The buccaneers, he writes, "came to anchor in a small port, at the distance of a league more or less from the castle. The next morning very early they went on shore, and marched through the woods, to attack the castle on that side. This march continued until two o'clock, afternoon, by reason of the difficulties of the way, and its mire and dirt. And although their guides served them exactly, notwithstanding they came so nigh the castle at first that they lost many of their men with the shot from the guns, they being in an open place where nothing could cover nor defend them. This much perplexed the Pirates ..." (but) "at last after many doubts and disputes among themselves they resolved to hazard the assault and their lives after a most desperate manner. Thus they advanced towards the castle, with their swords in one hand and fireballs in the other. The Spaniards defended themselves very briskly, ceasing not to fire at them with their great guns and muskets continually crying withal: 'Come on, ye English dogs, enemies to God and our King; let your other companions that are behind come on too, ye shall not go to Panama this bout.' After the Pirates had made some trial to climb up the walls, they were forced to retreat, which they accordingly did, resting themselves until night. This being done, they returned to the assault, to try if by the help of their fireballs they could overcome and pull down the pales before the wall. This they attempted to do, and while they were about it there happened a very remarkable accident, which gave them the opportunity of the victory. One of the Pirates was wounded with an arrow in his back, which pierced his body to the other side. This he instantly pulled out with great valour at the side of his breast; then taking a little cotton that he had about him, he wound it about the said arrow, and putting it into his musket, he shot it back into the castle. But the cotton being kindled by the powder, occasioned two or three houses that were within the castle, being thatched with palm-leaves, to take fire, which the Spaniards perceived not so soon as was necessary. For this fire meeting with a parcel of powder, blew it up and thereby caused great ruin, and no less consternation to the Spaniards, who were not able to account for this accident, not having seen the beginning thereof.

"Thus the Pirates perceiving the good effect of the arrow and the beginning of the misfortune of the Spaniards, were infinitely gladdened thereat. And while they were busied in extinguishing the fire, which caused great confusion in the whole castle, having not sufficient water wherewithal to do it, the Pirates made use of this opportunity, setting fire likewise to the palisades. Thus the fire was seen at the same time in several parts about the castle, which gave them huge advantage against the Spaniards. For many breaches were made at once by the fire among the pales, great heaps of earth falling down into the ditch. Upon these the Pirates climbed up, and got over into the castle, notwithstanding that some Spaniards, who were not busied about the fire, cast down upon them many flaming pots, full of combustible matter and odious smells, which occasioned the loss of many of the English.

"The Spaniards, notwithstanding the great resistance they made, could not hinder the palisades from being entirely burnt before midnight. Meanwhile the Pirates ceased not to persist in their intention of taking the castle. Unto which effect, although the fire was great, they would creep upon the ground, as nigh unto it as they could, and shoot amidst the flames, against the Spaniards they could perceive on the other side, and thus cause many to fall dead from the walls. When day was come, they observed all the moveable earth that lay between the pales to be fallen into the ditch in huge quantity. So that now those within the castle did in a manner lie equally exposed to them without, as had been on the contrary before. Whereupon the Pirates continued shooting very furiously against them, and killed great numbers of Spaniards. For the Governor had given them orders not to retire from those posts which corresponded to the heaps of earth fallen into the ditch, and caused the artillery to be transported unto the breaches.

"Notwithstanding, the fire within the castle still continued, and now the Pirates from abroad used what means they could to hinder its progress, by shooting incessantly against it. One party of the Pirates was employed only to this purpose, and another commanded to watch all the motions of the Spaniards, and take all opportunities against them. About noon the English happened to gain a breach, which the Governor himself defended with twenty-five soldiers. Here was performed a very courageous and warlike resistance by the Spaniards, both with muskets, pikes, stones and swords. Yet notwithstanding, through all these arms the Pirates forced and fought their way, till at last they gained the castle. The Spaniards who remained alive cast themselves down from the castle into the sea, choosing rather to die precipitated by their own selves (few or none surviving the fall) than to ask any quarter for their lives. The Governor himself retreated unto the corps du garde, before which were placed two pieces of cannon. Here he intended still to defend himself, neither would he demand any quarter. But at last he was killed with a musket shot, which pierced his skull into the brain.

"The Governor being dead, and the corps du garde surrendered, they found still remaining in it alive to the number of thirty men, whereof scarce ten were not wounded. These informed the Pirates that eight or nine of their soldiers had deserted their colours, and were gone to Panama to carry news of their arrival and invasion. These thirty men alone were remaining of three hundred and fourteen, wherewith the castle was garrisoned, among which number not one officer was found alive. These were all made prisoners, and compelled to tell whatsoever they knew of their designs and enterprises."[297]

Five days after the taking of the castle, Morgan arrived from Providence Island with the rest of the armament; but at the entrance to the Chagre river, in passing over the bar, his flagship and five or six smaller boats were wrecked, and ten men were drowned. After repairing and provisioning the castle, and leaving 300 men to guard it and the ships, Morgan, on 9th January 1671, at the head of 1400 men, began the ascent of the river in seven small vessels and thirty-six canoes.[298] The story of this brilliant march we will again leave to Exquemelin, who took part in it, to relate. The first day "they sailed only six leagues, and came to a place called De los Bracos. Here a party of his men went on shore, only to sleep some few hours and stretch their limbs, they being almost crippled with lying too much crowded in the boats. After they had rested awhile, they went abroad, to see if any victuals could be found in the neighbouring plantations. But they could find none, the Spaniards being fled and carrying with them all the provisions they had. This day, being the first of their journey, there was amongst them such scarcity of victuals that the greatest part were forced to pass with only a pipe of tobacco, without any other refreshment.

"The next day, very early in the morning, they continued their journey, and came about evening to a place called Cruz de Juan Gallego. Here they were compelled to leave their boats and canoes, by reason the river was very dry for want of rain, and the many obstacles of trees that were fallen into it. The guides told them that about two leagues farther on the country would be very good to continue the journey by land. Hereupon they left some companies, being in all one hundred and sixty men,[299] on board the boats to defend them, with intent they might serve for a place of refuge in case of necessity.

"The next morning, being the third day of their journey, they all went ashore, excepting those above-mentioned who were to keep the boats. Unto these Captain Morgan gave very strict orders, under great penalties, that no man, upon any pretext whatsoever, should dare to leave the boats and go ashore. This he did, fearing lest they should be surprised and cut off by an ambuscade of Spaniards, that might chance to lie thereabouts in the neighbouring woods, which appeared so thick as to seem almost impenetrable. Having this morning begun their march, they found the ways so dirty and irksome, that Captain Morgan thought it more convenient to transport some of the men in canoes (though it could not be done without great labour) to a place farther up the river, called Cedro Bueno. Thus they re-embarked, and the canoes returned for the rest that were left behind. So that about night they found themselves all together at the said place. The Pirates were extremely desirous to meet any Spaniards, or Indians, hoping to fill their bellies with what provisions they should take from them. For now they were reduced almost to the very extremity of hunger.

"On the fourth day, the greatest part of the Pirates marched by land, being led by one of the guides. The rest went by water, farther up with the canoes, being conducted by another guide, who always went before them with two of the said canoes, to discover on both sides the river the ambuscades of the Spaniards. These had also spies, who were very dextrous, and could at any time give notice of all accidents or of the arrival of the Pirates, six hours at least before they came to any place. This day about noon they found themselves nigh unto a post, called Torna Cavallos. Here the guide of the canoes began to cry aloud he perceived an ambuscade. His voice caused infinite joy unto all the Pirates, as persuading themselves they should find some provisions wherewith to satiate their hunger, which was very great. Being come unto the place, they found nobody in it, the Spaniards who were there not long before being every one fled, and leaving nothing behind unless it were a small number of leather bags, all empty, and a few crumbs of bread scattered upon the ground where they had eaten.[300] Being angry at this misfortune, they pulled down a few little huts which the Spaniards had made, and afterwards fell to eating the leathern bags, as being desirous to afford something to the ferment of their stomachs, which now was grown so sharp that it did gnaw their very bowels, having nothing else to prey upon. Thus they made a huge banquet upon those bags of leather, which doubtless had been more grateful unto them, if divers quarrels had not risen concerning who should have the greatest share. By the circumference of the place they conjectured five hundred Spaniards, more or less, had been there. And these, finding no victuals, they were now infinitely desirous to meet, intending to devour some of them rather than perish. Whom they would certainly in that occasion have roasted or boiled, to satisfy their famine, had they been able to take them.

"After they had feasted themselves with those pieces of leather, they quitted the place, and marched farther on, till they came about night to another post called Torna Munni. Here they found another ambuscade, but as barren and desert as the former. They searched the neighbouring woods, but could not find the least thing to eat. The Spaniards having been so provident as not to leave behind them anywhere the least crumb of sustenance, whereby the Pirates were now brought to the extremity aforementioned. Here again he was happy, that had reserved since noon any small piece of leather whereof to make his supper, drinking after it a good draught of water for his greatest comfort. Some persons who never were out of their mothers' kitchens may ask how these Pirates could eat, swallow and digest those pieces of leather, so hard and dry. Unto whom I only answer: That could they once experiment what hunger, or rather famine, is, they would certainly find the manner, by their own necessity, as the Pirates did. For these first took the leather, and sliced it in pieces. Then did they beat it between two stones and rub it, often dipping it in the water of the river, to render it by these means supple and tender. Lastly they scraped off the hair, and roasted or broiled it upon the fire. And being thus cooked they cut it into small morsels, and eat it, helping it down with frequent gulps of water, which by good fortune they had nigh at hand.

"They continued their march the fifth day, and about noon came unto a place called Barbacoa. Here likewise they found traces of another ambuscade, but the place totally as unprovided as the two precedent were. At a small distance were to be seen several plantations, which they searched very narrowly, but could not find any person, animal or other thing that was capable of relieving their extreme and ravenous hunger. Finally, having ranged up and down and searched a long time, they found a certain grotto which seemed to be but lately hewn out of a rock, in which they found two sacks of meal, wheat and like things, with two great jars of wine, and certain fruits called Platanos. Captain Morgan, knowing that some of his men were now, through hunger, reduced almost to the extremity of their lives, and fearing lest the major part should be brought into the same condition, caused all that was found to be distributed amongst them who were in greatest necessity. Having refreshed themselves with these victuals, they began to march anew with greater courage than ever. Such as could not well go for weakness were put into the canoes, and those commanded to land that were in them before. Thus they prosecuted their journey till late at night, at which time they came unto a plantation where they took up their rest. But without eating anything at all; for the Spaniards, as before, had swept away all manner of provisions, leaving not behind them the least signs of victuals.

"On the sixth day they continued their march, part of them by land through the woods, and part by water in the canoes. Howbeit they were constrained to rest themselves very frequently by the way, both for the ruggedness thereof and the extreme weakness they were under. Unto this they endeavoured to occur, by eating some leaves of trees and green herbs, or grass, such as they could pick, for such was the miserable condition they were in. This day, at noon, they arrived at a plantation, where they found a barn full of maize. Immediately they beat down the doors, and fell to eating of it dry, as much as they could devour. Afterwards they distributed great quantity, giving to every man a good allowance thereof. Being thus provided they prosecuted their journey, which having continued for the space of an hour or thereabouts, they met with an ambuscade of Indians. This they no sooner had discovered, but they threw away their maize, with the sudden hopes they conceived of finding all things in abundance. But after all this haste, they found themselves much deceived, they meeting neither Indians nor victuals, nor anything else of what they had imagined. They saw notwithstanding on the other side of the river a troop of a hundred Indians more or less, who all escaped away through the agility of their feet. Some few Pirates there were who leapt into the river, the sooner to reach the shore to see if they could take any of the said Indians prisoners. But all was in vain; for being much more nimble on their feet than the Pirates they easily baffled their endeavours. Neither did they only baffle them, but killed also two or three of the Pirates with their arrows, shooting at them at a distance, and crying: 'Ha! perros, a la savana, a la savana. Ha! ye dogs, go to the plain, go to the plain.'

"This day they could advance no further, by reason they were necessitated to pass the river hereabouts to continue their march on the other side. Hereupon they took up their repose for that night. Howbeit their sleep was not heavy nor profound, for great murmurings were heard that night in the camp, many complaining of Captain Morgan and his conduct in that enterprise, and being desirous to return home. On the contrary, others would rather die there than go back one step from what they had undertaken. But others who had greater courage than any of these two parties did laugh and joke at all their discourses. In the meanwhile they had a guide who much comforted them, saying: 'It would not now be long before they met with people, from whom they should reap some considerable advantage.'

"The seventh day in the morning they all made clean their arms, and every one discharged his pistol or musket without bullet, to examine the security of their firelocks. This being done, they passed to the other side of the river in the canoes, leaving the post where they had rested the night before, called Santa Cruz. Thus they proceeded on their journey till noon, at which time they arrived at a village called Cruz.[301] Being at a great distance as yet from the place, they perceived much smoke to arise out of the chimneys. The sight hereof afforded them great joy and hopes of finding people in the town, and afterwards what they most desired, which was plenty of good cheer. Thus they went on with as much haste as they could, making several arguments to one another upon those external signs, though all like castles built in the air. 'For,' said they, 'there is smoke coming out of every house, and therefore they are making good fires to roast and boil what we are to eat.' With other things to this purpose.

"At length they arrived there in great haste, all sweating and panting, but found no person in the town, nor anything that was eatable wherewith to refresh themselves, unless it were good fires to warm themselves, which they wanted not. For the Spaniards before their departure, had every one set fire to his own house, excepting only the storehouses and stables belonging to the King.

"They had not left behind them any beast whatsoever, either alive or dead. This occasioned much confusion in their minds, they not finding the least thing to lay hold on, unless it were some few cats and dogs, which they immediately killed and devoured with great appetite. At last in the King's stables they found by good fortune fifteen or sixteen jars of Peru wine, and a leather sack full of bread. But no sooner had they begun to drink of the said wine when they fell sick, almost every man. This sudden disaster made them think that the wine was poisoned, which caused a new consternation in the whole camp, as judging themselves now to be irrecoverably lost. But the true reason was, their huge want of sustenance in that whole voyage, and the manifold sorts of trash which they had eaten upon that occasion. Their sickness was so great that day as caused them to remain there till the next morning, without being able to prosecute their journey as they used to do, in the afternoon. This village is seated in the latitude in 9 degrees and 2 minutes, northern latitude, being distant from the river of Chagre twenty-six Spanish leagues, and eight from Panama. Moreover, this is the last place unto which boats or canoes can come; for which reason they built here store-houses, wherein to keep all sorts of merchandise, which from hence to and from Panama are transported upon the backs of mules.

"Here therefore Captain Morgan was constrained to leave his canoes and land all his men, though never so weak in their bodies. But lest the canoes should be surprised, or take up too many men for their defence, he resolved to send them all back to the place where the boats were, excepting one, which he caused to be hidden, to the intent it might serve to carry intelligence according to the exigency of affairs. Many of the Spaniards and Indians belonging to this village were fled to the plantations thereabouts. Hereupon Captain Morgan gave express orders that none should dare to go out of the village, except in whole companies of a hundred together. The occasion hereof was his fear lest the enemy should take an advantage upon his men, by any sudden assault. Notwithstanding, one party of English soldiers stickled not to contravene these commands, being thereunto tempted with the desire of finding victuals. But these were soon glad to fly into the town again, being assaulted with great fury by some Spaniards and Indians, who snatched up one of the Pirates, and carried him away prisoner. Thus the vigilance and care of Captain Morgan was not sufficient to prevent every accident that might happen.

"On the eighth day, in the morning, Captain Morgan sent two hundred men before the body of his army, to discover the way to Panama, and see if they had laid any ambuscades therein. Especially considering that the places by which they were to pass were very fit for that purpose, the paths being so narrow that only ten or twelve persons could march in a file, and oftentimes not so many. Having marched about the space of ten hours, they came unto a place called Quebrada Obscura. Here, all on a sudden, three or four thousand arrows were shot at them, without being able to perceive from whence they came, or who shot them. The place, from whence it was presumed they were shot was a high rocky mountain, excavated from one side to the other, wherein was a grotto that went through it, only capable of admitting one horse, or other beast laden. This multitude of arrows caused a huge alarm among the Pirates, especially because they could not discover the place from whence they were discharged. At last, seeing no more arrows to appear, they marched a little farther, and entered into a wood. Here they perceived some Indians to fly as fast as they could possible before them, to take the advantage of another post, and thence observe the march of the Pirates. There remained, notwithstanding one troop of Indians upon the place, with full design to fight and defend themselves. This combat they performed with huge courage, till such time as their captain fell to the ground wounded, who although he was now in despair of life, yet his valour being greater than his strength, would demand no quarter, but, endeavouring to raise himself, with undaunted mind laid hold of his azagaya, or javelin, and struck at one of the Pirates. But before he could second the blow, he was shot to death with a pistol. This was also the fate of many of his companions, who like good and courageous soldiers lost their lives with their captain, for the defence of their country.

"The Pirates endeavoured, as much as was possible, to lay hold on some of the Indians and take them prisoners. But they being infinitely swifter than the Pirates, every one escaped, leaving eight Pirates dead upon the place and ten wounded.[302] Yea, had the Indians been more dextrous in military affairs, they might have defended that passage, and not let one sole man to pass. Within a little while after they came to a large campaign field open and full of variegated meadows. From here they could perceive at a distance before them a parcel of Indians who stood on the top of a mountain, very nigh unto the way by which the Pirates were to pass. They sent a troop of fifty men, the nimblest they could pick out, to see if they could catch any of them, and afterwards force them to declare whereabouts their companions had their mansions. But all their industry was in vain, for they escaped through their nimbleness, and presently after showed themselves in another place, hallooing unto the English, and crying: 'A la savana, a la savana, cornudos, perros Ingleses;' that is, 'To the plain, to the plain, ye cockolds, ye English dogs!' While these things passed, the ten Pirates that were wounded a little before were dressed and plastered up.

"At this place there was a wood and on each side thereof a mountain. The Indians had possessed themselves of the one, and the Pirates took possession of the other that was opposite unto it. Captain Morgan was persuaded that in the wood the Spaniards had placed an ambuscade, as lying so conveniently for that purpose. Hereupon he sent before two hundred men to search it. The Spaniards and Indians, perceiving the Pirates to descend the mountain, did so too, as if they designed to attack them. But being got into the wood, out of sight of the Pirates, they disappeared, and were seen no more, leaving the passage open unto them.

"About night there fell a great rain, which caused the Pirates to march the faster and seek everywhere for houses wherein to preserve their arms from being wet. But the Indians had set fire to every one thereabouts, and transported all their cattle unto remote places, to the end that the Pirates, finding neither houses nor victuals, might be constrained to return homewards. Notwithstanding, after diligent search, they found a few little huts belonging to shepherds, but in them nothing to eat. These not being capable of holding many men, they placed in them out of every company a small number, who kept the arms of the rest of the army. Those who remained in the open field endured much hardship that night, the rain not ceasing to fall until the morning.

"The next morning, about break of day, being the ninth of this tedious journey, Captain Morgan continued his march while the fresh air of the morning lasted. For the clouds then hanging as yet over their heads were much more favourable unto them than the scorching rays of the sun, by reason the way was now more difficult and laborious than all the precedent. After two hours' march, they discovered a troop of about twenty Spaniards. who observed the motions of the Pirates. They endeavoured to catch some of them, but could lay hold on none, they suddenly disappearing, and absconding themselves in caves among the rocks, totally unknown to the Pirates. At last they came to a high mountain, which, when they ascended, they discovered from the top thereof the South Sea. This happy sight, as if it were the end of their labours, caused infinite joy among the Pirates. From hence they could descry also one ship and six boats, which were set forth from Panama, and sailed towards the islands of Tavoga and Tavogilla. Having descended this mountain, they came unto a vale, in which they found great quantity of cattle, whereof they killed good store. Here while some were employed in killing and flaying of cows, horses, bulls and chiefly asses, of which there was greatest number, others busied themselves in kindling of fires and getting wood wherewith to roast them. Thus cutting the flesh of these animals into convenient pieces, or gobbets, they threw them into the fire and, half carbonadoed or roasted, they devoured them with incredible haste and appetite. For such was their hunger that they more resembled cannibals than Europeans at this banquet, the blood many times running down from their beards to the middle of their bodies.

"Having satisfied their hunger with these delicious meats, Captain Morgan ordered them to continue the march. Here again he sent before the main body fifty men, with intent to take some prisoners, if possibly they could. For he seemed now to be much concerned that in nine days' time he could not meet one person who might inform him of the condition and forces of the Spaniards. About evening they discovered a troop of two hundred Spaniards, more or less, who hallooed unto the Pirates, but these could not understand what they said. A little while after they came the first time within sight of the highest steeple of Panama. This steeple they no sooner had discovered but they began to show signs of extreme joy, casting up their hats into the air, leaping for mirth, and shouting, even just as if they had already obtained the victory and entire accomplishment of their designs. All their trumpets were sounded and every drum beaten, in token of this universal acclamation and huge alacrity of their minds. Thus they pitched their camp for that night with general content of the whole army, waiting with impatience for the morning, at which time they intended to attack the city. This evening there appeared fifty horse who came out of the city, hearing the noise of the drums and trumpets of the Pirates, to observe, as it was thought, their motions. They came almost within musket-shot of the army, being preceded by a trumpet that sounded marvellously well. Those on horseback hallooed aloud unto the Pirates, and threatened them, saying, 'Perros! nos veremos,' that is,

'Ye dogs! we shall meet ye.' Having made this menace they returned to the city, excepting only seven or eight horsemen who remained hovering thereabouts, to watch what motions the Pirates made. Immediately after, the city began to fire and ceased not to play with their biggest guns all night long against the camp, but with little or no harm unto the Pirates, whom they could not conveniently reach. About this time also the two hundred Spaniards whom the Pirates had seen in the afternoon appeared again within sight, making resemblance as if they would block up the passages, to the intent no Pirates might escape the hands of their forces. But the Pirates, who were now in a manner besieged, instead of conceiving any fear of their blockades, as soon as they had placed sentries about their camp, began every one to open their satchels, and without any preparation of napkins or plates, fell to eating very heartily the remaining pieces of bulls' and horses' flesh which they had reserved since noon. This being done, they laid themselves down to sleep upon the grass with great repose and huge satisfaction, expecting only with impatience for the dawnings of the next day.

"On the tenth day, betimes in the morning, they put all their men in convenient order, and with drums and trumpets sounding, continued their march directly towards the city. But one of the guides desired Captain Morgan not to take the common highway that led thither, fearing lest they should find in it much resistance and many ambuscades. He presently took his advice, and chose another way that went through the wood, although very irksome and difficult. Thus the Spaniards, perceiving the Pirates had taken another way, which they scarce had thought on or believed, were compelled to leave their stops and batteries, and come out to meet them. The Governor of Panama put his forces in order, consisting of two squadrons, four regiments of foot, and a huge number of wild bulls, which were driven by a great number of Indians, with some negroes and others to help them.

"The Pirates being now upon their march, came unto the top of a little hill, from whence they had a large prospect of the city and campaign country underneath. Here they discovered the forces of the people of Panama, extended in battle array, which, when they perceived to be so numerous, they were suddenly surprised with great fear, much doubting the fortune of the day. Yea, few or none there were but wished themselves at home, or at least free from the obligation of that engagement, wherein they perceived their lives must be so narrowly concerned. Having been some time at a stand, in a wavering condition of mind, they at last reflected upon the straits they had brought themselves into, and that now they ought of necessity either to fight resolutely or die, for no quarter could be expected from an enemy against whom they had committed so many cruelties on all occasions. Hereupon they encouraged one another, and resolved either to conquer, or spend the very last drop of blood in their bodies. Afterwards they divided themselves into three battalions, or troops, sending before them one of two hundred buccaneers, which sort of people are infinitely dextrous at shooting with guns.[303] Thus the Pirates left the hill and descended, marching directly towards the Spaniards, who were posted in a spacious field, waiting for their coming. As soon as they drew nigh unto them, the Spaniards began to shout and cry, 'Viva el Rey! God save the King!' and immediately their horse began to move against the Pirates. But the field being full of quags and very soft under foot, they could not ply to and fro and wheel about, as they desired. The two hundred buccaneers who went before, every one putting one knee to the ground, gave them a full volley of shot, wherewith the battle was instantly kindled very hot. The Spaniards defended themselves very courageously, acting all they could possibly perform, to disorder the Pirates. Their foot, in like manner, endeavoured to second the horse, but were constrained by the Pirates to separate from them. Thus finding themselves frustrated of their designs, they attempted to drive the bulls against them at their backs, and by this means to put them into disorder. But the greatest part of that wild cattle ran away, being frightened with the noise of the battle. And some few that broke through the English companies did no other harm than to tear the colours in pieces; whereas the buccaneers, shooting them dead, left not one to trouble them thereabouts.

"The battle having now continued for the space of two hours, at the end thereof the greatest part of the Spanish horse was ruined and almost all killed. The rest fled away. Which being perceived by the foot, and that they could not possibly prevail, they discharged the shot they had in their muskets, and throwing them on the ground, betook themselves to flight, every one which way he could run. The Pirates could not possibly follow them, as being too much harassed and wearied with the long journey they had lately made. Many of them not being able to fly whither they desired, hid themselves for that present among the shrubs of the sea-side. But very unfortunately; for most of them being found out by the Pirates, were instantly killed, without giving quarter to any.[304] Some religious men were brought prisoners before Captain Morgan; but he being deaf to their cries and lamentations, commanded them all to be immediately pistoled, which was accordingly done. Soon after they brought a captain to his presence, whom he examined very strictly about several things, particularly wherein consisted the forces of those of Panama. Unto which he answered: Their whole strength did consist in four hundred horse, twenty-four companies of foot, each being of one hundred men complete, sixty Indians and some negroes, who were to drive two thousand wild bulls and cause them to run over the English camp, and thus by breaking their files put them into a total disorder and confusion.[305] He discovered more, that in the city they had made trenches and raised batteries in several places, in all which they had placed many guns. And that at the entry of the highway which led to the city they had built a fort, which was mounted with eight great guns of brass and defended by fifty men.

"Captain Morgan, having heard this information, gave orders instantly they should march another way. But before setting forth, he made a review of all his men, whereof he found both killed and wounded a considerable number, and much greater than he had believed. Of the Spaniards were found six hundred dead upon the place, besides the wounded and prisoners.[306] The Pirates were nothing discouraged, seeing their number so much diminished, but rather filled with greater pride than before, perceiving what huge advantage they had obtained against their enemies. Thus having rested themselves some while, they prepared to march courageously towards the city, plighting their oaths to one another in general they would fight till never a man was left alive. With this courage they recommenced their march, either to conquer or be conquered, carrying with them all the prisoners.

"They found much difficulty in their approach unto the city. For within the town the Spaniards had placed many great guns, at several quarters thereof, some of which were charged with small pieces of iron, and others with musket bullets. With all these they saluted the Pirates, at their drawing nigh unto the place, and gave them full and frequent broadsides, firing at them incessantly. Whence it came to pass that unavoidably they lost, at every step they advanced, great numbers of men. But neither these manifest dangers of their lives, nor the sight of so many of their own as dropped down continually at their sides, could deter them from advancing farther, and gaining ground every moment upon the enemy. Thus, although the Spaniards never ceased to fire and act the best they could for their defence, yet notwithstanding they were forced to deliver the city after the space of three hours' combat.[307] And the Pirates, having now possessed themselves thereof, both killed and destroyed as many as attempted to make the least opposition against them. The inhabitants had caused the best of their goods to be transported to more remote and occult places. Howbeit they found within the city as yet several warehouses, very well stocked with all sorts of merchandise, as well silks and cloths as linen, and other things of considerable value. As soon as the first fury of their entrance into the city was over, Captain Morgan assembled all his men at a certain place which he assigned, and there commanded them under very great penalties that none of them should dare to drink or taste any wine. The reason he gave for this injunction was, because he had received private intelligence that it had been all poisoned by the Spaniards. Howbeit it was the opinion of many he gave these prudent orders to prevent the debauchery of his people, which he foresaw would be very great at the beginning, after so much hunger sustained by the way. Fearing withal lest the Spaniards, seeing them in wine, should rally their forces and fall upon the city, and use them as inhumanly as they had used the inhabitants before."

Exquemelin accuses Morgan of setting fire to the city and endeavouring to make the world believe that it was done by the Spaniards. Wm. Frogge, however, who was also present, says distinctly that the Spaniards fired the town, and Sir William Godolphin, in a letter from Madrid to Secretary Arlington on 2nd June 1671, giving news of the exploit which must have come from a Spanish source, says that the President of Panama left orders that the city if taken should be burnt.[308] Moreover the President of Panama himself, in a letter to Spain describing the event which was intercepted by the English, admits that not the buccaneers but the slaves and the owners of the houses set fire to the city.[309] The buccaneers tried in vain to extinguish the flames, and the whole town, which was built mostly of wood, was consumed by twelve o'clock midnight. The only edifices which escaped were the government buildings, a few churches, and about 300 houses in the suburbs. The freebooters remained at Panama twenty-eight days seeking plunder and indulging in every variety of excess. Excursions were made daily into the country for twenty leagues round about to search for booty, and 3000 prisoners were brought in. Exquemelin's story of the sack is probably in the main true. In describing the city he writes: "There belonged to this city (which is also the head of a bishopric) eight monasteries, whereof seven were for men and one for women, two stately churches and one hospital. The churches and monasteries were all richly adorned with altar-pieces and paintings, huge quantity of gold and silver, with other precious things; all which the ecclesiastics had hidden and concealed. Besides which ornaments, here were to be seen two thousand houses of magnificent and prodigious building, being all or the greatest part inhabited by merchants of that country, who are vastly rich. For the rest of the inhabitants of lesser quality and tradesmen, this city contained five thousand houses more. Here were also great numbers of stables, which served for the horses and mules, that carry all the plate, belonging as well unto the King of Spain as to private men, towards the coast of the North Sea. The neighbouring fields belonging to this city are all cultivated with fertile plantations and pleasant gardens, which afford delicious prospects unto the inhabitants the whole year long."[310] The day after the capture, continues Exquemelin, "Captain Morgan dispatched away two troops of Pirates of one hundred and fifty men each, being all very stout soldiers and well armed with orders to seek for the inhabitants of Panama who were escaped from the hands of their enemies. These men, having made several excursions up and down the campaign fields, woods and mountains, adjoining to Panama, returned after two days' time bringing with them above 200 prisoners, between men, women and slaves. The same day returned also the boat …which Captain Morgan had sent into the South Sea, bringing with her three other boats, which they had taken in a little while. But all these prizes they could willingly have given, yea, although they had employed greater labour into the bargain, for one certain galleon, which miraculously escaped their industry, being very richly laden with all the King's plate and great quantity of riches of gold, pearl, jewels and other most precious goods, of all of the best and richest merchants of Panama. On board of this galleon were also the religious women, belonging to the nunnery of the said city, who had embarked with them all the ornaments of their church, consisting in great quantity of gold, plate, and other things of great value....

"Notwithstanding the Pirates found in the ports of the islands of Tavoga and Tavogilla several boats that were laden with many sorts of very good merchandise; all which they took and brought unto Panama; where being arrived, they made an exact relation of all that had passed while they were abroad to Captain Morgan. The prisoners confirmed what the Pirates had said, adding thereto, that they undoubtedly knew whereabouts the said galleon might be at that present, but that it was very probable they had been relieved before now from other places. These relations stirred up Captain Morgan anew to send forth all the boats that were in the port of Panama, with design to seek and pursue the said galleon till they could find her. The boats aforesaid being in all four, set sail from Panama, and having spent eight days in cruising to and fro, and searching several ports and creeks, they lost all their hopes of finding what they so earnestly sought for. Hereupon they resolved to return unto the isles of Tavoga and Tavogilla. Here they found a reasonable good ship, that was newly come from Payta, being laden with cloth, soap, sugar and biscuit, with twenty thousand pieces of eight in ready money. This vessel they instantly seized, not finding the least resistance from any person within her. Nigh unto the said ship was also a boat whereof in like manner they possessed themselves. Upon the boat they laded great part of the merchandises they had found in the ship, together with some slaves they had taken in the said islands. With this purchase they returned to Panama, something better satisfied of their voyage, yet withal much discontented they could not meet with the galleon....

"Captain Morgan used to send forth daily parties of two hundred men, to make inroads into all the fields and country thereabouts, and when one party came back, another consisting of two hundred more was ready to go forth. By this means they gathered in a short time huge quantity of riches, and no lesser number of prisoners. These being brought into the city, were presently put unto the most exquisite tortures imaginable, to make them confess both other people's goods and their own. Here it happened, that one poor and miserable wretch was found in the house of a gentleman of great quality, who had put on, amidst that confusion of things, a pair of taffety breeches belonging to his master with a little silver key hanging at the strings thereof. This being perceived by the Pirates they immediately asked him where was the cabinet of the said key? His answer was: he knew not what was become of it, but only that finding those breeches in his master's house, he had made bold to wear them. Not being able to extort any other confession out of him, they first put him upon the rack, wherewith they inhumanly disjointed his arms. After this they twisted a cord about his forehead, which they wrung so hard, that his eyes appeared as big as eggs, and were ready to fall out of his skull. But neither with these torments could they obtain any positive answer to their demands. Whereupon they soon after hung him up, giving him infinite blows and stripes, while he was under that intolerable pain and posture of body. Afterwards they cut off his nose and ears, and singed his face with burning straw, till he could speak nor lament his misery no longer. Then losing all hopes of hearing any confession from his mouth, they commanded a negro to run him through with a lance, which put an end to his life and a period to their cruel and inhuman tortures. After this execrable manner did many others of those miserable prisoners finish their days, the common sport and recreation of these Pirates being these and other tragedies not inferior to these.

"They spared in these their cruelties no sex nor condition whatsoever. For as to religious persons and priests, they granted them less quarter than unto others, unless they could produce a considerable sum of money, capable of being a sufficient ransom. Women themselves were no better used ... and Captain Morgan, their leader and commander, gave them no good example in this point....[311]

"Captain Morgan having now been at Panama the full space of three weeks, commanded all things to be put in order for his departure. Unto this effect he gave orders to every company of his men, to seek out for so many beasts of carriage as might suffice to convey the whole spoil of the city unto the river where his canoes lay. About this time a great rumour was spread in the city, of a considerable number of Pirates who intended to leave Captain Morgan; and that, by taking a ship which was in the port, they determined to go and rob upon the South Sea till they had got as much as they thought fit, and then return homewards by the way of the East Indies into Europe. For which purpose they had already gathered great quantity of provisions which they had hidden in private places, with sufficient store of powder, bullets and all other sorts of ammunition; likewise some great guns belonging to the town, muskets and other things, wherewith they designed not only to equip the said vessel but also to fortify themselves and raise batteries in some island or other, which might serve them for a place of refuge.

"This design had certainly taken effect as they intended, had not Captain Morgan had timely advice thereof given him by one of their comrades. Hereupon he instantly commanded the mainmast of the said ship should be cut down and burnt, together with all the other boats that were in the port. Hereby the intentions of all or most of his companions were totally frustrated. After this Captain Morgan sent forth many of the Spaniards into the adjoining fields and country, to seek for money wherewith to ransom not only themselves but also all the rest of the prisoners, as likewise the ecclesiastics, both secular and regular. Moreover, he commanded all the artillery of the town to be spoiled, that is to say, nailed and stopped up. At the same time he sent out a strong company of men to seek for the Governor of Panama, of whom intelligence was brought that he had laid several ambuscades in the way, by which he ought to pass at his return. But those who were sent upon this design returned soon after, saying they had not found any sign or appearance of any such ambuscades. For a confirmation whereof they brought with them some prisoners they had taken, who declared how that the said Governor had had an intention of making some opposition by the way, but that the men whom he had designed to effect it were unwilling to undertake any such enterprise; so that for want of means he could not put his design into execution.[312]

"On the 24th of February of the year 1671,[313] Captain Morgan departed from the city of Panama, or rather from the place where the said city of Panama did stand. Of the spoils whereof he carried with him one hundred and seventy-five beasts of carriage, laden with silver, gold and other precious things, besides 600 prisoners, more or less, between men, women, children and slaves. That day they came unto a river that passeth through a delicious campaign field, at the distance of a league from Panama. Here Captain Morgan put all his forces into good order of martial array in such manner that the prisoners were in the middle of the camp, surrounded on all sides with Pirates. At which present conjuncture nothing else was to be heard but lamentations, cries, shrieks and doleful sighs, of so many women and children, who were persuaded Captain Morgan designed to transport them all, and carry them into his own country for slaves. Besides that, among all those miserable prisoners, there was extreme hunger and thirst endured at that time. Which hardship and misery Captain Morgan designedly caused them to sustain, with intent to excite them more earnestly to seek for money wherewith to ransom themselves, according to the tax he had set upon every one. Many of the women begged of Captain Morgan upon their knees, with infinite sighs and tears, he would permit them to return unto Panama, there to live in company of their dear husbands and children, in little huts of straw which they would erect, seeing they had no houses until the rebuilding of the city. But his answer was: he came not thither to hear lamentations and cries, but rather to seek money. Therefore, they ought to seek out for that in the first place, wherever it were to be had, and bring it to him, otherwise he would assuredly transport them all to such places whither they cared not to go....

"As soon as Captain Morgan arrived, upon his march, at the town called Cruz, seated on the banks of the river Chagre, as was mentioned before, he commanded an order to be published among the prisoners, that within the space of three days every one of them should bring in their ransom, under the penalty aforementioned, of being transported unto Jamaica. In the meanwhile he gave orders for so much rice and maize to be collected thereabouts as was necessary for the victualling all his ships. At this place some of the prisoners were ransomed, but many others could not bring in their moneys in so short a time. Hereupon he continued his voyage ... carrying with him all the spoil that ever he could transport. From this village he likewise led away some new prisoners, who were inhabitants of the said place. So that these prisoners were added to those of Panama who had not as yet paid their ransoms, and all transported.... About the middle of the way unto the Castle of Chagre, Captain Morgan commanded them to be placed in due order, according to their custom, and caused every one to be sworn, that they had reserved nor concealed nothing privately to themselves, even not so much as the value of sixpence. This being done, Captain Morgan having had some experience that those lewd fellows would not much stickle to swear falsely in points of interest, he commanded them every one to be searched very strictly, both in their clothes and satchels and everywhere it might be presumed they had reserved anything. Yea, to the intent this order might not be ill taken by his companions, he permitted himself to be searched, even to the very soles of his shoes. To this effect by common consent, there was assigned one out of every company to be the searchers of all the rest. The French Pirates that went on this expedition with Captain Morgan were not well satisfied with this new custom of searching. Yet their number being less than that of the English, they were forced to submit unto it, as well as the others had done before them. The search being over, they re-embarked in their canoes and boats, which attended them on the river, and arrived at the Castle of Chagre.[314] ... Here they found all things in good order, excepting the wounded men, whom they had left there at the time of their departure. For of these the greatest number were dead, through the wounds they had received.

"From Chagre, Captain Morgan sent presently after his arrival, a great boat unto Porto Bello, wherein were all the prisoners he had taken at the Isle of St. Catherine, demanding by them a considerable ransom for the Castle of Chagre, where he then was, threatening otherwise to ruin and demolish it even to the ground. To this message those of Porto Bello made answer: they would not give one farthing towards the ransom of the said castle, and that the English might do with it as they pleased. This answer being come, the dividend was made of all the spoil they had purchased in that voyage. Thus every company and every particular person therein included received their portion of what was gotten; or rather what part thereof Captain Morgan was pleased to give them. For so it was, that the rest of his companions, even of his own nation, complained of his proceedings in this particular, and feared not to tell him openly to his face, that he had reserved the best jewels to himself. For they judged it impossible that no greater share should belong unto them than two hundred pieces of eight per capita, of so many valuable purchases and robberies as they had obtained. Which small sum they thought too little reward for so much labour and such huge and manifest dangers as they had so often exposed their lives unto. But Captain Morgan was deaf to all these and many other complaints of this kind, having designed in his mind to cheat them of as much as he could."[315]

On 6th March 1671, Morgan, after demolishing the fort and other edifices at Chagre and spiking all the guns, got secretly on board his own ship, if we are to believe Exquemelin, and followed by only three or four vessels of the fleet, returned to Port Royal. The rest of the fleet scattered, most of the ships having "much ado to find sufficient victuals and provisions for their voyage to Jamaica." At the end of August not more than ten vessels of the original thirty-six had made their way back to the English colony. Morgan, with very inadequate means, accomplished a feat which had been the dream of Drake and other English sailors for a century or more, and which Admiral Vernon in 1741 with a much greater armament feared even to attempt. For display of remarkable leadership and reckless bravery the expedition against Panama has never been surpassed. Its brilliance was only clouded by the cruelty and rapacity of the victors —a force levied without pay and little discipline, and unrestrained, if not encouraged, in brutality by Morgan himself. Exquemelin's accusation against Morgan, of avarice and dishonesty in the division of the spoil amongst his followers, is, unfortunately for the admiral's reputation, too well substantiated. Richard Browne, the surgeon-general of the fleet, estimated the plunder at over £70,000 "besides other rich goods," of which the soldiers were miserably cheated, each man receiving but £10 as his share. At Chagre, he writes, the leaders gave what they pleased "for which ... we must be content or else be clapped in irons." The wronged seamen were loud in their complaints against Morgan, Collier and the other captains for starving, cheating and deserting them; but so long as Modyford was governor they could obtain no redress. The commanders "dared but seldom appear," writes Browne, "the widows, orphans and injured inhabitants who had so freely advanced upon the hopes of a glorious design, being now ruined through fitting out the privateers."[316] The Spaniards reckoned their whole loss at 6,000,000 crowns.[317]

On 31st May 1671, the Council of Jamaica extended a vote of thanks to Morgan for the execution of his late commission, and formally expressed their approval of the manner in which he had conducted himself.[318] There can be no question but that the governor had full knowledge of Morgan's intentions before the fleet sailed from Cape Tiburon. After the decision of the council of officers on 2nd December to attack Panama, a boat was dispatched to Jamaica to inform Modyford, and in a letter written to Morgan ten days after the arrival of the vessel the governor gave no countermand to the decision.[319] Doubtless the defence made, that the governor and council were trying to forestall an impending invasion of Jamaica by the Spaniards, was sincere. But it is also very probable that they were in part deceived into this belief by Morgan and his followers, who made it their first object to get prisoners, and obtain from them by force a confession that at Cartagena, Porto Bello or some other Spanish maritime port the Spaniards were mustering men and fitting a fleet to invade the island.

By a strange irony of fate, on 8th-18th July 1670 a treaty was concluded at Madrid by Sir William Godolphin for "composing differences, restraining depredations and establishing peace" in America. No trading privileges in the West Indies were granted by either crown, but the King of Spain acknowledged the sovereignty of the King of England over all islands, colonies, etc., in America then in possession of the English, and the ships of either nation, in case of distress, were to have entertainment and aid in the ports of the other. The treaty was to be published in the West Indies simultaneously by English and Spanish governors within eight months after its ratification.[320] In May of the following year, a messenger from San Domingo arrived in Port Royal with a copy of the articles of peace, to propose that a day be fixed for their publication, and to offer an exchange of prisoners,[321] Modyford had as yet received no official notice from England of the treaty, and might with justice complain to the authorities at home of their neglect.[322] Shortly after, however, a new governor came to relieve him of further responsibility. Charles II. had probably placated the Spanish ambassador in 1670 by promising the removal of Modyford and the dispatch of another governor well-disposed to the Spaniards.[323] At any rate, a commission was issued in September 1670, appointing Colonel Thomas Lynch Lieutenant-Governor of Jamaica, to command there in the "want, absence or disability" of the governor;[324] and on 4th January following, in spite of a petition of the officers, freeholders and inhabitants of Jamaica in favour of Modyford,[325] the commission of the governor was revoked.[326] Lynch arrived in Jamaica on 25th June with instructions, as soon as he had possession of the government and forts, to arrest Sir Thomas Modyford and send him home under guard to answer charges laid against him.[327] Fearing to exasperate the friends of the old governor, Lynch hesitated to carry out his instructions until 12th August, when he invited Modyford on board the frigate "Assistance," with several members of the council, and produced the royal orders for his arrest. Lynch assured him, however, that his life and fortune were not in danger, the proceeding being merely a sop to the indignant Spaniards.[328] Modyford arrived in England in November, and on the 17th of the month was committed to the Tower.[329]

The indignation of the Spaniards, when the news of the sack of Panama reached Spain, rose to a white heat. "It is impossible for me to paint to your Lordship," wrote Godolphin to Lord Arlington, "the face of Madrid upon the news of this action … nor to what degree of indignation the queen and ministers of State, the particular councils and all sorts of people here, have taken it to heart."[330] It seems that the ambassador or the Spanish consul in London had written to Madrid that this last expedition was made by private intimation, if not orders, from London, and that Godolphin had been commanded to provide in the treaty for a long term before publication, so as to give time for the execution of the design. Against these falsehoods the English ambassador found it difficult to make headway, although he assured the queen of the immediate punishment of the perpetrators, and the arrest and recall of the Governor of Jamaica. Only by the greatest tact and prudence was he able to stave off, until an official disavowal of the expedition came from England, an immediate embargo on all the goods of English merchants in Spain. The Spanish government decided to send a fleet of 10,000 men with all speed to the Indies; and the Dukes of Albuquerque and Medina Coeli vied with each other in offering to raise the men at their own charge from among their own vassals. After Godolphin had presented his official assurance to the queen, however, nothing more was heard of this armament. "God grant," wrote the English ambassador, "that Sir Thomas Modyford's way of defending Jamaica (as he used to call it) by sending out the forces thereof to pillage, prove an infallible one; for my own part, I do not think it hath been our interest to awaken the Spaniards so much as this last action hath done."[331]

Chapter VI

The Government Suppresses the Buccaneers

The new Lieutenant-Governor of Jamaica, Sir Thomas Lynch, brought with him instructions to publish and carefully observe the articles of 1670 with Spain, and at the same time to revoke all commissions issued by his predecessor "to the prejudice of the King of Spain or any of his subjects." When he proclaimed the peace he was likewise to publish a general pardon to privateers who came in and submitted within a reasonable time, of all offences committed since June 1660, assuring to them the possession of their prize-goods (except the tenths and the fifteenths which were always reserved to the crown as a condition of granting commissions), and offering them inducements to take up planting, trade, or service in the royal navy. But he was not to insist positively on the payment of the tenths and fifteenths if it discouraged their submission; and if this course failed to bring in the rovers, he was to use every means in his power "by force or persuasion" to make them submit.[332] Lynch immediately set about to secure the good-will of his Spanish neighbours and to win back the privateers to more peaceful pursuits. Major Beeston was sent to Cartagena with the articles of peace, where he was given every satisfaction and secured the release of thirty-two English prisoners.[333] On the 15th August the proclamation of pardon to privateers was issued at Port Royal;[334] and those who had railed against their commanders for cheating them at Panama, were given an opportunity of resorting to the law-courts.[335] Similar proclamations were sent by the governor "to all their haunts," intimating that he had written to Bermuda, the Caribbees, New England, New York and Virginia for their apprehension, had sent notices to all Spanish ports declaring them pirates, and intended to send to Tortuga to prevent their reception there.[336] However, although the governor wrote home in the latter part of the month that the privateers were entirely suppressed, he soon found that the task was by no means a simple one. Two buccaneers with a commission from Modyford, an Englishman named Thurston and a mulatto named Diego, flouted his offer of pardon, continued to prey upon Spanish shipping, and carried their prizes to Tortuga.[337] A Dutchman named Captain Yallahs (or Yellowes) fled to Campeache, sold his frigate for 7000 pieces of eight to the Spanish governor, and entered into Spanish service to cruise against the English logwood-cutters. The Governor of Jamaica sent Captain Wilgress in pursuit, but Wilgress devoted his time to chasing a Spanish vessel ashore, stealing logwood and burning Spanish houses on the coast.[338] A party of buccaneers, English and French, landed upon the north side of Cuba and burnt two towns, carrying away women and inflicting many cruelties on the inhabitants; and when the governors of Havana and St. Jago complained to Lynch, the latter could only disavow the English in the marauding party as rebels and pirates, and bid the Spanish governors hang all who fell into their power.[339] The governor, in fact, was having his hands full, and wrote in January 1672 that "this cursed trade has been so long followed, and there is so many of it, that like weeds or hydras, they spring up as fast as we can cut them down."[340]

Some of the recalcitrant freebooters, however, were captured and brought to justice. Major Beeston, sent by the governor in January 1672, with a frigate and four smaller vessels, to seize and burn some pirate ships careening on the south cays of Cuba, fell in instead with two other vessels, one English and one French, which had taken part in the raids upon Cuba, and carried them to Jamaica. The French captain was offered to the Governor of St. Jago, but the latter refused to punish him for fear of his comrades in Tortuga and Hispaniola. Both captains were therefore tried and condemned to death at Port Royal. As the Spaniards, however, had refused to punish them, and as there was no reason why the Jamaicans should be the executioners, the captains of the port and some of the council begged for a reprieve, and the English prisoner, Francis Witherborn, was sent to England.[341] Captain Johnson, one of the pirates after whom Beeston had originally been sent, was later in the year shipwrecked by a hurricane upon the coast of Jamaica. Johnson, immediately after the publication of the peace by Sir Thomas Lynch, had fled from Port Royal with about ten followers, and falling in with a Spanish ship of eighteen guns, had seized it and killed the captain and twelve or fourteen of the crew. Then gathering about him a party of a hundred or more, English and French, he had robbed Spanish vessels round Havana and the Cuban coast. Finally, however, he grew weary of his French companions, and sailed for Jamaica to make terms with the governor, when on coming to anchor in Morant Bay he was blown ashore by the hurricane. The governor had him arrested, and gave a commission to Colonel Modyford, the son of Sir Thomas, to assemble the justices and proceed to trial and immediate execution. He adjured him, moreover, to see to it that the pirate was not acquitted. Colonel Modyford, nevertheless, sharing perhaps his father's sympathy with the sea-rovers, deferred the trial, acquainted none of the justices with his orders, and although Johnson and two of his men "confessed enough to hang a hundred honester persons," told the jury they could not find against the prisoner. Half an hour after the dismissal of the court, Johnson "came to drink with his judges." The baffled governor thereupon placed Johnson a second time under arrest, called a meeting of the council, from which he dismissed Colonel Modyford, and "finding material errors," reversed the judgment. The pirate was again tried-Lynch himself this time presiding over the court-and upon making a full confession, was condemned and executed, though "as much regretted," writes Lynch, "as if he had been as pious and as innocent as one of the primitive martyrs." The second trial was contrary to the fundamental principles of English law, howsoever guilty the culprit may have been, and the king sent a letter to Lynch reproving him for his rashness. He commanded the governor to try all pirates thereafter by maritime law, and if a disagreement arose to remit the case to the king for re-judgment. Nevertheless he ordered Lynch to suspend from all public employments in the island, whether civil or military, both Colonel Modyford and all others guilty with him of designedly acquitting Johnson.[342]

The Spaniards in the West Indies, notwithstanding the endeavours of Sir Thomas Lynch to clear their coasts of pirates, made little effort to co-operate with him. The governors of Cartagena and St. Jago de Cuba, pretending that they feared being punished for allowing trade, had forbidden English frigates to come into their ports, and refused them provisions and water; and the Governor of Campeache had detained money, plate and negroes taken out of an English trading-vessel, to the value of 12,000 pieces of eight. When Lynch sent to demand satisfaction, the governor referred him to Madrid for justice, "which to me that have been there," writes Lynch, "seems worse than the taking it away."[343] The news also of the imposing armament, which the Spanish grandees made signs of preparing to send to the Indies on learning of the capture of Panama, was in November 1671 just beginning to filter into Jamaica; and the governor and council, fearing that the fleet was directed against them, made vigorous efforts, by repairing the forts, collecting stores and marshalling the militia, to put the island in a state of defence. The Spanish fleet never appeared, however, and life on the island soon subsided into its customary channels.[344] Sir Thomas Lynch, meanwhile, was all the more careful to observe the peace with Spain and yet refrain from alienating the more troublesome elements of the population. It had been decided in England that Morgan, too, like Modyford, was to be sacrificed, formally at least, to the remonstrances of the Spanish Government; yet Lynch, because Morgan himself was ill, and fearing perhaps that two such arrests might create a disturbance among the friends of the culprits, or at least deter the buccaneers from coming in under the declaration of amnesty, did not send the admiral to England until the following spring. On 6th April 1672 Morgan sailed from Jamaica a prisoner in the frigate "Welcome."[345] He sailed, however, with the universal respect and sympathy of all parties in the colony. Lynch himself calls him "an honest, brave fellow," and Major James Banister in a letter to the Secretary of State recommends him to the esteem of Arlington as "a very well deserving person, and one of great courage and conduct, who may, with his Majesty's pleasure, perform good service at home, and be very advantageous to the island if war should break forth with the Spaniard."[346]

Indeed Morgan, the buccaneer, was soon in high favour at the dissolute court of Charles II., and when in January 1674 the Earl of Carlisle was chosen Governor of Jamaica, Morgan was selected as his deputy[347] —an act which must have entirely neutralized in Spanish Councils the effect of his arrest a year and a half earlier. Lord Carlisle, however, did not go out to Jamaica until 1678, and meanwhile in April a commission to be governor was issued to Lord Vaughan,[348] and several months later another to Morgan as lieutenant-governor.[349] Vaughan arrived in Jamaica in the middle of March 1675; but Morgan, whom the king in the meantime had knighted, sailed ahead of Vaughan, apparently in defiance of the governor's orders, and although shipwrecked on the Isle la Vache, reached Jamaica a week before his superior.[350] It seems that Sir Thomas Modyford sailed for Jamaica with Morgan, and the return of these two arch-offenders to the West Indies filled the Spanish Court with new alarms. The Spanish ambassador in London presented a memorial of protest to the English king,[351] and in Spain the Council of War blossomed into fresh activity to secure the defence of the West Indies and the coasts of the South Sea.[352] Ever since 1672, indeed, the Spaniards moved by some strange infatuation, had persisted in a course of active hostility to the English in the West Indies. Could the Spanish Government have realized the inherent weakness of its American possessions, could it have been informed of the scantiness of the population in proportion to the large extent of territory and coast-line to be defended, could it have known how in the midst of such rich, unpeopled countries abounding with cattle, hogs and other provisions, the buccaneers could be extirpated only by co-operation with its English and French neighbours, it would have soon fallen back upon a policy of peace and good understanding with England. But the news of the sack of Panama, following so close upon the conclusion of the treaty of 1670, and the continued depredations of the buccaneers of Tortuga and the declared pirates of Jamaica, had shattered irrevocably the reliance of the Spaniards upon the good faith of the English Government. And when Morgan was knighted and sent back to Jamaica as lieutenant-governor, their suspicions seemed to be confirmed. A ketch, sent to Cartagena in 1672 by Sir Thomas Lynch to trade in negroes, was seized by the general of the galleons, the goods burnt in the market-place, and the negroes sold for the Spanish King's account.[353] An Irish papist, named Philip Fitzgerald, commanding a Spanish man-of-war of twelve guns belonging to Havana, and a Spaniard called Don Francisco with a commission from the Governor of Campeache, roamed the West Indian seas and captured English vessels sailing from Jamaica to London, Virginia and the Windward Islands, barbarously ill-treating and sometimes massacring the English mariners who fell into their hands.[354] The Spanish governors, in spite of the treaty and doubtless in conformity with orders from home,[355] did nothing to restrain the cruelties of these privateers. At one time eight English sailors who had been captured in a barque off Port Royal and carried to Havana, on attempting to escape from the city were pursued by a party of soldiers, and all of them murdered, the head of the master being set on a pole before the governor's door.[356] At another time Fitzgerald sailed into the harbour of Havana with five Englishmen tied ready to hang, two at the main-yard arms, two at the fore-yard arms, and one at the mizzen peak, and as he approached the castle he had the wretches swung off, while he and his men shot at the dangling corpses from the decks of the vessel.[357] The repeated complaints and demands for reparation made to the Spanish ambassador in London, and by Sir William Godolphin to the Spanish Court, were answered by counter-complaints of outrages committed by buccaneers who, though long ago disavowed and declared pirates by the Governor of Jamaica, were still charged by the Spaniards to the account of the English.[358] Each return of the fleet from Porto Bello or Vera Cruz brought with it English prisoners from Cartagena and other Spanish fortresses, who were lodged in the dungeons of Seville and often condemned to the galleys or to the quicksilver mines. The English ambassador sometimes secured their release, but his efforts to obtain redress for the loss of ships and goods received no satisfaction. The Spanish Government, believing that Parliament was solicitous of Spanish trade and would not supply Charles II. with the necessary funds for a war,[359] would disburse nothing in damages. It merely granted to the injured parties despatches directed to the Governor of Havana, which ordered him to restore the property in dispute unless it was contraband goods. Godolphin realized that these delays and excuses were only the prelude to an ultimate denial of any reparation whatever, and wrote home to the Secretary of State that "England ought rather to provide against future injuries than to depend on satisfaction here, till they have taught the Spaniards their own interest in the West Indies by more efficient means than friendship."[360] The aggrieved merchants and shipowners, often only too well acquainted with the dilatory Spanish forms of procedure, saw that redress at Havana was hopeless, and petitioned Charles II. for letters of reprisal.[361] Sir Leoline Jenkins, Judge of the Admiralty, however, in a report to the king gave his opinion that although he saw little hope of real reparation, the granting of reprisals was not justified by law until the cases had been prosecuted at Havana according to the queen-regent's orders.[362] This apparently was never done, and some of the cases dragged on for years without the petitioners ever receiving satisfaction.

The excuse of the Spaniards for most of these seizures was that the vessels contained logwood, a dyewood found upon the coasts of Campeache, Honduras and Yucatan, the cutting and removal of which was forbidden to any but Spanish subjects. The occupation of cutting logwood had sprung up among the English about ten years after the seizure of Jamaica. In 1670 Modyford writes that a dozen vessels belonging to Port Royal were concerned in this trade alone, and six months later he furnished a list of thirty-two ships employed in logwood cutting, equipped with seventy-four guns and 424 men.[363] The men engaged in the business had most of them been privateers, and as the regions in which they sought the precious wood were entirely uninhabited by Spaniards, Modyford suggested that the trade be encouraged as an outlet for the energies of the buccaneers. By such means, he thought, these "soldiery men" might be kept within peaceable bounds, and yet be always ready to serve His Majesty in event of any new rupture. When Sir Thomas Lynch replaced Modyford, he realized that this logwood-cutting would be resented by the Spaniards and might neutralize all his efforts to effect a peace. He begged repeatedly for directions from the council in England. "For God's sake," he writes, "give your commands about the logwood."[364] In the meantime, after consulting with Modyford, he decided to connive at the business, but he compelled all who brought the wood into Port Royal to swear that they had not stolen it or done any violence to the Spaniards.[365] Secretary Arlington wrote to the governor, in November 1671, to hold the matter over until he obtained the opinion of the English ambassador at Madrid, especially as some colour was lent to the pretensions of the logwood cutters by the article of the peace of 1670 which confirmed the English King in the possession and sovereignty of all territory in America occupied by his subjects at that date.[366] In May 1672 Ambassador Godolphin returned his answer. "The wood," he writes, "is brought from Yucatan, a large province of New Spain, about 100 leagues in length, sufficiently peopled, having several great towns, as Merida, Valladolid, San Francisco de Campeache, etc., and the government one of the most considerable next to Peru and Mexico....So that Spain has as well too much right as advantage not to assert the propriety of these woods, for though not all inhabited, these people may as justly pretend to make use of our rivers, mountains and commons, as we can to enjoy any benefit to those woods." So much for the strict justice of the matter. But when the ambassador came to give his own opinion on the trade, he advised that if the English confined themselves to cutting wood alone, and in places remote from Spanish settlements, the king might connive at, although not authorize, their so doing.[367] Here was the kernel of the whole matter. Spain was too weak and impotent to take any serious revenge. So let us rob her quietly but decently, keeping the theft out of her sight and so sparing her feelings as much as possible. It was the same piratical motive which animated Drake and Hawkins, which impelled Morgan to sack Maracaibo and Panama, and which, transferred to the dignified council chambers of England, took on a more humane but less romantic guise. On 8th October 1672, the Council for the Plantations dispatched to Governor Lynch their approval of his connivance at the business, but they urged him to observe every care and prudence, to countenance the cutting only in desolate and uninhabited places, and to use every endeavour to prevent any just complaints by the Spaniards of violence and depredation.[368]

The Spaniards nevertheless did, as we have seen, engage in active reprisal, especially as they knew the cutting of logwood to be but the preliminary step to the growth of English settlements upon the coasts of Yucatan and Honduras, settlements, indeed, which later crystallized into a British colony. The Queen-Regent of Spain sent orders and instructions to her governors in the West Indies to encourage privateers to take and punish as pirates all English and French who robbed and carried away wood within their jurisdictions; and three small frigates from Biscay were sent to clear out the intruders.[369] The buccaneer Yallahs, we have seen, was employed by the Governor of Campeache to seize the logwood-cutters; and although he surprised twelve or more vessels, the Governor of Jamaica, not daring openly to avow the business, could enter no complaint. On 3rd November 1672, however, he was compelled to issue a proclamation ordering all vessels sailing from Port Royal for the purpose of cutting dye-wood to go in fleets of at least four as security against surprise and capture. Under the governorship of Lord Vaughan, and after him of Lord Carlisle, matters continued in this same uncertain course, the English settlements in Honduras gradually increasing in numbers and vitality, and the Spaniards maintaining their right to take all ships they found at sea laden with logwood, and indeed, all English and French ships found upon their coasts. Each of the English governors in turn had urged that some equitable adjustment of the trade be made with the Spanish Crown, if peace was to be preserved in the Indies and the buccaneers finally suppressed; but the Spaniards would agree to no accommodation, and in March 1679 the king wrote to Lord Carlisle bidding him discourage, as far as possible, the logwood-cutting in Campeache or any other of the Spanish dominions, and to try and induce the buccaneers to apply themselves to planting instead.[370]

The reprisals of the Spaniards on the score of logwood-cutting were not the only difficulties with which Lord Vaughan as governor had to contend. From the day of his landing in Jamaica he seems to have conceived a violent dislike of his lieutenant, Sir Henry Morgan, and this antagonism was embittered by Morgan's open or secret sympathy with the privateers, a race with whom Vaughan had nothing in common. The ship on which Morgan had sailed from England, and which was cast away upon the Isle la Vache, had contained the military stores for Jamaica, most of which were lost in the wreck. Morgan, contrary to Lord Vaughan's positive and written orders, had sailed before him, and assumed the authority in Jamaica a week before the arrival of the governor at Port Royal. This the governor seems to have been unable to forgive. He openly blamed Morgan for the wreck and the loss of the stores; and only two months after his coming to Jamaica, in May 1675, he wrote to England that for the good of His Majesty's service he thought Morgan ought to be removed, and the charge of so useless an officer saved.[371] In September he wrote that he was "every day more convinced of (Morgan's) imprudence and unfitness to have anything to do in the Civil Government, and of what hazards the island may run by so dangerous a succession." Sir Henry, he continued, had made himself and his authority so cheap at the Port, drinking and gaming in the taverns, that the governor intended to remove thither speedily himself for the reputation of the island and the security of the place.[372] He recommended that his predecessor, Sir Thomas Lynch, whom he praises for "his prudent government and conduct of affairs," be appointed his deputy instead of Morgan in the event of the governor's death or absence.[373] Lord Vaughan's chief grievance, however, was the lieutenant-governor's secret encouragement of the buccaneers. "What I most resent," he writes again, "is ... that I find Sir Henry, contrary to his duty and trust, endeavours to set up privateering, and has obstructed all my designs and purposes for the reducing of those that do use this course of life."[374] When he had issued proclamations, the governor continued, declaring as pirates all the buccaneers who refused to submit, Sir Henry had encouraged the English freebooters to take French commissions, had himself fitted them out for sea, and had received authority from the French Governor of Tortuga to collect the tenths on prize goods brought into Jamaica under cover of these commissions. The quarrel came to a head over the arrest and trial of a buccaneer named John Deane, commander of the ship "St. David." Deane was accused of having stopped a ship called the "John Adventure," taken out several pipes of wine and a cable worth £100, and forcibly carried the vessel to Jamaica. He was also reported to be wearing Dutch, French and Spanish colours without commission.[375] When the "John Adventure" entered Port Royal it was seized by the governor for landing goods without entry, contrary to the Acts of Navigation, and on complaint of the master of the vessel that he had been robbed by Deane and other privateers, Sir Henry Morgan was ordered to imprison the offenders. The lieutenant-governor, however, seems rather to have encouraged them to escape,[376] until Deane made so bold as to accuse the governor of illegal seizure. Deane was in consequence arrested by the governor, and on 27th April 1676, in a Court of Admiralty presided over by Lord Vaughan as vice-admiral, was tried and condemned to suffer death as a pirate.[377] The proceedings, however, were not warranted by legal practice, for according to statutes of the twenty-seventh and twenty-eighth years of Henry VIII., pirates might not be tried in an Admiralty Court, but only under the Common Law of England by a Commission of Oyer and Terminer under the great seal.[378] After obtaining an opinion to this effect from the Judge of the Admiralty, the English Council wrote to Lord Vaughan staying the execution of Deane, and ordering a new trial to be held under a proper commission about to be forwarded to him.[379] The Governor of Jamaica, however, upon receiving a confession from Deane and frequent petitions for pardon, had reprieved the pirate a month before the letter from the council reached him.[380] The incident had good effect in persuading the freebooters to come in, and that result assured, the governor could afford to bend to popular clamour in favour of the culprit. In the latter part of 1677 a standing commission of Oyer and Terminer for the trial of pirates in Jamaica was prepared by the attorney-general and sent to the colony.[381]

After the trial of Deane, the lieutenant-governor, according to Lord Vaughan, had openly expressed himself, both in the taverns and in his own house, in vindication of the condemned man and in disparagement of Vaughan himself.[382] The quarrel hung fire, however, until on 24th July when the governor, in obedience to orders from England,[383] cited Morgan and his brother-in-law, Colonel Byndloss, to appear before the council. Against Morgan he brought formal charges of using the governor's name and authority without his orders in letters written to the captains of the privateers, and Byndloss he accused of unlawfully holding a commission from a foreign governor to collect the tenths on condemned prize goods.[384] Morgan in his defence to Secretary Coventry flatly denied the charges, and denounced the letters written to the privateers as forgeries; and Byndloss declared his readiness "to go in this frigate with a tender of six or eight guns and so to deal with the privateers at sea, and in their holes (sic) bring in the chief of them to His Majesty's obedience or bring in their heads and destroy their ships."[385] There seems to be little doubt that letters were written by Morgan to certain privateers soon after his arrival in Jamaica, offering them, in the name of the governor, favour and protection in Port Royal. Copies of these letters, indeed, still exist;[386] but whether they were actually used is not so certain. Charles Barre, secretary to Sir Henry Morgan, confessed that such letters had been written, but with the understanding that the governor lent them his approval, and that when this was denied Sir Henry refused to send them.[387] It is natural to suppose that Morgan should feel a bond of sympathy with his old companions in the buccaneer trade, and it is probable that in 1675, in the first enthusiasm of his return to Jamaica, having behind him the openly-expressed approbation of the English Court for what he had done in the past, and feeling uncertain, perhaps, as to Lord Vaughan's real attitude toward the sea-rovers, Morgan should have done some things inconsistent with the policy of stern suppression pursued by the government. It is even likely that he was indiscreet in some of his expressions regarding the governor and his actions. His bluff, unconventional, easygoing manners, natural to men brought up in new countries and intensified by his early association with the buccaneers, may have been distasteful to a courtier accustomed to the urbanities of Whitehall. It is also clear, however, that Lord Vaughan from the first conceived a violent prejudice against his lieutenant, and allowed this prejudice to colour the interpretation he put upon all of Sir Henry's actions. And it is rather significant that although the particulars of the dispute and of the examination before the Council of Jamaica were sent to the Privy Council in England, the latter body did not see fit to remove Morgan from his post until six years later.

As in the case of Modyford and Lynch, so with Lord Vaughan, the thorn in his side was the French colony on Hispaniola and Tortuga. The English buccaneers who would not come in under the proclamation of pardon published at Port Royal, still continued to range the seas with French commissions, and carried their prizes into French ports. The governor protested to M. d'Ogeron and to his successor, M. de Pouançay, declaring that any English vessels or subjects caught with commissions against the Spaniards would be treated as pirates and rebels; and in December 1675, in compliance with the king's orders of the previous August, he issued a public proclamation to that effect.[388] In April 1677 an act was passed by the assembly, declaring it felony for any English subject belonging to the island to serve under a foreign prince or state without licence under the hand and seal of the governor;[389] and in the following July the council ordered another proclamation to be issued, offering ample pardon to all men in foreign service who should come in within twelve months to claim the benefit of the act.[390] These measures seem to have been fairly successful, for on 1st August Peter Beckford, Clerk of the Council in Jamaica, wrote to Secretary Williamson that since the passing of the law at least 300 privateers had come in and submitted, and that few men would now venture their lives to serve the French.[391]

Even with the success of this act, however, the path of the governor was not all roses. Buccaneering had always been so much a part of the life of the colony that it was difficult to stamp it out entirely. Runaway servants and others from the island frequently recruited the ranks of the freebooters; members of the assembly, and even of the council, were interested in privateering ventures; and as the governor was without a sufficient naval force to deal with the offenders independently of the council and assembly, he often found his efforts fruitless. In the early part of 1677 a Scotchman, named James Browne, with a commission from M. d'Ogeron and a mixed crew of English, Dutch and French, seized a Dutch ship trading in negroes off the coast of Cartagena, killed the Dutch captain and several of his men, and landed the negroes, about 150 in number, in a remote bay of Jamaica. Lord Vaughan sent a frigate which seized about 100 of the negroes, and when Browne and his crew fell into the governor's hands he had them all tried and condemned for piracy. Browne was ordered to be executed, but his men, eight in number, were pardoned. The captain petitioned the assembly to have the benefit of the Act of Privateers, and the House twice sent a committee to the governor to endeavour to obtain a reprieve. Lord Vaughan, however, refused to listen and gave orders for immediate execution. Half an hour after the hanging, the provost-marshal appeared with an order signed by the speaker to observe the Chief-Justice's writ of Habeas Corpus, whereupon Vaughan, resenting the action, immediately dissolved the Assembly.[392]

The French colony on Hispaniola was an object of concern to the Jamaicans, not only because it served as a refuge for privateers from Port Royal, but also because it threatened soon to overwhelm the old Spanish colony and absorb the whole island. Under the conciliatory, opportunist regime of M. d'Ogeron, the French settlements in the west of the island had grown steadily in number and size;[393] while the old Spanish towns seemed every year to become weaker and more open to attack. D'Ogeron, who died in France in 1675, had kept always before him the project of capturing the Spanish capital, San Domingo; but he was too weak to accomplish so great a design without aid from home, and this was never vouchsafed him. His policy, however, was continued by his nephew and successor, M. de Pouançay, and every defection from Jamaica seemed so much assistance to the French to accomplish their ambition. Yet it was manifestly to the English interest in the West Indies not to permit the French to obtain a pre-eminence there. The Spanish colonies were large in area, thinly populated, and ill-supported by the home government, so that they were not likely to be a serious menace to the English islands. With their great wealth and resources, moreover, they had few manufactures and offered a tempting field for exploitation by English merchants. The French colonies, on the other hand, were easily supplied with merchandise from France, and in event of a war would prove more dangerous as neighbours than the Spaniards. To allow the French to become lords of San Domingo would have been to give them an undisputed predominance in the West Indies and make them masters of the neighbouring seas.

In the second war of conquest waged by Louis XIV. against Holland, the French in the West Indies found the buccaneers to be useful allies, but as usually happened at such times, the Spaniards paid the bill. In the spring of 1677 five or six English privateers surprised the town of Santa Marta on the Spanish Main. According to the reports brought to Jamaica, the governor and the bishop, in order to save the town from being burnt, agreed with the marauders for a ransom; but the Governor of Cartagena, instead of contributing with pieces of eight, despatched a force of 500 men by land and three vessels by sea to drive out the invaders. The Spanish troops, however, were easily defeated, and the ships, seeing the French colours waving over the fort and the town, sailed back to Cartagena. The privateers carried away the governor and the bishop and came to Jamaica in July. The plunder amounted to only £20 per man. The English in the party, about 100 in number and led by Captains Barnes and Coxon, submitted at Port Royal under the terms of the Act against Privateers, and delivered up the Bishop of Santa Marta to Lord Vaughan. Vaughan took care to lodge the bishop well, and hired a vessel to send him to Cartagena, at which "the good old man was exceedingly pleased." He also endeavoured to obtain the custody of the Spanish governor and other prisoners, but without success, "the French being obstinate and damnably enraged the English had left them" and submitted to Lord Vaughan.[394]

In the beginning of the following year, 1678, Count d'Estrées, Vice-Admiral of the French fleet in the West Indies, was preparing a powerful armament to go against the Dutch on Curaçao, and sent two frigates to Hispaniola with an order from the king to M. de Pouançay to join him with 1200 buccaneers. De Pouançay assembled the men at Cap François, and embarking on the frigates and on some filibustering ships in the road, sailed for St. Kitts. There he was joined by a squadron of fifteen or more men-of-war from Martinique under command of Count d'Estrées. The united fleet of over thirty vessels sailed for Curaçao on 7th May, but on the fourth day following, at about eight o'clock in the evening, was wrecked upon some coral reefs near the Isle d'Aves.[395] As the French pilots had been at odds among themselves as to the exact position of the fleet, the admiral had taken the precaution to send a fire-ship and three buccaneering vessels several miles in advance of the rest of the squadron. Unfortunately these scouts drew too little water and passed over the reefs without touching them. A buccaneer was the first to strike and fired three shots to warn the admiral, who at once lighted fires and discharged cannon to keep off the rest of the ships. The latter, however, mistaking the signals, crowded on sail, and soon most of the fleet were on the reefs. Those of the left wing, warned in time by a shallop from the flag-ship, succeeded in veering off. The rescue of the crews was slow, for the seas were heavy and the boats approached the doomed ships with difficulty. Many sailors and marines were drowned, and seven men-of-war, besides several buccaneering ships, were lost on the rocks. Count d'Estrées himself escaped, and sailed with the remnant of his squadron to Petit Goave and Cap François in Hispaniola, whence on 18th June he departed for France.[396]

The buccaneers were accused in the reports which reached Barbadoes of deserting the admiral after the accident, and thus preventing the reduction of Curaçao, which d'Estrées would have undertaken in spite of the shipwreck.[397] However this may be, one of the principal buccaneer leaders, named de Grammont, was left by de Pouançay at the Isle d'Aves to recover what he could from the wreck, and to repair some of the privateering vessels.[398] When he had accomplished this, finding himself short of provisions, he sailed with about 700 men to make a descent on Maracaibo; and after spending six months in the lake, seizing the shipping and plundering all the settlements in that region, he re-embarked in the middle of December. The booty is said to have been very small.[399] Early in the same year the Marquis de Maintenon, commanding the frigate "La Sorcière," and aided by some French filibusters from Tortuga, was on the coast of Caracas, where he ravaged the islands of Margarita and Trinidad. He had arrived in the West Indies from France in the latter part of 1676, and when he sailed from Tortuga was at the head of 700 or 800 men. His squadron met with little success, however, and soon scattered.[400] Other bands of filibusters pillaged Campeache, Puerto Principe in Cuba, Santo Tomas on the Orinoco, and Truxillo in the province of Honduras; and de Pouançay, to console the buccaneers for their losses at the Isle d'Aves, sent 800 men under the Sieur de Franquesnay to make a descent upon St. Jago de Cuba, but the expedition seems to have been a failure.[401]

On 1st March 1678 a commission was again issued to the Earl of Carlisle, appointing him governor of Jamaica.[402] Carlisle arrived in his new government on 18th July,[403] but Lord Vaughan, apparently because of ill-health, had already sailed for England at the end of March, leaving Sir Henry Morgan, who retained his place under the new governor, deputy in his absence.[404] Lord Carlisle, immediately upon his arrival, invited the privateers to come in and encouraged them to stay, hoping, according to his own account, to be able to wean them from their familiar courses, and perhaps to use them in the threatened war with France, for the island then had "not above 4000 whites able to bear arms, a secret not fit to be made public."[405] If the governor was sincere in his intentions, the results must have been a bitter disappointment. Some of the buccaneers came in, others persevered in the old trade, and even those who returned abused the pardon they had received. In the autumn of 1679, several privateering vessels under command of Captains Coxon, Sharp and others who had come back to Jamaica, made a raid in the Gulf of Honduras, plundered the royal storehouses there, carried off 500 chests of indigo,[406] besides cocoa, cochineal, tortoiseshell, money and plate, and returned with their plunder to Jamaica. Not knowing what their reception might be, one of the vessels landed her cargo of indigo in an unfrequented spot on the coast, and the rest sent word that unless they were allowed to bring their booty to Port Royal and pay the customs duty, they would sail to Rhode Island or to one of the Dutch plantations. The governor had taken security for good behaviour from some of the captains before they sailed from Jamaica; yet in spite of this they were permitted to enter the indigo at the custom house and divide it in broad daylight; and the frigate "Success" was ordered to coast round Jamaica in search of other privateers who failed to come in and pay duty on their plunder at Port Royal. The glut of indigo in Jamaica disturbed trade considerably, and for a time the imported product took the place of native sugar and indigo as a medium of exchange. Manufacture on the island was hindered, prices were lowered, and only the king's customs received any actual benefit.[407]

These same privateers, however, were soon out upon a much larger design. Six captains, Sharp, Coxon, Essex, Allison, Row, and Maggott, in four barques and two sloops, met at Point Morant in December 1679, and on 7th January set sail for Porto Bello. They were scattered by a terrible storm, but all eventually reached their rendezvous in safety. There they picked up another barque commanded by Captain Cooke, who had sailed from Jamaica on the same design, and likewise a French privateering vessel commanded by Captain Lessone. They set out for Porto Bello in canoes with over 300 men, and landing twenty leagues from the town, marched for four days along the seaside toward the city. Coming to an Indian village about three miles from Porto Bello, they were discovered by the natives, and one of the Indians ran to the city, crying, "Ladrones! ladrones!" The buccaneers, although "many of them were weak, being three days without any food, and their feet cut with the rocks for want of shoes," made all speed for the town, which they entered without difficulty on 17th February 1680. Most of the inhabitants sought refuge in the castle, whence they made a counter-attack without success upon the invaders. On the evening of the following day, the buccaneers retreated with their prisoners and booty down to a cay or small island about three and a half leagues from Porto Bello, where they were joined by their ships. They had just left in time to avoid a force of some 700 Spanish troops who were sent from Panama and arrived the day after the buccaneers departed. After capturing two Spanish vessels bound for Porto Bello with provisions from Cartagena, they divided the plunder, of which each man received 100 pieces of eight, and departed for Boca del Toro some fifty leagues to the north. There they careened and provisioned, and being joined by two other Jamaican privateers commanded by Sawkins and Harris, sailed for Golden Island, whence on 5th April 1680, with 334 men, they began their march across the Isthmus of Darien to the coasts of Panama and the South Seas.[408]

Lord Carlisle cannot escape the charge of culpable negligence for having permitted these vessels in the first place to leave Jamaica. All the leaders in the expedition were notorious privateers, men who had repeatedly been concerned in piratical outrages against the Dutch and Spaniards. Coxon and Harris had both come in after taking part in the expedition against Santa Marta; Sawkins had been caught with his vessel by the frigate "Success" and sent to Port Royal, where on 1st December 1679 he seems to have been in prison awaiting trial;[409] while Essex had been brought in by another frigate, the "Hunter," in November, and tried with twenty of his crew for plundering on the Jamaican coast, two of his men being sentenced to death.[410] The buccaneers themselves declared that they had sailed with permission from Lord Carlisle to cut logwood.[411] This was very likely true; yet after the exactly similar ruse of these men when they went to Honduras, the governor could not have failed to suspect their real intentions.

At the end of May 1680 Lord Carlisle suddenly departed for England in the frigate "Hunter," leaving Morgan again in charge as lieutenant-governor.[412] On his passage home the governor met with Captain Coxon, who, having quarrelled with his companions in the Pacific, had returned across Darien to the West Indies and was again hanging about the shores of Jamaica. The "Hunter" gave chase for twenty-four hours, but being outsailed was content to take two small vessels in the company of Coxon which had been deserted by their crews.[413] In England Samuel Long, whom the governor had suspended from the council and dismissed from his post as chief justice of the colony for his opposition to the new Constitution, accused the governor before the Privy Council of collusion with pirates and encouraging them to bring their plunder to Jamaica. The charges were doubtless conceived in a spirit of revenge; nevertheless the two years during which Carlisle was in Jamaica were marked by an increased activity among the freebooters, and by a lukewarmness and negligence on the part of the government, for which Carlisle alone must be held responsible. To accuse him of deliberately supporting and encouraging the buccaneers, however, may be going too far. Sir Henry Morgan, during his tenure of the chief command of the island, showed himself very zealous in the pursuit of the pirates, and sincerely anxious to bring them to justice; and as Carlisle and Morgan always worked together in perfect harmony, we may be justified in believing that Carlisle's mistakes were those of negligence rather than of connivance. The freebooters who brought goods into Jamaica increased the revenues of the island, and a governor whose income was small and tastes extravagant, was not apt to be too inquisitive about the source of the articles which entered through the customs. There is evidence, moreover, that French privateers, being unable to obtain from the merchants on the coast of San Domingo the cables, anchors, tar and other naval stores necessary for their armaments, were compelled to resort to other islands to buy them, and that Jamaica came in for a share of this trade. Provisions, too, were more plentiful at Port Royal than in the cul-de-sac of Hispaniola, and the French governors complained to the king that the filibusters carried most of their money to foreign plantations to exchange for these commodities. Such French vessels if they came to Jamaica were not strictly within the scope of the laws against piracy which had been passed by the assembly, and their visits were the more welcome as they paid for their goods promptly and liberally in good Spanish doubloons.[414]

A general warrant for the apprehension of Coxon, Sharp and the other men who had plundered Porto Bello had been issued by Lord Carlisle in May 1680, just before his departure for England. On 1st July a similar warrant was issued by Morgan, and five days later a proclamation was published against all persons who should hold any correspondence whatever with the outlawed crews.[415] Three men who had taken part in the expedition were captured and clapped into prison until the next meeting of the court. The friends of Coxon, however, including, it seems, almost all the members of the council, offered to give £2000 security, if he was allowed to come to Port Royal, that he would never take another commission except from the King of England; and Morgan wrote to Carlisle seeking his approbation.[416] At the end of the following January Morgan received word that a notorious Dutch privateer, named Jacob Everson, commanding an armed sloop, was anchored on the coast with a brigantine which he had lately captured. The lieutenant-governor manned a small vessel with fifty picked men and sent it secretly at midnight to seize the pirate. Everson's sloop was boarded and captured with twenty-six prisoners, but Everson himself and several others escaped by jumping overboard and swimming to the shore. The prisoners, most of whom were English, were tried six weeks later, convicted of piracy and sentenced to death; but the lieutenant-governor suspended the execution and wrote to the king for instructions. On 16th June 1681, the king in council ordered the execution of the condemned men.[417]

The buccaneers who, after plundering Porto Bello, crossed the Isthmus of Darien to the South Seas, had a remarkable history. For eighteen months they cruised up and down the Pacific coast of South America, burning and plundering Spanish towns, giving and taking hard blows with equal courage, keeping the Spanish provinces of Equador, Peru and Chili in a fever of apprehension, finally sailing the difficult passage round Cape Horn, and returning to the Windward Islands in January of 1682. Touching at the island of Barbadoes, they learned that the English frigate "Richmond" was lying in the road, and fearing seizure they sailed on to Antigua. There the governor, Colonel Codrington, refused to give them leave to enter the harbour. So the party, impatient of their dangerous situation, determined to separate, some landing on Antigua, and Sharp and sixteen others going to Nevis where they obtained passage to England. On their arrival in England several, including Sharp, were arrested at the instance of the Spanish ambassador, and tried for committing piracy in the South Seas; but from the defectiveness of the evidence produced they escaped conviction.[418] Four of the party came to Jamaica, where they were apprehended, tried and condemned. One of the four, who had given himself up voluntarily, turned State's evidence; two were represented by the judges as fit objects of the king's mercy; and the other, "a bloody and notorious villein," was recommended to be executed as an example to the rest.[419]

The recrudescence of piratical activity between the years 1679 and 1682 had, through its evil effects, been strongly felt in Jamaica; and public opinion was now gradually changing from one of encouragement and welcome to the privateers and of secret or open opposition to the efforts of the governors who tried to suppress them, to one of distinct hostility to the old freebooters. The inhabitants were beginning to realize that in the encouragement of planting, and not of buccaneering, lay the permanent welfare of the island. Planting and buccaneering, side by side, were inconsistent and incompatible, and the colonists chose the better course of the two. In spite of the frequent trials and executions at Port Royal, the marauders seemed to be as numerous as ever, and even more troublesome. Private trade with the Spaniards was hindered; runaway servants, debtors and other men of unfortunate or desperate condition were still, by every new success of the buccaneers, drawn from the island to swell their ranks; and most of all, men who were now outlawed in Jamaica, driven to desperation turned pirate altogether, and began to wage war indiscriminately on the ships of all nationalities, including those of the English. Morgan repeatedly wrote home urging the dispatch of small frigates of light draught to coast round the island and surprise the freebooters, and he begged for orders for himself to go on board and command them, for "then I shall not much question," he concludes, "to reduce them or in some time to leave them shipless."[420] "The governor," wrote the Council of Jamaica to the Lords of Trade and Plantations in May 1680, "can do little from want of ships to reduce the privateers, and of plain laws to punish them"; and they urged the ratification of the Act passed by the assembly two years before, making it felony for any British subject in the West Indies to serve under a foreign prince without leave from the governor.[421] This Act, and another for the more effectual punishment of pirates, had been under consideration in the Privy Council in February 1678, and both were returned to Jamaica with certain slight amendments. They were again passed by the assembly as one Act in 1681, and were finally incorporated into the Jamaica Act of 1683 "for the restraining and punishing of privateers and pirates."[422]

Chapter VII
The Buccaneers Turn Pirate

On 25th May 1682, Sir Thomas Lynch returned to Jamaica as governor of the colony.[423] Of the four acting governors since 1671, Lynch stood apart as the one who had endeavoured with singleness and tenacity of purpose to clear away the evils of buccaneering. Lord Vaughan had displayed little sympathy for the corsairs, but he was hampered by an irascible temper, and according to some reports by an avarice which dimmed the lustre of his name. The Earl of Carlisle, if he did not directly encourage the freebooters, had been grossly negligent in the performance of his duty of suppressing them; while Morgan, although in the years 1680 and 1681 he showed himself very zealous in punishing his old associates, cannot escape the suspicion of having secretly aided them under the governorship of Lord Vaughan. The task of Sir Thomas Lynch in 1671 had been a very difficult one. Buccaneering was then at flood-tide; three wealthy Spanish cities on the mainland had in turn been plundered, and the stolen riches carried to Jamaica; the air was alive with the exploits of these irregular warriors, and the pockets of the merchants and tavern-keepers of Port Royal were filled with Spanish doubloons, with emeralds and pearls from New Granada and the coasts of Rio de la Hacha, and with gold and silver plate from the Spanish churches and cathedrals of Porto Bello and Panama. The old governor, Sir Thomas Modyford, had been popular in his person, and his policy had been more popular still. Yet Lynch, by a combination of tact and firmness, and by an untiring activity with the small means at his disposal, had inaugurated a new and revolutionary policy in the island, which it was the duty of his successors merely to continue. In 1682 the problem before him, although difficult, was much simpler. Buccaneering was now rapidly being transformed into pure piracy. By laws and repeated proclamations, the freebooters had been offered an opportunity of returning to civilized pursuits, or of remaining ever thereafter outlawed. Many had come in, some to remain, others to take the first opportunity of escaping again. But many entirely refused to obey the summons, trusting to the protection of the French in Hispaniola, or so hardened to their cruel, remorseless mode of livelihood that they preferred the dangerous risks of outlawry. The temper of the inhabitants of the island, too, had changed. The planters saw more clearly the social and economic evils which the buccaneers had brought upon the island. The presence of these freebooters, they now began to realize, had discouraged planting, frightened away capital, reduced the number of labourers, and increased drunkenness, debauchery and every sort of moral disorder. The assembly and council were now at one with the governor as to the necessity of curing this running sore, and Lynch could act with the assurance which came of the knowledge that he was backed by the conscience of his people.

One of the earliest and most remarkable cases of buccaneer turning pirate was that of "La Trompeuse." In June 1682, before Governor Lynch's arrival in Jamaica, a French captain named Peter Paine (or Le Pain), commander of a merchant ship called "La Trompeuse" belonging to the French King, came to Port Royal from Cayenne in Guiana. He told Sir Henry Morgan and the council that, having heard of the inhuman treatment of his fellow Protestants in France, he had resolved to send back his ship and pay what was due under his contract; and he petitioned for leave to reside with the English and have English protection. The Council, without much inquiry as to the petitioner's antecedents, allowed him to take the oath of allegiance and settle at St. Jago, while his cargo was unloaded and entered customs-free. The ship was then hired by two Jamaican merchants and sent to Honduras to load logwood, with orders to sail eventually for Hamburg and be delivered to the French agent.[424] The action of the Council had been very hasty and ill-considered, and as it turned out, led to endless trouble. It soon transpired that Paine did not own the cargo, but had run away with it from Cayenne, and had disposed of both ship and goods in his own interest. The French ambassador in London made complaints to the English King, and letters were sent out to Sir Thomas Lynch and to Governor Stapleton of the Leeward Isles to arrest Paine and endeavour to have the vessel lade only for her right owners.[425] Meanwhile a French pirate named Jean Hamlin, with 120 desperadoes at his back, set out in a sloop in pursuit of "La Trompeuse," and coming up with her invited the master and mate aboard his own vessel, and then seized the ship. Carrying the prize to some creek or bay to careen her and fit her up as a man-of-war, he then started out on a mad piratical cruise, took sixteen or eighteen Jamaican vessels, barbarously ill-treated the crews, and demoralized the whole trade of the island.[426] Captain Johnson was dispatched by Lynch in a frigate in October 1682 to find and destroy the pirate; but after a fruitless search of two months round Porto Rico and Hispaniola, he returned to Port Royal. In December Lynch learned that "La Trompeuse" was careening in the neighbourhood of the Isle la Vache, and sent out another frigate, the "Guernsey," to seize her; but the wary pirate had in the meantime sailed away. On 15th February the "Guernsey" was again dispatched with positive orders not to stir from the coast of Hispaniola until the pirate was gone or destroyed; and Coxon, who seems to have been in good odour at Port Royal, was sent to offer to a privateer named "Yankey," men, victuals, pardon and naturalization, besides £200 in money for himself and Coxon, if he would go after "La Trompeuse."[427] The next news of Hamlin was from the Virgin Islands, where he was received and entertained by the Governor of St. Thomas, a small island belonging to the King of Denmark.[428] Making St. Thomas his headquarters, he robbed several English vessels that came into his way, and after first obtaining from the Danish governor a promise that he would find shelter at St. Thomas on his return, stood across for the Gulf of Guinea. In May 1683 Hamlin arrived on the west side of Africa disguised as an English man-of-war, and sailing up and down the coast of Sierra Leone captured or destroyed within several weeks seventeen ships, Dutch and English, robbing them of gold-dust and negroes.[429] The pirates then quarrelled over the division of their plunder and separated into two companies, most of the English following a Captain Morgan in one of the prizes, and the rest returning in "La Trompeuse" to the West Indies. The latter arrived at Dominica in July, where forty of the crew deserted the ship, leaving but sixteen white men and twenty-two negroes on board. Finally on the 27th the pirates dropped anchor at St. Thomas. They were admitted and kindly received by the governor, and allowed to bring their plunder ashore.[430] Three days later Captain Carlile of H.M.S. "Francis," who had been sent out by Governor Stapleton to hunt for pirates, sailed into the harbour, and on being assured by the pilot and by an English sloop lying at anchor there that the ship before him was the pirate "La Trompeuse," in the night of the following day he set her on fire and blew her up. Hamlin and some of the crew were on board, but after firing a few shots, escaped to the shore. The pirate ship carried thirty-two guns, and if she had not been under-manned Carlile might have encountered a formidable resistance. The Governor of St. Thomas sent a note of protest to Carlile for having, as he said, secretly set fire to a frigate which had been confiscated to the King of Denmark.[431] Nevertheless he sent Hamlin and his men for safety in a boat to another part of the island, and later selling him a sloop, let him sail away to join the French buccaneers in Hispaniola.[432]

The Danish governor of St. Thomas, whose name was Adolf Esmit, had formerly been himself a privateer, and had used his popularity on the island to eject from authority his brother Nicholas Esmit, the lawful governor. By protecting and encouraging pirates-for a consideration, of course-he proved a bad neighbour to the surrounding English islands. Although he had but 300 or 350 people on St. Thomas, and most of these British subjects, he laid claim to all the Virgin Islands, harboured runaway servants, seamen and debtors, fitted out pirate vessels with arms and provisions, and refused to restore captured ships and crews which the pirates brought into his port.[433] The King of Denmark had sent out a new governor, named Everson, to dispossess Esmit, but he did not arrive in the West Indies until October 1684, when with the assistance of an armed sloop which Sir William Stapleton had been ordered by the English Council to lend him, he took possession of St. Thomas and its pirate governor.[434]

A second difficulty encountered by Sir Thomas Lynch, in the first year of his return, was the privateering activity of Robert Clarke, Governor of New Providence, one of the Bahama Islands. Governor Clarke, on the plea of retaliating Spanish outrages, gave letters of marque to several privateers, including Coxon, the same famous chief who in 1680 had led the buccaneers into the South Seas. Coxon carried his commission to Jamaica and showed it to Governor Lynch, who was greatly incensed and wrote to Clarke a vigorous note of reproof.[435] To grant such letters of marque was, of course, contrary to the Treaty of Madrid, and by giving the pirates only another excuse for their actions, greatly complicated the task of the Governor of Jamaica. Lynch forwarded Coxon's commission to England, where in August 1682 the proprietors of the Bahama Islands were ordered to attend the council and answer for the misdeeds of their governor.[436] The proprietors, however, had already acted on their own initiative, for on 29th July they issued instructions to a new governor, Robert Lilburne, to arrest Clarke and keep him in custody till he should give security to answer accusations in England, and to recall all commissions against the Spaniards.[437] The whole trouble, it seems, had arisen over the wreck of a Spanish galleon in the Bahamas, to which Spaniards from St. Augustine and Havana were accustomed to resort to fish for ingots of silver, and from which they had been driven away by the governor and inhabitants of New Providence. The Spaniards had retaliated by robbing vessels sailing to and from the Bahamas, whereupon Clarke, without considering the illegality of his action, had issued commissions of war to privateers.

The Bahamas, however, were a favourite resort for pirates and other men of desperate character, and Lilburne soon discovered that his place was no sinecure. He found it difficult moreover to refrain from hostilities against a neighbour who used every opportunity to harm and plunder his colony. In March 1683, a former privateer named Thomas Pain[438] had entered into a conspiracy with four other captains, who were then fishing for silver at the wreck, to seize St. Augustine in Florida. They landed before the city under French colours, but finding the Spaniards prepared for them, gave up the project and looted some small neighbouring settlements. On the return of Pain and two others to New Providence, Governor Lilburne tried to apprehend them, but he failed for lack of means to enforce his authority. The Spaniards, however, were not slow to take their revenge. In the following January they sent 250 men from Havana, who in the early morning surprised and plundered the town and shipping at New Providence, killed three men, and carried away money and provisions to the value of £14,000.[439] When Lilburne in February sent to ask the Governor of Havana whether the plunderers had acted under his orders, the Spaniard not only acknowledged it but threatened further hostilities against the English settlement. Indeed, later in the same year the Spaniards returned, this time, it seems, without a commission, and according to report burnt all the houses, murdered the governor in cold blood, and carried many of the women, children and negroes to Havana.[440] About 200 of the inhabitants made their way to Jamaica, and a number of the men, thirsting for vengeance, joined the English pirates in the Carolinas.[441]

In French Hispaniola corsairing had been forbidden for several years, yet the French governor found the problem of suppressing the evil even more difficult than it was in Jamaica. M. de Pouançay, the successor of d'Ogeron, died toward the end of 1682 or the beginning of 1683, and in spite of his efforts to establish order in the colony he left it in a deplorable condition. The old fraternity of hunters or cow-killers had almost disappeared; but the corsairs and the planters were strongly united, and galled by the oppression of the West India Company, displayed their strength in a spirit of indocility which caused great embarrassment to the governor. Although in time of peace the freebooters kept the French settlements in continual danger of ruin by reprisal, in time of war they were the mainstay of the colony. As the governor, therefore, was dependent upon them for protection against the English, Spanish and Dutch, although he withdrew their commissions he dared not punish them for their crimes. The French buccaneers, indeed, occupied a curious and anomalous position. They were not ordinary privateers, for they waged war without authority; and they were still less pirates, for they had never been declared outlaws, and they confined their attentions to the Spaniards. They served under conditions which they themselves imposed, or which they deigned to accept, and were always ready to turn against the representatives of authority if they believed they had aught of which to complain.[442]

The buccaneers almost invariably carried commissions from the governors of French Hispaniola, but they did not scruple to alter the wording of their papers, so that a permission to privateer for three months was easily transformed into a licence to plunder for three years. These papers, moreover, were passed about from one corsair to another, until long after the occasion for their issue had ceased to exist. Thus in May or June of 1680, de Grammont, on the strength of an old commission granted him by de Pouançay before the treaty of Nimuegen, had made a brilliant night assault upon La Guayra, the seaport of Caracas. Of his 180 followers only forty-seven took part in the actual seizure of the town, which was amply protected by two forts and by cannon upon the walls. On the following day, however, he received word that 2000 men were approaching from Caracas, and as the enemy were also rallying in force in the vicinity of the town he was compelled to retire to the ships. This movement was executed with difficulty, and for two hours de Grammont with a handful of his bravest companions covered the embarkation from the assaults of the Spaniards. Although he himself was dangerously wounded in the throat, he lost only eight or nine men in the whole action. He carried away with him the Governor of La Guayra and many other prisoners, but the booty was small. De Grammont retired to the Isle d'Aves to nurse his wound, and after a long convalescence returned to Petit Goave.[443]

In 1683, however, these filibusters of Hispaniola carried out a much larger design upon the coasts of New Spain. In April of that year eight buccaneer captains made a rendezvous in the Gulf of Honduras for the purpose of attacking Vera Cruz. The leaders of the party were two Dutchmen named Vanhorn and Laurens de Graff. Of the other six captains, three were Dutch, one was French, and two were English. Vanhorn himself had sailed from England in the autumn of 1681 in command of a merchant ship called the "Mary and Martha," *alias* the "St. Nicholas." He soon, however, revealed the rogue he was by turning two of his merchants ashore at Cadiz and stealing four Spanish guns. He then sailed to the Canaries and to the coast of Guinea, plundering ships and stealing negroes, and finally, in November 1682, arrived at the city of San Domingo, where he tried to dispose of his black cargo. From San Domingo he made for Petit Goave picked up 300 men, and sailed to join Laurens in the Gulf of Honduras.[444] Laurens, too, had distinguished himself but a short time before by capturing a Spanish ship bound from Havana for San Domingo and Porto Rico with about 120,000 pieces of eight to pay off the soldiers. The freebooters had shared 700 pieces of eight per man, and carrying their prize to Petit Goave had compounded with the French governor for a part of the booty.[445]

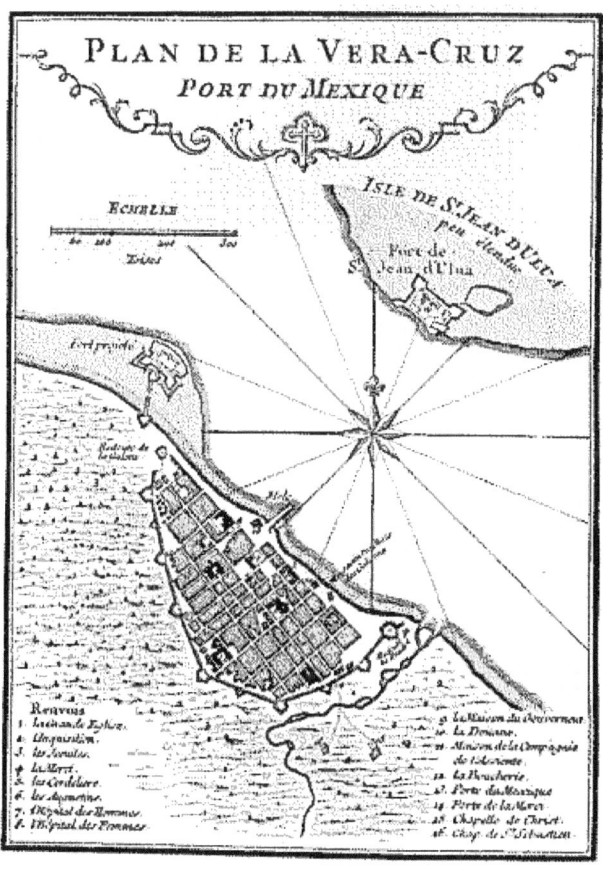

Plan of Vera-Cruz, From Charlevoix' *Histoire de S. Domingue*, 1730.

The buccaneers assembled near Cape Catoche to the number of about 1000 men, and sailed in the middle of May for Vera Cruz. Learning from some prisoners that the Spaniards on shore were expecting two ships from Caracas, they crowded the landing party of about 800 upon two of their vessels, displayed the Spanish colours, and stood in for the city. The unfortunate inhabitants mistook them for their own people, and even lighted fires to pilot them in. The pirates landed at midnight on 17th May about two miles from the town, and by daybreak had possession of the city and its forts. They found the soldiers and sentinels asleep, and "all the people in the houses as quiet and still as if in their graves." For four days they held the place, plundering the churches, houses and convents; and not finding enough plate and jewels to meet their expectations, they threatened to burn the cathedral and all the prisoners within it, unless a ransom was brought in from the surrounding country. The governor, Don Luis de Cordova, was on the third day discovered by an Englishman hidden in the hay in a stable, and was ransomed for 70,000 pieces of eight. Meanwhile the Spanish Flota of twelve or fourteen ships from Cadiz had for two days been lying outside the harbour and within sight of the city; yet it did not venture to land or to attack the empty buccaneer vessels. The proximity of such an armament, however, made the freebooters uneasy, especially as the Spanish viceroy was approaching with an army from the direction of Mexico. On the fourth day, therefore, they sailed away in the very face of the Flota to a neighbouring cay, where they divided the pillage into a thousand or more shares of 800 pieces of eight each. Vanhorn alone is said to have received thirty shares for himself and his two ships. He and Laurens, who had never been on good terms, quarrelled and fought over the division, and Vanhorn was wounded in the wrist. The wound seemed very slight, however, and he proposed to return and attack the Spanish fleet, offering to board the "Admiral" himself; but Laurens refused, and the buccaneers sailed away, carrying with them over 1000 slaves. The invaders, according to report, had lost but four men in the action. About a fortnight later Vanhorn died of gangrene in his wound, and de Grammont, who was then acting as his lieutenant, carried his ship back to Petit Goave, where Laurens and most of the other captains had already arrived.[446]

The Mexican fleet, which returned to Cadiz on 18th December, was only half its usual size because of the lack of a market after the visit of the corsairs; and the Governor of Vera Cruz was sentenced to lose his head for his remissness in defending the city.[447] The Spanish ambassador in London, Ronquillo, requested Charles II. to command Sir Thomas Lynch to co-operate with a commissioner whom the Spanish Government was sending to the West Indies to inquire into this latest outrage of the buccaneers, and such orders were dispatched to Lynch in April 1684.[448]

M. de Cussy, who had been appointed by the French King to succeed his former colleague, de Pouançay, arrived at Petit Goave in April 1684, and found the buccaneers on the point of open revolt because of the efforts of de Franquesnay, the temporary governor, to enforce the strict orders from France for their suppression.[449] De Cussy visited all parts of the colony, and by tact, patience and politic concessions succeeded in restoring order. He knew that in spite of the instructions from France, so long as he was surrounded by jealous neighbours, and so long as the peace in Europe remained precarious, the safety of French Hispaniola depended on his retaining the presence and good-will of the sea-rovers; and when de Grammont and several other captains demanded commissions against the Spaniards, the governor finally consented on condition that they persuade all the freebooters driven away by de Franquesnay to return to the colony. Two commissioners, named Begon and St. Laurent, arrived in August 1684 to aid him in reforming this dissolute society, but they soon came to the same conclusions as the governor, and sent a memoir to the French King advising less severe measures. The king did not agree with their suggestion of compromise, and de Cussy, compelled to deal harshly with the buccaneers, found his task by no means an easy one.[450] Meanwhile, however, many of the freebooters, seeing the determined attitude of the established authorities, decided to transfer their activities to the Pacific coasts of America, where they would be safe from interference on the part of the English or French Governments. The expedition of Harris, Coxon, Sharp and their associates across the isthmus in 1680 had kindled the imaginations of the buccaneers with the possibilities of greater plunder and adventure in these more distant regions. Other parties, both English and French, speedily followed in their tracks, and after 1683 it became the prevailing practice for buccaneers to make an excursion into the South Seas. The Darien Indians and their fiercer neighbours, the natives of the Mosquito Coast, who were usually at enmity with the Spaniards, allied themselves with the freebooters, and the latter, in their painful marches through the dense tropical wilderness of these regions, often owed it to the timely aid and friendly offices of the natives that they finally succeeded in reaching their goal.

In the summer of 1685, a year after the arrival of de Cussy in Hispaniola, de Grammont and Laurens de Graff united their forces again at the Isle la Vache, and in spite of the efforts of the governor to persuade them to renounce their project, sailed with 1100 men for the coasts of Campeache. An attempt on Merida was frustrated by the Spaniards, but Campeache itself was occupied after a feeble resistance, and remained in possession of the French for six weeks. After reducing the city to ashes and blowing up the fortress, the invaders retired to Hispaniola.[451] According to Charlevoix, before the buccaneers sailed away they celebrated the festival of St. Louis by a huge bonfire in honour of the king, in which they burnt logwood to the value of 200,000 crowns, representing the greater part of their booty. The Spaniards of Hispaniola, who kept up a constant desultory warfare with their French neighbours, were incited by the ravages of the buccaneers in the South Seas, and by the sack of Vera Cruz and Campeache, to renewed hostilities; and de Cussy, anxious to attach to himself so enterprising and daring a leader as de Grammont, obtained for him, in September 1686, the commission of "Lieutenant de Roi" of the coast of San Domingo. Grammont, however, on learning of his new honour, wished to have a last fling at the Spaniards before he settled down to respectability. He armed a ship, sailed away with 180 men, and was never heard of again.[452] At the same time Laurens de Graff was given the title of "Major," and he lived to take an active part in the war against the English between 1689 and 1697.[453]

These semi-pirates, whom the French governor dared not openly support yet feared to disavow, were a constant source of trouble to the Governor of Jamaica. They did not scruple to attack English traders and fishing sloops, and when pursued took refuge in Petit Goave, the port in the *cul-de-sac* at the west end of Hispaniola which had long been a sanctuary of the freebooters, and which paid little respect to the authority of the royal governor.[454] In Jamaica they believed that the corsairs acted under regular commissions from the French authorities, and Sir Thomas Lynch sent repeated complaints to de Pouançay and to his successor. He also wrote to England begging the Council to ascertain from the French ambassador whether these governors had authority to issue commissions of war, so that his frigates might be able to distinguish between the pirate and the lawful privateer.[455] Except at Petit Goave, however, the French were really desirous of preserving peace with Jamaica, and did what they could to satisfy the demands of the English without unduly irritating the buccaneers. They were in the same position as Lynch in 1671, who, while anxious to do justice to the Spaniards, dared not immediately alienate the freebooters who plundered them, and who might, if driven away, turn their arms against Jamaica. Vanhorn himself, it seems, when he left Hispaniola to join Laurens in the Gulf of Honduras, had been sent out by de Pouançay really to pursue "La Trompeuse" and other pirates, and his lieutenant, de Grammont, delivered letters to Governor Lynch to that effect; but once out of sight he steered directly for Central America, where he anticipated a more profitable game than pirate-hunting.[456]

On the 24th of August 1684 Sir Thomas Lynch died in Jamaica, and Colonel Hender Molesworth, by virtue of his commission as lieutenant-governor, assumed the authority.[457] Sir Henry Morgan, who had remained lieutenant-governor when Lynch returned to Jamaica, had afterwards been suspended from the council and from all other public employments on charges of drunkenness, disorder, and encouraging disloyalty to the government. His brother-in-law, Byndloss, was dismissed for similar reasons, and Roger Elletson, who belonged to the same faction, was removed from his office as attorney-general of the island. Lynch had had the support of both the assembly and the council, and his actions were at once confirmed in England.[458]   The governor, however, although he had enjoyed the confidence of most of the inhabitants, who looked upon him as the saviour of the island, left behind in the persons of Morgan, Elletson and their roystering companions, a group of implacable enemies, who did all in their power to vilify his memory to the authorities in England. Several of these men, with Elletson at their head, accused the dead governor of embezzling piratical goods which had been confiscated to the use of the king; but when inquiry was made by Lieutenant-Governor Molesworth, the charges fell to the ground. Elletson's information was found to be second-hand and defective, and Lynch's name was more than vindicated. Indeed, the governor at his death had so little ready means that his widow was compelled to borrow £500 to pay for his funeral.[459]

The last years of Sir Thomas Lynch's life had been troublous ones. Not only had the peace of the island been disturbed by "La Trompeuse" and other French corsairs which hovered about Hispaniola; not only had his days been embittered by strife with a small, drunken, insolent faction which tried to belittle his attempts to introduce order and sobriety into the colony; but the hostility of the Spanish governors in the West Indies still continued to neutralize his efforts to root out buccaneering. Lynch had in reality been the best friend of the Spaniards in America. He had strictly forbidden the cutting of logwood in Campeache and Honduras, when the Spaniards were outraging and enslaving every Englishman they found upon those coasts;[460] he had sent word to the Spanish governors of the intended sack of Vera Cruz;[461] he had protected Spanish merchant ships with his own men-of-war and hospitably received them in Jamaican ports. Yet Spanish corsairs continued to rob English vessels, and Spanish governors refused to surrender English ships and goods which were carried into their ports.[462] On the plea of punishing interlopers they armed small galleys and ordered them to take all ships which had on board any products of the Indies.[463] Letters to the governors at Havana and St. Jago de Cuba were of no avail. English trade routes were interrupted and dangerous, the turtling, trading and fishing sloops, which supplied a great part of the food of Jamaica, were robbed and seized, and Lynch was compelled to construct a galley of fifty oars for their protection.[464] Pirates, it is true, were frequently brought into Port Royal by the small frigates employed by the governor, and there were numerous executions;[465] yet the outlaws seemed to increase daily. Some black vessel was generally found hovering about the island ready to pick up any who wished to join it, and when the runaways were prevented from returning by the statute against piracy, they retired to the Carolinas or to New England to dispose of their loot and refit their ships.[466] When such retreats were available the laws against piracy did not reduce buccaneering so much as they depopulated Jamaica of its white inhabitants.

After 1680, indeed, the North American colonies became more and more the resort of the pirates who were being driven from West Indian waters by the stern measures of the English governors. Michel Landresson, *alias* Breha, who had accompanied Pain in his expedition against St. Augustine in 1683, and who had been a constant source of worriment to the Jamaicans because of his attacks on the fishing sloops, sailed to Boston and disposed of his booty of gold, silver, jewels and cocoa to the godly New England merchants, who were only too ready to take advantage of so profitable a trade and gladly fitted him out for another cruise.[467] Pain himself appeared in Rhode Island, displayed the old commission to hunt for pirates given him by Sir Thomas Lynch, and was protected by the governor against the deputy-collector of customs, who endeavoured to seize him and his ship.[468] The chief resort of the pirates, however, was the colony of Carolina. Indented by numerous harbours and inlets, the shores of Carolina had always afforded a safe refuge for refitting and repairing after a cruise, and from 1670 onwards, when the region began to be settled by colonists from England, the pirates found in the new communities a second Jamaica, where they could sell their cargoes and often recruit their forces. In the latter part of 1683 Sir Thomas Lynch complained to the Lords of the Committee for Trade and Plantations;[469] and in February of the following year the king, at the suggestion of the committee, ordered that a draft of the Jamaican law against pirates be sent to all the plantations in America, to be passed and enforced in each as a statute of the province.[470] On 12th

March 1684 a general proclamation was issued by the king against pirates in America, and a copy forwarded to all the colonial governors for publication and execution.[471] Nevertheless in Massachusetts, in spite of these measures and of a letter from the king warning the governors to give no succour or aid to any of the outlaws, Michel had been received with open arms, the proclamation of 12th March was torn down in the streets, and the Jamaica Act, though passed, was never enforced.[472] In the Carolinas, although the Lords Proprietors wrote urging the governors to take every care that no pirates were entertained in the colony, the Act was not passed until November 1685.[473] There were few, if any, convictions, and the freebooters plied their trade with the same security as before. Toward the end of 1686 three galleys from St. Augustine landed about 150 men, Spaniards, Indians and mulattos, a few leagues below Charleston, and laid waste several plantations, including that of Governor Moreton. The enemy pushed on to Port Royal, completely destroyed the Scotch colony there, and retired before a force could be raised to oppose them. To avenge this inroad the inhabitants immediately began preparations for a descent upon St. Augustine; and an expedition consisting of two French privateering vessels and about 500 men was organized and about to sail, when a new governor, James Colleton, arrived and ordered it to disband.[474] Colleton was instructed to arrest Governor Moreton on the charge of encouraging piracy, and to punish those who entertained and abetted the freebooters;[475] and on 12th February 1687 he had a new and more explicit law to suppress the evil enacted by the assembly.[476] On 22nd May of the same year James II. renewed the proclamation for the suppression of pirates, and offered pardon to all who surrendered within a limited time and gave security for future good behaviour.[477] The situation was so serious, however, that in August the king commissioned Sir Robert Holmes to proceed with a squadron to the West Indies and make short work of the outlaws;[478] and in October he issued a circular to all the governors in the colonies, directing the most stringent enforcement of the laws, "a practice having grown up of bringing pirates to trial before the evidence was ready, and of using other evasions to insure their acquittal."[479] On the following 20th January another proclamation was issued by James to insure the co-operation of the governors with Sir Robert Holmes and his agents.[480] The problem, however, was more difficult than the king had anticipated. The presence of the fleet upon the coast stopped the evil for a time, but a few years later, especially in the Carolinas under the administration of Governor Ludwell (1691-1693), the pirates again increased in numbers and in boldness, and Charleston was completely overrun with the freebooters, who, with the connivance of the merchants and a free display of gold, set the law at defiance.

In Jamaica Lieutenant-Governor Molesworth continued in the policy and spirit of his predecessor. He sent a frigate to the Bay of Darien to visit Golden Isle and the Isle of Pines (where the buccaneers were accustomed to make their rendezvous when they crossed over to the South Seas), with orders to destroy any piratical craft in that vicinity, and he made every exertion to prevent recruits from leaving Jamaica.[481] The stragglers who returned from the South Seas he arrested and executed, and he dealt severely with those who received and entertained them.[482] By virtue of the king's proclamation of 1684, he had the property in Port Royal belonging to men then in the South Seas forfeited to the crown.[483] A Captain Bannister, who in June 1684 had run away from Port Royal on a privateering venture with a ship of thirty guns, had been caught and brought back by the frigate "Ruby," but when put on trial for piracy was released by the grand jury on a technicality. Six months later Bannister managed to elude the forts a second time, and for two years kept dodging the frigates which Molesworth sent in pursuit of him. Finally, in January 1687, Captain Spragge sailed into Port Royal with the buccaneer and three of his companions hanging at the yard-arms, "a spectacle of great satisfaction to all good people, and of terror to the favourers of pirates."[484] It was during the government of Molesworth that the "Biscayners" began to appear in American waters. These privateers from the Bay of Biscay seem to have been taken into the King of Spain's service to hunt pirates, but they interrupted English trade more than the pirates did. They captured and plundered English merchantmen right and left, and carried them to Cartagena, Vera Cruz, San Domingo and other Spanish ports, where the governors took charge of their prisoners and allowed them to dispose of their captured goods. They held their commissions, it seems, directly from the Crown, and so pretended to be outside the pale of the authority of the Spanish governors. The latter, at any rate, declared that they could give no redress, and themselves complained to the authorities in Jamaica of the independence of these marauders.[485] In December 1688 the king issued a warrant to the Governor of Jamaica authorizing him to suppress the Biscayans with the royal frigates.[486]

On 28th October 1685 the governorship of the island was assigned to Sir Philip Howard,[487] but Howard died shortly after, and the Duke of Albemarle was appointed in his stead.[488] Albemarle, who arrived at Port Royal in December 1687,[489] completely reversed the policy of his predecessors, Lynch and Molesworth. Even before he left England he had undermined his health by his intemperate habits, and when he came to Jamaica he leagued himself with the most unruly and debauched men in the colony. He seems to have had no object but to increase his fortune at the expense of the island. Before he sailed he had boldly petitioned for powers to dispose of money without the advice and consent of his council, and, if he saw fit, to reinstate into office Sir Henry Morgan and Robert Byndloss. The king, however, decided that the suspension of Morgan and Byndloss should remain until Albemarle had reported on their case from Jamaica.[490] When the Duke entered upon his new government, he immediately appointed Roger Elletson to be Chief Justice of the island in the place of Samuel Bernard. Three assistant-judges of the Supreme Court thereupon resigned their positions on the bench, and one was, in revenge, dismissed by the governor from the council. Several other councillors were also suspended, contrary to the governor's instructions against arbitrary dismissal of such officers, and on 18th January 1688 Sir Henry Morgan, upon the king's approval of the Duke's recommendation, was re-admitted to the council-chamber.[491] The old buccaneer, however, did not long enjoy his restored dignity. About a month later he succumbed to a sharp illness, and on 26th August was buried in St. Catherine's Church in Port Royal.[492]

In November 1688 a petition was presented to the king by the planters and merchants trading to Jamaica protesting against the new régime introduced by Lord Albemarle: —"The once flourishing island of Jamaica is likely to be utterly undone by the irregularities of some needy persons lately set in power. Many of the most considerable inhabitants are deserting it, others are under severe fines and imprisonments from little or no cause.... The provost-marshal has been dismissed and an indebted person put in his place; and all the most substantial officers, civil and military, have been turned out and necessitous persons set up in their room. The like has been done in the judicial offices, whereby the benefit of appeals and prohibitions is rendered useless. Councillors are suspended without royal order and without a hearing. Several persons have been forced to give security not to leave the island lest they should seek redress; others have been brought before the council for trifling offences and innumerable fees taken from them; money has been raised twenty per cent. over its value to defend creditors. Lastly, the elections have been tampered with by the indebted provost-marshal, and since the Duke of Albemarle's death are continued without your royal authority."[493] The death of Albemarle, indeed, at this opportune time was the greatest service he rendered to the colony. Molesworth was immediately commanded to return to Jamaica and resume authority. The duke's system was entirely reversed, and the government restored as it had been under the administration of Sir Thomas Lynch. Elletson was removed from the council and from his position as chief justice, and Bernard returned in his former place. All of the rest of Albemarle's creatures were dismissed from their posts, and the supporters of Lynch's régime again put in control of a majority in the council.[494] This measure of plain justice was one of the last acts of James II. as King of England. On 5th November 1688 William of Orange landed in England at Torbay, and on 22nd December James escaped to France to live as a pensioner of Louis XIV. The new king almost immediately wrote to Jamaica confirming the reappointment of Molesworth, and a commission to the latter was issued on 25th July 1689.[495] Molesworth, unfortunately for the colony, died within a few days,[496] and the Earl of Inchiquin was appointed on 19th September to succeed him.[497] Sir Francis Watson, President of the Council in Jamaica, obeyed the instructions of William III., although he was a partizan of Albemarle; yet so high was the feeling between the two factions that the greatest confusion reigned in the government of the island until the arrival of Inchiquin in May 1690.[498]

The Revolution of 1688, by placing William of Orange on the English throne, added a powerful kingdom to the European coalition which in 1689 attacked Louis XIV. over the question of the succession of the Palatinate. That James II. should accept the hospitality of the French monarch and use France as a basis for attack on England and Ireland was, quite apart from William's sympathy with the Protestants on the Continent, sufficient cause for hostilities against France. War broke out in May 1689, and was soon reflected in the English and French colonies in the West Indies. De Cussy, in Hispaniola, led an expedition of 1000 men, many of them filibusters, against St. Jago de los Cavalleros in the interior of the island, and took and burnt the town. In revenge the Spaniards, supported by an English fleet which had just driven the French from St. Kitts, appeared in January 1691 before Cap François, defeated and killed de Cussy in an engagement near the town, and burned and sacked the settlement. Three hundred French filibusters were killed in the battle. The English fleet visited Leogane and Petit Goave in the *cul-de-sac* of Hispaniola, and then sailed to Jamaica. De Cussy before his death had seized the opportunity to provide the freebooters with new commissions for privateering, and English shipping suffered severely.[499] Laurens with 200 men touched at Montego Bay on the north coast in October, and threatened to return and plunder the whole north side of the island. The people were so frightened that they sent their wives and children to Port Royal; and the council armed several vessels to go in pursuit of the Frenchmen.[500] It was a new experience to feel the danger of invasion by a foreign foe. The Jamaicans had an insight into the terror which their Spanish neighbours felt for the buccaneers, whom the English islanders had always been so ready to fit out, or to shield from the arm of the law. Laurens in the meantime was as good as his word. He returned to Jamaica in the beginning of December with several vessels, seized eight or ten English trading sloops, landed on the north shore and plundered a plantation.[501] War with France was formally proclaimed in Jamaica on the 13th of January 1690.[502]

Two years later, in January 1692, Lord Inchiquin also succumbed to disease in Jamaica, and in the following June Colonel William Beeston was chosen by the queen to act as lieutenant-governor.[503] Inchiquin before he left England had solicited for the power to call in and pardon pirates, so as to strengthen the island during the war by adding to its forces men who would make good fighters on both land and sea. The Committee on Trade and Plantations reported favourably on the proposal, but the power seems never to have been granted.[504] In January 1692, however, the President of the Council of Jamaica began to issue commissions to privateers, and in a few months the surrounding seas were full of armed Jamaican sloops.[505] On 7th June of the same year the colony suffered a disaster which almost proved its destruction. A terrible earthquake overwhelmed Port Royal and "in ten minutes threw down all the churches, dwelling-houses and sugar-works in the island. Two-thirds of Port Royal were swallowed up by the sea, all the forts and fortifications demolished and great part of its inhabitants miserably knocked on the head or drowned."[506] The French in Hispaniola took advantage of the distress caused by the earthquake to invade the island, and nearly every week hostile bands landed and plundered the coast of negroes and other property.[507] In December 1693 a party of 170 swooped down in the night upon St. Davids, only seven leagues from Port Royal, plundered the whole parish, and got away again with 370 slaves.[508] In the following April Ducasse, the new French governor of Hispaniola, sent 400 buccaneers in six small vessels to repeat the exploit, but the marauders met an English man-of-war guarding the coast, and concluding "that they would only get broken bones and spoil their men for any other design," they retired whence they had come.[509] Two months later, however, a much more serious incursion was made. An expedition of twenty-two vessels and 1500 men, recruited in France and instigated, it is said, by Irish and Jacobite refugees, set sail under Ducasse on 8th June with the intention of conquering the whole of Jamaica. The French landed at Point Morant and Cow Bay, and for a month cruelly desolated the whole south-eastern portion of the island. Then coasting along the southern shore they made a feint on Port Royal, and landed in Carlisle Bay to the west of the capital. After driving from their breastworks the English force of 250 men, they again fell to ravaging and burning, but finding they could make no headway against the Jamaican militia, who were now increased to 700 men, in the latter part of July they set sail with their plunder for Hispaniola.[510] Jamaica had been denuded of men by the earthquake and by sickness, and Lieutenant-Governor Beeston had wisely abandoned the forts in the east of the island and concentrated all his strength at Port Royal.[511] It was this expedient which doubtless saved the island from capture, for Ducasse feared to attack the united Jamaican forces behind strong intrenchments. The harm done to Jamaica by the invasion, however, was very great. The French wholly destroyed fifty sugar works and many plantations, burnt and plundered about 200 houses, and killed every living thing they found. Thirteen hundred negroes were carried off besides other spoil. In fighting the Jamaicans lost about 100 killed and wounded, but the loss of the French seems to have been several times that number. After the French returned home Ducasse reserved all the negroes for himself, and many of the freebooters who had taken part in the expedition, exasperated by such a division of the spoil, deserted the governor and resorted to buccaneering on their own account.[512]

Colonel, now become Sir William, Beeston, from his first arrival in Jamaica as lieutenant-governor, had fixed his hopes upon a joint expedition with the Spaniards against the French at Petit Goave; but the inertia of the Spaniards, and the loss of men and money caused by the earthquake, had prevented his plans from being realized.[513] In the early part of 1695, however, an army of 1700 soldiers on a fleet of twenty-three ships sailed from England under command of Commodore Wilmot for the West Indies. Uniting with 1500 Spaniards from San Domingo and the Barlovento fleet of three sail, they captured and sacked Cap François and Port de Paix in the French end of the island. It had been the intention of the allies to proceed to the *cul-de-sac* and destroy Petit Goave and Leogane, but they had lost many men by sickness and bad management, and the Spaniards, satisfied with the booty already obtained, were anxious to return home. So the English fleet sailed away to Port Royal.[514] These hostilities so exhausted both the French in Hispaniola and the English in Jamaica that for a time the combatants lay back to recover their strength.

The last great expedition of this war in the West Indies serves as a fitting close to the history of the buccaneers. On 26th September 1696 Ducasse received from the French Minister of Marine, Pontchartrain, a letter informing him that the king had agreed to the project of a large armament which the Sieur de Pointis, aided by private capital, was preparing for an enterprise in the Mexican Gulf.[515] Ducasse, although six years earlier he had written home urging just such an enterprise against Vera Cruz or Cartagena, now expressed his strong disapproval of the project, and dwelt rather on the advantages to be gained by the capture of Spanish Hispaniola, a conquest which would give the French the key to the Indies. A second letter from Pontchartrain in January 1697, however, ordered him to aid de Pointis by uniting all the freebooters and keeping them in the colony till 15th February. It was a difficult task to maintain the buccaneers in idleness for two months and prohibit all cruising, especially as de Pointis, who sailed from Brest in the beginning of January, did not reach Petit Goave till about 1st March.[516] The buccaneers murmured and threatened to disband, and it required all the personal ascendancy of Ducasse to hold them together. The Sieur de Pointis, although a man of experience and resource, capable of forming a large design and sparing nothing to its success, suffered from two very common faults-vanity and avarice. He sometimes allowed the sense of his own merits to blind him to the merits of others, and considerations of self-interest to dim the brilliance of his achievements. Of Ducasse he was insanely jealous, and during the whole expedition he tried in every way to humiliate him. Unable to bring himself to conciliate the unruly spirit of the buccaneers, he told them plainly that he would lead them not as a companion in fortune but as a military superior, and that they must submit themselves to the same rules as the men on the king's ships. The freebooters rebelled under the haughtiness of their commander, and only Ducasse's influence was able to bring them to obedience.[517] On 18th March the ships were all gathered at the rendezvous at Cape Tiburon, and on the 13th of the following month anchored two leagues to the east of Cartagena.[518] De Pointis had under his command about 4000 men, half of them seamen, the rest soldiers. The reinforcements he had received from Ducasse numbered 1100, and of these 650 were buccaneers commanded by Ducasse himself. He had nine frigates, besides seven vessels belonging to the buccaneers, and numerous smaller boats.[519] The appearance of so formidable an armament in the West Indies caused a great deal of concern both in England and in Jamaica. Martial law was proclaimed in the colony and every means taken to put Port Royal in a state of defence.[520] Governor Beeston, at the first news of de Pointis' fleet, sent advice to the governors of Porto Bello and Havana, against whom he suspected that the expedition was intended.[521] A squadron of thirteen vessels was sent out from England under command of Admiral Nevill to protect the British islands and the Spanish treasure fleets, for both the galleons and the Flota were then in the Indies.[522] Nevill touched at Barbadoes on 17th April,[523] and then sailed up through the Leeward Islands towards Hispaniola in search of de Pointis. The Frenchman, however, had eluded him and was already before Cartagena.

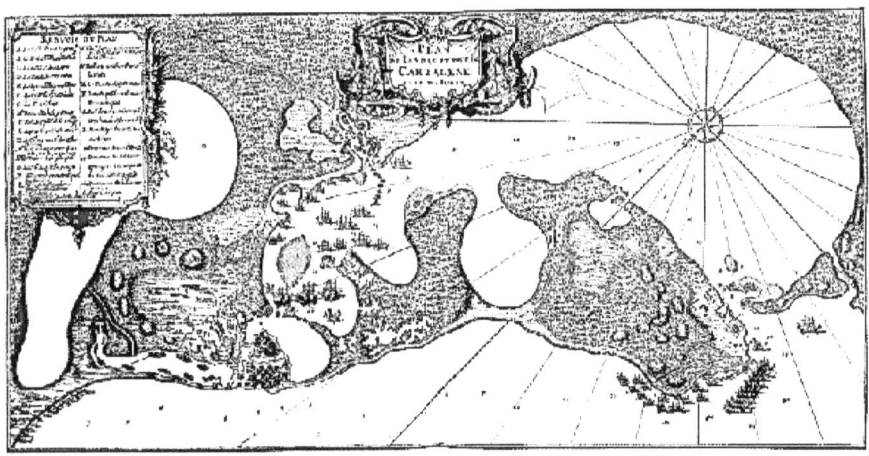

Plan of the Town and Roadstead of Cartegena and of the Forts, From Baron de Pontis' Relation de ce qui c'est fait la prise de Carthagene, Bruxelles, 1698.

Cartagena, situated at the eastward end of a large double lagoon, was perhaps the strongest fortress in the Indies, and the Spaniards within opposed a courageous defence.[524] After a fortnight of fighting and bombardment, however, on the last day of April the outworks were carried by a brilliant assault, and on 6th May the small Spanish garrison, followed by the *Cabildo* or municipal corporation, and by many of the citizens of the town, in all about 2800 persons, marched out with the honours of war. Although the Spaniards had been warned of the coming of the French, and before their arrival had succeeded in withdrawing the women and some of their riches to Mompos in the interior, the treasure which fell into the hands of the invaders was enormous, and has been variously estimated at from six million crowns to twenty millions sterling. Trouble soon broke out between de Pointis and the buccaneers, for the latter wanted the whole of the plunder to be divided equally among the men, as had always been their custom, and they expected, according to this arrangement, says de Pointis in his narrative, about a quarter of all the booty. De Pointis, however, insisted upon the order which he had published before the expedition sailed from Petit Goave, that the buccaneers should be subject to the same rule in the division of the spoil as the sailors in the fleet, *i.e.*, they should receive one-tenth of the first million and one-thirtieth of the rest. Moreover, fearing that the buccaneers would take matters into their own hands, he had excluded them from the city while his officers gathered the plunder and carried it to the ships. On the repeated remonstrances of Ducasse, de Pointis finally announced that the share allotted to the men from Hispaniola was 40,000 crowns. The buccaneers, finding themselves so miserably cheated, broke out into open mutiny, but were restrained by the influence of their leader and the presence of the king's frigates. De Pointis, meanwhile, seeing his own men decimated by sickness, put all the captured guns on board the fleet and made haste to get under sail for France. South of Jamaica he fell in with the squadron of Admiral Nevill, to which in the meantime had been joined some eight Dutch men-of-war; but de Pointis, although inferior in numbers, outsailed the English ships and lost but one or two of his smaller vessels. He then manœuvred past Cape S. Antonio, round the north of Cuba and through the Bahama Channel to Newfoundland, where he stopped for fresh wood and water, and after a brush with a small English squadron under Commodore Norris, sailed into the harbour of Brest on 19th August 1697.[525]

The buccaneers, even before de Pointis sailed for France, had turned their ships back toward Cartagena to reimburse themselves by again plundering the city. De Pointis, indeed, was then very ill, and his officers were in no condition to oppose them. After the fleet had departed the freebooters re-entered Cartagena, and for four days put it to the sack, extorting from the unfortunate citizens, and from the churches and monasteries, several million more in gold and silver. Embarking for the Isle la Vache, they had covered but thirty leagues when they met with the same allied fleet which had pursued de Pointis. Of the nine buccaneer vessels, the two which carried most of the booty were captured, two more were driven ashore, and the rest succeeded in escaping to Hispaniola. Ducasse, who had returned to Petit Goave when de Pointis sailed for France, sent one of his lieutenants on a mission to the French Court to complain of the ill-treatment he had received from de Pointis, and to demand his own recall; but the king pacified him by making him a Chevalier of St. Louis, and allotting 1,400,000 francs to the French colonists who had aided in the expedition. The money, however, was slow in reaching the hands of those to whom it was due, and much was lost through the malversations of the men charged with its distribution.[526]

With the capture of Cartagena in 1697 the history of the buccaneers may be said to end. More and more during the previous twenty years they had degenerated into mere pirates, or had left their libertine life for more civilised pursuits. Since 1671 the English government had been consistent in its policy of suppressing the freebooters, and with few exceptions the governors sent to Jamaica had done their best to uphold and enforce the will of the councils at home. Ten years or more had to elapse before the French Court saw the situation in a similar light, and even then the exigencies of war and defence in French Hispaniola prevented the governors from taking any effective measures toward suppression. The problem, indeed, had not been an easy one. The buccaneers, whatever their origin, were intrepid men, not without a sense of honour among themselves, wedded to a life of constant danger which they met and overcame with surprising hardiness. When an expedition was projected against their traditional foes, the Spaniards, they calculated the chances of profit, and taking little account of the perils to be run, or indeed of the flag under which they sailed, English, French and Dutch alike became brothers under a chief whose courage they perfectly recognised and whom they servilely obeyed. They lived at a time when they were in no danger of being overhauled by ubiquitous cruisers with rifled guns, and so long as they confined themselves to His Catholic Majesty's ships and settlements, they had trusted in the immunity arising from the traditional hostility existing between the English and the Spaniards of that era. And for the Spaniards the record of the buccaneers had been a terrible one. Between the years 1655 and 1671 alone, the corsairs had sacked eighteen cities, four towns and more than thirty-five villages-Cumana once, Cumanagote twice, Maracaibo and Gibraltar twice, Rio de la Hacha five times, Santa Marta three times, Tolu eight times, Porto Bello once, Chagre twice, Panama once, Santa Catalina twice, Granada in Nicaragua twice, Campeache three times, St. Jago de Cuba once, and other towns and villages in Cuba and Hispaniola for thirty leagues inland innumerable times. And this fearful tale of robbery and outrage does not embrace the various expeditions against Porto Bello, Campeache, Cartagena and other Spanish ports made after 1670. The Marquis de Barinas in 1685 estimated the losses of the Spaniards at the hands of the buccaneers since the accession of Charles II. to be sixty million crowns; and these figures covered merely the destruction of towns and treasure, without including the loss of more than 250 merchant ships and frigates.[527] If the losses and suffering of the Spaniards had been terrible, the advantages accruing to the invaders, or to the colonies which received and supported them, scarcely compensated for the effort it cost them. Buccaneering had denuded Jamaica of its bravest men, lowered the moral tone of the island, and retarded the development of its natural resources. It was estimated that there were lost to the island between 1668 and 1671, in the designs against Tobago, Curaçao, Porto Bello, Granada and Panama, about 2600 men,[528] which was a large number for a new and very weak colony surrounded by powerful foes. Says the same writer later on: "People have not married, built or settled as they would in time of peace-some for fear of being destroyed, others have got much suddenly by privateers bargains and are gone. War carries away all freemen, labourers and planters of provisions, which makes work and victuals dear and scarce. Privateering encourages all manner of disorder and dissoluteness; and if it succeed, does but enrich the worst sort of people and provoke and alarm the Spaniards."[529]

The privateers, moreover, really injured English trade as much as they injured Spanish navigation; and if the English in the second half of the seventeenth century had given the Spaniards as little cause for enmity in the West Indies as the Dutch had done, they perhaps rather than the Dutch would have been the convoys and sharers in the rich Flotas. The Spaniards, moreover, if not in the court at home, at least in the colonies, would have readily lent themselves to a trade, illicit though it be, with the English islands, a trade, moreover, which it was the constant aim of English diplomacy to encourage and maintain, had they been able to assure themselves that their English neighbours were their friends. But when outrage succeeded upon outrage, and the English Governors seemed, in spite of their protestations of innocence, to make no progress toward stopping them, the Spaniards naturally concluded that the English government was the best of liars and the worst of friends. From another point of view, too, the activity of the buccaneers was directly opposed to the commercial interests of Great Britain. Of all the nations of Europe the Spaniards were those who profited least from their American possessions. It was the English, the French and the Dutch who carried their merchandize to Cadiz and freighted the Spanish-American fleets, and who at the return of these fleets from Porto Bello and Vera Cruz appropriated the greater part of the gold, silver and precious stuffs which composed their cargoes. And when the buccaneers cut off a Spanish galleon, or wrecked the Spanish cities on the Main, it was not so much the Spaniards who suffered as the foreign merchants interested in the trade between Spain and her colonies. If the policy of the English and French Governments toward the buccaneers gradually changed from one of connivance or encouragement to one of hostility and suppression, it was because they came to realise that it was easier and more profitable to absorb the trade and riches of Spanish America through the peaceful agencies of treaty and concession, than by endeavouring to enforce a trade in the old-fashioned way inaugurated by Drake and his Elizabethan contemporaries.

The pirate successors of the buccaneers were distinguished from their predecessors mainly by the fact that they preyed on the commerce of all flags indiscriminately, and were outlawed and hunted down by all nations alike. They, moreover, widely extended their field of operations. No longer content with the West Indies and the shores of the Caribbean Sea, they sailed east to the coast of Guinea and around Africa to the Indian Ocean. They haunted the shores of Madagascar, the Red Sea and the Persian Gulf, and ventured even as far as the Malabar Coast, intercepting the rich trade with the East, the great ships from Bengal and the Islands of Spice. And not only did the outlaws of all nations from America and the West Indies flock to these regions, but sailors from England were fired by reports of the rich spoils obtained to imitate their example. One of the most remarkable instances was that of Captain Henry Avery, *alias* Bridgman. In May 1694 Avery was on an English merchantman, the "Charles II.," lying near Corunna. He persuaded the crew to mutiny, set the captain on shore, re-christened the ship the "Fancy," and sailed to the East Indies. Among other prizes he captured, in September 1695, a large vessel called the "Gunsway," belonging to the Great Mogul-an exploit which led to reprisals and the seizure of the English factories in India. On application of the East India Company, proclamations were issued on 17th July, 10th and 21st August 1696, by the Lords Justices of England, declaring Avery and his crew pirates and offering a reward for their apprehension.[530] Five of the crew were seized on their return to England in the autumn of the same year, were tried at the Old Bailey and hanged, and several of their companions were arrested later.[531]

In the North American colonies these new pirates still continued to find encouragement and protection. Carolina had long had an evil reputation as a hot-bed of piracy, and deservedly so. The proprietors had removed one governor after another for harbouring the freebooters, but with little result. In the Bahamas, which belonged to the same proprietors, the evil was even more flagrant. Governor Markham of the Quaker colony of Pennsylvania allowed the pirates to dispose of their goods and to refit upon the banks of the Delaware, and William Penn, the proprietor, showed little disposition to reprimand or remove him. Governor Fletcher of New York was in open alliance with the outlaws, accepted their gifts and allowed them to parade the streets in broad daylight. The merchants of New York, as well as those of Rhode Island and Massachusetts, who were prevented by the Navigation Laws from engaging in legitimate trade with other nations, welcomed the appearance of the pirate ships laden with goods from the East, provided a ready market for their cargoes, and encouraged them to repeat their voyages.

In 1699 an Act was passed through Parliament of such severity as to drive many of the outlaws from American waters. It was largely a revival of the Act of 28, Henry VIII., was in force for seven years, and was twice renewed. The war of the Spanish Succession, moreover, gave many men of piratical inclinations an opportunity of sailing under lawful commissions as privateers against the French and Spaniards. In this long war, too, the French filibusters were especially numerous and active. In 1706 there were 1200 or 1300 who made their headquarters in Martinique alone.[532] While keeping the French islands supplied with provisions and merchandise captured in their prizes, they were a serious discouragement to English commerce in those regions, especially to the trade with the North American colonies. Occasionally they threatened the coasts of Virginia and New England, and some combined with their West Indian cruises a foray along the coasts of Guinea and into the Red Sea. These corsairs were not all commissioned privateers, however, for some of them seized French shipping with as little compunction as English or Dutch. Especially after the Treaty of Utrecht there was a recrudescence of piracy both in the West Indies and in the East, and it was ten years or more thereafter before the freebooters were finally suppressed.

Appendix I

An account of the English buccaneers belonging to Jamaica and Tortuga in 1663, found among the Rawlinson MSS., makes the number of privateering ships fifteen, and the men engaged in the business nearly a thousand. The list is as follows: —

Captain	Ship	Men	Guns
Sir Thomas Whetstone	a Spanish prize	60	7
Captain Smart	Griffon, frigate	100	14
Captain Guy	James, frigate	90	14
Captain James	American, frigate	70	6
Captain Cooper	his frigate	80	10
Captain Morris	a brigantine	60	7
Captain Brenningham	his frigate	70	6

Captain Mansfield	a brigantine	60	4
Captain Goodly	a pink	60	6
Captain Blewfield, belonging to Cape Gratia de Dios	a barque	50	3
Captain Herdue	a frigate	40	4

There were four more belonging to Jamaica, of which no account was available. The crews were mixed of English, French and Dutch.

Appendix II

List of filibusters and their vessels on the coasts of French San Domingo in 1684: —

Captain	Ship	Men	Guns
Le sieur Grammont	le Hardy	300	52
Le capitaine Laurens de Graff	Le Neptune	210	54
Le capitaine Michel	la Mutine	200	44
Le capitaine Janquais	la Dauphine	180	30
Le capitaine le Sage	le Tigre	130	30
Le capitaine Dedran	le Chasseur	120	20
Le sieur du Mesnil	la Trompeuse	100	14
Le capitaine Jocard	l'Irondelle	120	18
Le capitaine Brea	la Fortune	100	14
La prise du cap^{ne}. Laurens	—	80	18
Le sieur de Bernanos	la Schitie	60	8
Le capitaine Cachemarée	le St Joseph	70	6
Le capitaine Blot	la Quagone	90	8
Le capitaine Vigeron	la Louse (barque)	30	4
Le capitaine Petit	le Ruzé (bateau)	40	4
Le capitaine Lagarde	la Subtille	30	2
Le capitaine Verpre	le Postilion	25	2

(Paris, Archives Coloniales, Corresp. gén. de St. Dom., vol. i. —Mémoire sur l'estat de Saint Domingue à M. de Seignelay par M. de Cussy.)

Sources and Bibliography

Manuscript Sources in England

Public Record Office:
State Papers. Foreign. Spain. Vols. 34-72. (Abbreviated in the footnotes as S.P. Spain.)
British Museum:
Additional MSS. Vols. 11,268; 11,410-11; 12,410; 12,423; 12,429-30; 13,964; 13,975; 13,977; 13,992; 18,273; 22,676; 36,314-53.
Egerton MSS. Vol. 2395.
Sloane MSS. Vols. 793 or 894; 2724; 2752; 4020.
Stowe MSS. Vols. 305f; 205b.
Bodleian Library:
Rawlinson MSS. Vols. a. 26, 31, 32, 175, 347. Tanner MSS. Vols. xlvii.; li.

Manuscript Sources in France

Archives du ministère des Colonies:
Correspondance générale de Saint-Domingue. Vols. i.-ix.
Historique de Saint-Domingue. Vols. i.-iii.
Correspondance générale de Martinique. Vols. i.-xix.
Archives du ministère des affaires étrangères:
Mémoires et documents. Fonds divers. Amérique. Vols. v., xiii., xlix., li.
Correspondance politique. Angleterre.
Bibliothèque nationale:
Manuscrits, nouvelles acquisitions. Vols. 9325; 9334.
Renaudat MSS.

Printed Sources

Calendar of State Papers. Colonial series. America and the West Indies. 1574-1699. (Abbreviated in the footnotes as C.S.P. Colon.)

Calendar of State Papers. Venetian. 1603-1617. (Abbreviated in the footnotes as C.S.P. Ven.)

Dampier, William: Voyages. Edited by J. Masefield. 2 vols. London, 1906.

Gage, Thomas: The English American ... or a new survey of the West Indies, etc. London, 1648.

Historical Manuscripts Commission: Reports. London, 1870 (in progress).

Margry, Pierre: Relations et mémoires inédits pour servir à l'histoire de la France dans les pays d'outremer. Paris, 1867.

Pacheco, Cardenas, y Torres de Mendoza: Coleccion de documentos relativos al describrimiento, conquista y colonizacion de las posesiones españoles en América y Oceania. 42 vols. Madrid, 1864-83; *continued as* Coleccion de documentos ineditos ... de ultramar. 13 vols. Madrid, 1885-1900.

Pointis, Jean Bernard Desjeans, sieur de: Relation de l'expedition de Carthagène faite par les François en 1697. Amsterdam, 1698.

Present state of Jamaica ... to which is added an exact account of Sir Henry Morgan's voyage to ... Panama, etc. London, 1683.

Recopilacion de leyes de los reynos de las Indias, mandadas imprimir y publicar por rey Carlos II. 4 vols. Madrid, 1681.

Sharp, Bartholomew: The voyages and adventures of Captain B. Sharp ... in the South Sea ... Also Captain Van Horn with his buccanieres surprising of la Vera Cruz, etc. London, 1684.

Thurloe, John. A collection of the State papers of, etc. Edited by Thomas Birch. 7 vols. London, 1742.

Venables, General. The narrative of, etc. Edited by C.H. Firth. London, 1900.

Wafer, Lionel: A new voyage and description of the Isthmus of America, etc. London, 1699.

Winwood, Sir Ralph. Memorials of affairs of State ... collected from the original papers of, etc. Edited by Edmund Sawyer. London, 1725.

Among the printed sources one of the earliest and most important is the well-known history of the buccaneers written by Alexander Olivier Exquemelin (corrupted by the English into Esquemeling, by the French into Oexmelin). Of the author himself very little is known. Though sometimes claimed as a native of France, he was probably a Fleming or a Hollander, for the first edition of his works was written in the Dutch language. He came to Tortuga in 1666 as an *engagé* of the French West India Company, and after serving three years under a cruel master was rescued by the governor, M. d'Ogeron, joined the filibusters, and remained with them till 1674, taking part in most of their exploits. He seems to have exercised among them the profession of barber-surgeon. Returning to Europe in 1674, he published a narrative of the exploits in which he had taken part, or of which he at least had a first-hand knowledge. This "history" is the oldest and most elaborate chronicle we possess of the extraordinary deeds and customs of these freebooters who played so large a part in the history of the West Indies in the seventeenth century, and it forms the basis of all the popular modern accounts of Morgan and other buccaneer captains. Exquemelin, although he sadly confuses his dates, seems to be a perfectly honest witness, and his accounts of such transactions as fell within his own experience are closely corroborated by the official narratives.

(Biographies of Exquemelin are contained in the "Biographie Universelle" of Michaud, vol. xxxi. p. 201, and in the "Nouvelle Biographie Générale" of Hoefer, vol. xxxviii. p. 544. But both are very unsatisfactory and display a lamentable ignorance of the bibliography of his history of the buccaneers. According to the preface of a French edition of the work published at Lyons in 1774 and cited in the "Nouvelle Biographie," Exquemelin was born about 1645 and died after 1707.)

The first edition of the book, now very rare, is entitled:

> De Americaensche Zee-Roovers. Behelsende eene pertinente en waerachtige Beschrijving van alle de voornaemste Roveryen en onmenschliycke wreend heden die Englese en France Rovers tegens de Spanjaerden in America gepleeght hebben; Verdeelt in drie deelen ... Beschreven door A. O. Exquemelin ... t'Amsterdam, by Jan ten Hoorn, anno 1678, in 4°.

(Brit. Mus., 1061. *Cf.* 20 (2). The date, 1674, of the first Dutch edition cited by Dampierre ("Essai sur les sources de l'histoire des Antilles Françaises," p. 151) is doubtless a misprint.)

(Both Dampierre (*op. cit.*, p. 152) and Sabin ("Dict. of Books relating to America," vi. p. 310) cite, as the earliest separate account of the buccaneers, Claes G. Campaen's "Zee-Roover," Amsterdam, 1659. This little volume, however, does not deal with the buccaneers in the West Indies, but with privateering along the coasts of Europe and Africa.)

This book was reprinted several times and numerous translations were made, one on the top of the other. What appears to be a German translation of Exquemelin appeared in 1679 with the title:

> Americanische Seeräuber. Beschreibung der grössesten durch die Französische und Englische Meer-Beuter wider die Spanier in Amerika verübten Raubery Grausamheit ... Durch A. O. Nürnberg, 1679. 12°.

("Historie der Boecaniers of Vrybuyters van America ... Met Figuuren, 3 Deel. t'Amsterdam, 1700," 4°. —Brit. Mus., 9555. c. 19.)

This was followed two years later by a Spanish edition, also taken from the Dutch original:

> Piratas de la America y luz a la defensa de las costas de Indias Occidentales. Dedicado a Don Bernadino Antonio de Pardinas Villar de Francos ... por el zelo y cuidado de Don Antonio Freyre ... Traducido de la lingua Flamenca en Espanola por el Dor. de Buena-Maison ... Colonia Agrippina, en casa de Lorenzo Struickman. Ano de 1681. 12°.

(Brit. Mus., G. 7179. The appended description of the Spanish Government in America was omitted and a few Spanish verses were added in one or two places, but otherwise the translation seems to be trustworthy. The portraits and the map of the isthmus of Panama are the same as in the Dutch edition, but the other plates are different and better. In the Bibl. Nat. there is another Spanish edition of 1681 in quarto.)

This Spanish text, which seems to be a faithful rendering of the Dutch, was reprinted with a different dedication in 1682 and in 1684, and again in Madrid in 1793. It is the version on which the first English edition was based. The English translation is entitled:

> Bucaniers of America; or a true account of the ... assaults committed ... upon the coasts of the West Indies, by the Bucaniers of Jamaica and Tortuga ... especially the ... exploits of Sir Henry Morgan ... written originally in Dutch by J. Esquemeling ... now ... rendered into English. W. Crooke; London, 1684. 4º.

(Brit. Mus., 1198, a. 12 (or) 1197, h. 2.; G. 7198.)

The first English edition of Exquemelin was so well received that within three months a second was published, to which was added the account of a voyage by Captain Cook and a brief chapter on the exploits of Barth. Sharp in the Pacific Ocean. In the same year, moreover, there appeared an entirely different English version, with the object of vindicating the character of Morgan from the charges of brutality and lust which had appeared in the first translation and in the Dutch original. It was entitled:

> The History of the Bucaniers; being an impartial relation of all the battels, sieges, and other most eminent assaults committed for several years upon the coasts of the West Indies by the pirates of Jamaica and Tortuga. More especially the unparalleled achievements of Sir Henry Morgan ... very much corrected from the errors of the original, by the relations of some English gentlemen, that then resided in those parts. *Den Engelseman is een Duyvil voor een Mensch.* London, printed for Thomas Malthus at the Sun in the Poultry. 1684.

(Brit. Mus., G. 13,674.)

The first edition of 1684 was reprinted with a new title-page in 1695, and again in 1699. The latter included, in addition to the text of Exquemelin, the journals of Basil Ringrose and Raveneau de Lussan, both describing voyages in the South Seas, and the voyage of the Sieur de Montauban to Guinea in 1695. This was the earliest of the composite histories of the buccaneers and became the model for the Dutch edition of 1700 and the French editions published at Trevoux in 1744 and 1775.

The first French translation of Exquemelin appeared two years after the English edition of 1684. It is entitled:

> Histoire des Aventuriers qui se sont signalez dans les Indes contenant ce qu'ils ont fait de plus remarquable depuis vingt années. Avec la vie, les Moeurs, les Coutumes des Habitans de Saint Domingue et de la Tortuë et une Description exacte de ces lieux; ... Le tout enrichi de Cartes Geographiques et de Figures en Taille-douce. Par Alexandre Olivier Oexmelin. A Paris, chez Jacques Le Febre. MDCLXXXVI., 2 vols. 12º.

(Brit. Mus., 9555, aa. 4.)

This version may have been based on the Dutch original; although the only indication we have of this is the fact that the work includes at the end a description of the government and revenues of the Spanish Indies, a description which is found in none of the earlier editions of Exquemelin, except in the Dutch original of 1678. The French text, however, while following the outline of Exquemelin's narrative, is greatly altered and enlarged. The history of Tortuga and French Hispaniola is elaborated with details from another source, as are also the descriptions of the manners and customs of the cattle-hunters and the freebooters. Accounts of two other buccaneers, Montbars and Alexandre Bras-le-Fer, are inserted, but d'Ogeron's shipwreck on

Porto Rico and the achievements of Admiral d'Estrees against the Dutch are omitted. In general the French editor, the Sieur de Frontignières, has re-cast the whole story. A similar French edition appeared in Paris in 1688, (Brit. Mus., 278, a. 13, 14.) and in 1713 a facsimile of this last was published at Brussels by Serstevens (Dampierre, p. 153). Sabin (*op. cit.*, vi. 312) mentions an edition of 1699 in three volumes which included the journal of Raveneau de Lussan. In 1744, and again in 1775, another French edition was published in four volumes at Trevoux, to which was added the voyage of Montauban to the Guinea Coast, and the expeditions against Vera Cruz in 1683, Campeache in 1685, and Cartagena in 1697. The third volume contained the journal of R. de Lussan, and the fourth a translation of Johnson's "History of the Pirates." (Brit. Mus., 9555, aa. 1.) A similar edition appeared at Lyons in 1774, but I have had no opportunity of examining a copy. (Nouvelle Biographie Générale, tom. xxxviii. 544. The best bibliography of Exquemelin is in Sabin, *op. cit.*, vi. 309.)

Secondary Works

Of the secondary works concerned with the history of the buccaneers, the oldest are the writings of the French Jesuit historians of the seventeenth and eighteenth centuries. Dutertre (Histoire générale des Antilles. Paris, 1667-71), a chronicler of events within his own experience as well as a reliable historian, unfortunately brings his narrative to a close in 1667, but up to that year he is the safest guide to the history of the French Antilles. Labat, in his "Nouveau Voyage aux Isles de l'Amerique" (Paris, 1722), gives an account of eleven years, between 1694 and 1705, spent in Martinique and Guadeloupe, and although of little value as an historian, he supplies us with a fund of the most picturesque and curious details about the life and manners of the people in the West Indies at the end of the seventeenth century. A much more important and accurate work is Charlevoix's "Histoire de l'Isle Espagnole ou de S. Domingue" (Paris, 1732), and this I have used as a general introduction to the history of the French buccaneers. Raynal's "Histoire philosophique et politique des établissements et du commerce européen dans les deux Indes" (Amsterdam, 1770) is based for the origin of the French Antilles upon Dutertre and Labat and is therefore negligible for the period of the buccaneers. Adrien Dessalles, who in 1847 published his "Histoire générale des Antilles," preferred, like Labat and Raynal, to depend on the historians who had preceded him rather than endeavour to gain an intimate knowledge of the sources.

In the English histories of Jamaica written by Long, Bridges, and Gardner, whatever notice is taken of the buccaneers is meagre and superficial, and the same is true of Bryan Edwards' "History, civil and commercial, of the British colonies in the West Indies." Thomas Southey, in his "Chronological History of the West Indies" (Lond. 1827), devotes considerable space to their achievements, but depends entirely upon the traditional sources. In 1803 J.W. von Archenholz published "Die Geschichte der Flibustier," a superficial, diffuse and even puerile narrative, giving no references whatever to authorities. (It was translated into French (Paris, 1804), and into English by Geo. Mason (London, 1807).) In 1816 a "History of the Buccaneers in America" was published by James Burney as the fourth volume of "A chronological History of the Discoveries in the South Seas or Pacific Ocean." Burney casts but a rapid glance over the West Indies, devoting most of the volume to an account of the voyages of the freebooters along the coast of South America and in the East Indies. Walter Thornbury in 1858 wrote "The Buccaneers, or the Monarchs of the Main," a hasty compilation, florid and overdrawn, and without historical judgment or accuracy. In 1895 M. Henri Lorin presented a Latin thesis to the Faculty of History in Paris, entitled: —"De praedonibus Insulam Santi Dominici celebrantibus saeculo septimo decimo," but he seems to have confined himself to Exquemelin, Le Pers, Labat, Dutertre and a few documents drawn from the French colonial archives. The best summary account in English of the history and significance of the buccaneers in the West Indies is contained in Hubert H. Bancroft's "History of Central America" (ii. chs. 26, 28-30). Within the past year there has appeared an excellent volume by M. Pierre de Vaissière describing creole life and manners in the French colony of San Domingo in the century and a half preceding the Revolution. (Vaissière, Pierre de: Saint Domingue. (1629-1789). Paris, 1909.) It is a reliable monograph, and like his earlier volume, "Gentilshommes campagnards de l'ancienne France," is written in a most entertaining style. De Vaissière contributes much valuable information, especially in the first chapter, about the origins and customs of the French "flibustiers."

I have been able to find only two Spanish works which refer at all to the buccaneers. One is entitled:

> Piraterias y agresiones de los ingleses y de otros pueblos de Europa en la America espanola desde el siglo XVI. al XVIII., deducidas de las obras de D. Dionisio de Alcedo y Herrera. Madrid, 1883. 4º.

Except for a long introduction by Don Justo Zaragoza based upon Exquemelin and Alcedo, it consists of a collection of extracts referring to freebooters on the coasts of Peru and Chili, and deals chiefly with the eighteenth century. The other Spanish work is an elaborate history of the Spanish navy lately published in nine volumes by Cesareo Fernandez Duro, and entitled: —

> Armada espanola desde la union de los reinos de Castilla y de Aragon. Madrid, 1895.

There are numerous chapters dealing with the outrages of the French and English freebooters in the West Indies, some of them based upon Spanish sources to which I have had no access. But upon comparison of Duro's narrative, which in so far as it relates to the buccaneers is often meagre, with the sources available to me, I find that he adds little to what may be learned on the subject here in England.

One of the best English descriptions of the Spanish colonial administration and commercial system is still that contained in book viii. of Robertson's "History of America" (Lond. 1777). The latest and best summary account, however, is in French, in the introduction to vol. i. of "La traite négrière aux Indes de Castille" (Paris, 1906), by Georges Scelle. Weiss, in vol. ii. of his history of "L'Espagne depuis Philippe II. jusqu'aux Bourbons" (Paris, 1844), treats of the causes of the economic decadence of Spain, and gives an account of the contraband trade in Spanish America, drawn largely from Labat. On this general subject Leroy-Beaulieu, "De la colonization chez les peuples modernes" (Paris, 1874), has been especially consulted.

The best account of the French privateers of the sixteenth century in America is in an essay entitled: "Les corsairs français au XVIᵉ siècle dans les Antilles" (Paris, 1902), by Gabriel Marcel. It is a short monograph based on the collections of Spanish documents brought together by Pacheco and Navarrete. The volume by E. Ducéré entitled, "Les corsairs sous l'ancien regîme" (Bayonne, 1895), is also valuable for the history of privateering. For the history of the Elizabethan mariners I have made use of the two works by J. S. Corbett: "Drake and the Tudor Navy" (Lond. 1898), and "The successors of Drake" (Lond. 1900). Other works consulted were:

Arias de Miranda, José: Examen critico-historico del influyo que tuvo en el comercio, industria y poblacion de Espana su dominacion en America. Madrid, 1854.

Blok, Pieter Johan: History of the people of the Netherlands. Translated by C. A. Bierstadt and Ruth Putnam. 4 vols. New York, 1898.

Brown, Alex.: The Genesis of the United States. 2 vols. Lond., 1890.

Crawford, James Ludovic Lindsay, 26th Earl of: Bibliotheca Lindesiana. Handlist of proclamations. 3 vols. Aberdeen, 1893-1901.

Dumont, Jean: Corps universel diplomatique. 13 vols. Hague, 1726-39.

Froude, James Anthony: History of England from the fall of Wolsey to the defeat of the Spanish armada. 12 vols. 1870-75. English seamen in the sixteenth century. Lond., 1901.

Gardiner, Samuel Rawson: History of the Commonwealth and Protectorate, 1649-1660. 3 vols. Lond., 1894-1903.

Geographical and historical description of ... Cartagena, Porto Bello, La Vera Cruz, the Havana and San Augustin. Lond., 1741.

Gibbs, Archibald R.: British Honduras ... from ... 1670. Lond., 1883.

Hakluyt, Richard: The principal navigations ... of the English nation, etc. 3 vols. Lond., 1598-1600.

Herrera y Tordesillas, Antonio: Historia general de las Indias. 4 vols. Madrid, 1601-15.

Hughson, Shirley C.: The Carolina pirates and colonial commerce. Baltimore, 1894.

Lucas, C. P.: A historical geography of the British colonies. 4 vols. Oxford, 1905. Vol. ii. The West Indies.

Monson, Sir William: The naval tracts of ... Edited ... by M. Oppenheim. Vols. i. and ii. Lond., 1902 —(in progress).

Oviedo y Valdes, Gonzalo Fernandez de: Historia general de las Indias. Salamanca, 1547.

Peytraud, Lucien: L'Esclavage aux Antilles françaises avant 1789, etc. Paris, 1897.

Saint-Yves, G.: Les compagnes de Jean d'Estrées dans la mer des Antilles, 1676-78. Paris, 1900.

Strong, Frank: Causes of Cromwell's West Indian expedition. (Amer. Hist. Review. Jan. 1899).

Veitia Linaje, Josef de: Norte de la Contratacion de las Indias Occidentales. Sevilla, 1672.

Vignols, Leon: La piraterie sur l'Atlantique au XVIIIᵉ siècle. Rennes, 1891.

Footnotes

1. Herrera: Decades II. 1, p. 4, cited in Scelle: la Traite Négrière, I. p. 6. Note 2.

2. Scelle, *op. cit.*, i. pp. 6-9.

3. "Por cuanto los pacificaciones no se han de hacer con ruido de armas, sino con caridad y buen modo." —Recop. de leyes ... de las Indias, lib. vii. tit. 1.

4. Scelle, *op. cit.*, i. p. 35.

5. Weiss: L'Espagne depuis Philippe II. jusqu'aux Bourbons., II. pp. 204 and 215. Not till 1722 was legislative sanction given to this practice. M. Lemonnet wrote to Colbert in 1670 concerning this commerce: —"Quelque perquisition qu'on ait faite dans ce dernier temps aux Indes pour découvrir les biens des François, ils ont plustost souffert la prison que de rien déclarer ... toute les merchandises qu'on leur donne à porter aux Indes sont chargées sous le nom d'Espagnols, que bien souvent n'en ont pas connaissance, ne jugeant pas à propos de leur en parler, afin de tenir les affaires plus secrètes et qu'il n'y ait que le commissionaire à le savoir, lequel en rend compte à son retour des Indes, directement à celui qui en a donne la cargaison en confiance sans avoir nul egard pour ceux au nom desquels le chargement à été fait, et lorsque ces commissionaires reviennent des Indes soit sur le flottes galions ou navires particuliers, ils apportent leur argent dans leurs coffres, la pluspart entre pont et sans connoissement." (Margry: Relations et mémoires inédits pour servir à l'histoire de la France dans les pays d'outremer, p. 185.) The importance to the maritime powers of preserving and protecting this clandestine trade is evident, especially as the Spanish government frequently found it a convenient instrument for retaliating upon those nations against which it harboured some grudge. All that was necessary was to sequester the vessels and goods of merchants belonging to the nation at which it wished to strike. This happened frequently in the course of the seventeenth century. Thus Lerma in 1601 arrested the French merchants in Spain to revenge himself on Henry IV. In 1624 Olivares seized 160 Dutch vessels. The goods of Genoese merchants were sequestered by Philip IV. in 1644; and in 1684 French merchandize was again seized, and Mexican traders whose storehouses contained such goods were fined 500,000 ecus, although the same storehouses contained English and Dutch goods which were left unnoticed. The fine was later restored upon Admiral d'Estrées' threat to bombard Cadiz. The solicitude of the French government for this trade is expressed in a letter of Colbert to the Marquis de Villars, ambassador at Madrid, dated 5th February 1672: —"Il est tellement necessaire d'avoir soin d'assister les particuliers qui font leur trafic en Espagne, pour maintenir le plus important commerce que nous ayons, que je suis persuadé que vous ferez toutes les instances qui pourront dépendre de vous ... en sorte que cette protection produira des avantages considérables au commerce des sujets de Sa Majesté" (*ibid.*, p. 188). *Cf.* also the instructions of Louis XIV. to the Comte d'Estrées, 1st April 1680. The French admiral was to visit all the ports of the Spaniards in the West Indies, especially Cartagena and San Domingo; and to be always informed of the situation and advantages of these ports, and of the facilities and difficulties to be met with in case of an attack upon them; so that the Spaniards might realise that if they failed to do justice to the French merchants on the return of the galleons, his Majesty was always ready to force them to do so, either by attacking these galleons, or by capturing one of their West Indian ports (*ibid.*).

6. Weiss, *op. cit.*, II. p. 205.

7. *Ibid.*, II. p. 206.

8.   Oppenheim: The Naval Tracts of Sir Wm. Monson. Vol. II. Appendix B., p. 316.

9.   In 1509, owing to the difficulties experienced by merchants in ascending the Guadalquivir, ships were given permission to load and register at Cadiz under the supervision of an inspector or "visitador," and thereafter commerce and navigation tended more and more to gravitate to that port. After 1529, in order to facilitate emigration to America, vessels were allowed to sail from certain other ports, notably San Sebastian, Bilboa, Coruna, Cartagena and Malaga. The ships might register in these ports, but were obliged always to make their return voyage to Seville. But either the *cedula* was revoked, or was never made use of, for, according to Scelle, there are no known instances of vessels sailing to America from those towns. The only other exceptions were in favour of the Company of Guipuzcoa in 1728, to send ships from San Sebastian to Caracas, and of the Company of Galicia in 1734, to send two vessels annually to Campeache and Vera Cruz. (Scelle, *op. cit.*, i. pp. 48-49 and notes.)

10.   Scelle, *op. cit.*, i. p. 36 *ff.*

11.   In Nov. 1530 Charles V., against the opposition of the *Contratacion*, ordered the Council of the Indies to appoint a resident judge at Cadiz to replace the officers of the *Casa* there. This institution, called the "Juzgado de Indias," was, until the removal of the *Casa* to Cadiz in 1717, the source of constant disputes and irritation.

12.   Scelle, *op. cit.*, i. p. 52 and note; Duro: Armada Espanola, I. p. 204.

13.   The distinction between the Flota or fleet for New Spain and the galleons intended for Terra Firma only began with the opening of the great silver mines of Potosi, the rich yields of which after 1557 made advisable an especial fleet for Cartagena and Nombre de Dios. (Oppenheim, II. Appendix B., p. 322.)

14.   Memoir of MM. Duhalde and de Rochefort to the French king, 1680 (Margry, *op. cit.*, p. 192 *ff.*).

15.   Memoir of MM. Duhalde and de Rochefort to the French king, 1680 (Margry, *op. cit.*, p. 192 *ff.*)

16.   Scelle, *op. cit.*, i. p. 64; Dampier: Voyages, *ed.* 1906, i. p. 200.

17.   Gage: A New Survey of the West Indies, *ed.* 1655, pp. 185-6. When Gage was at Granada, in February 1637, strict orders were received from Gautemala that the ships were not to sail that year, because the President and Audiencia were informed of some Dutch and English ships lying in wait at the mouth of the river.

18.   Scelle, *op. cit.*, i. pp. 64-5; Duhalde and de Rochefort. There were two ways of sending goods from Panama to Porto Bello. One was an overland route of 18 leagues, and was used only during the summer. The other was by land as far as Venta Cruz, 7 leagues from Panama, and thence by water on the river Chagre to its mouth, a distance of 26 leagues. When the river was high the transit might be accomplished in two or three days, but at other times from six to twelve days were required. To transfer goods from Chagre to Porto Bello was a matter of only eight or nine hours. This route was used in winter when the roads were rendered impassable by the great rains and floods. The overland journey, though shorter, was also more difficult and expensive. The goods were carried on long mule-trains, and the "roads, so-called, were merely bridle paths ... running through swamps and jungles, over hills and rocks, broken by unbridged rivers, and situated in one of the deadliest climates in the world." The project of a canal to be cut through the isthmus was often proposed to the Councils in Spain, but was never acted upon. (Descript. ... of Cartagena; Oppenheim, i. p. 333.)

19.   Nombre de Dios, a few leagues to the east of Porto Bello, had formerly been the port where the galleons received the treasure brought from Panama, but in 1584 the King of Spain ordered the settlement to be abandoned on account of its unhealthiness, and because the harbour, being open to the sea, afforded little shelter to shipping. Gage says that in his time Nombre de Dios was almost forsaken because of its climate. Dampier, writing thirty years later, describes the site as a waste. "Nombre de Dios," he says, "is now nothing but a name. For I have lain ashore in the place where that City stood, but it is all overgrown with Wood, so as to have no sign that any Town hath been there." (Voyages, *ed.* 1906, i. p. 81.)

20.   Gage, *ed.* 1655, pp. 196-8.

21.   Scelle, *op. cit.*, i. p. 65.

22.   Oppenheim, ii. p. 338.

23.   When the Margarita patache failed to meet the galleons at Cartagena, it was given its clearance and allowed to sail alone to Havana —a tempting prey to buccaneers hovering in those seas.

24.   Duhalde and de Rochefort.

25.   Rawl. MSS., A. 175, 313 b; Oppenheim, ii. p. 338.

26.   Here I am following the MSS. quoted by Oppenheim (ii. pp. 335 *ff.*). Instead of watering in Hispaniola, the fleet sometimes stopped at Dominica, or at Aguada in Porto Rico.

27.   Duhalde and de Rochefort.

28.   Quintal=about 100 pounds.

29.   These "vaisseaux de registre" were supposed not to exceed 300 tons, but through fraud were often double that burden.

30.   Duhalde and de Rochefort; Scelle, *op. cit.*, i. p. 54.

31.   Gage, *ed.* 1655, pp. 199-200.

32.   Duhalde and de Rochefort; Oppenheim, ii. p. 318.

33.   Scelle, *op. cit.*, i. p. 45; Recop., t. i. lib. iii. tit. viii.

34.   There seems to have been a contraband trade carried on at Cadiz itself. Foreign merchants embarked their goods upon the galleons directly from their own vessels in the harbour, without registering them with the *Contratacion*; and on the return of the fleets received the price of their goods in ingots of gold and silver by the same fraud. It is scarcely possible that this was done without the tacit authorization of the Council of the Indies at Madrid, for if the Council had insisted upon a rigid execution of the laws regarding registration, detection would have been inevitable.

35.   Weiss, *op. cit.*, ii. p. 226.

36.   Most of the offices in the Spanish Indies were venal. No one obtained a post without paying dearly for it, except the viceroys of Mexico and Peru, who were grandees, and received their places through favour at court. The governors of the ports, and the presidents of the Audiencias established at Panama, San Domingo, and Gautemala, bought their posts in Spain. The offices in the interior were in the gift of the viceroys and sold to the highest bidder. Although each port had three corregidors who audited the finances, as they also paid for their places, they connived with the governors. The consequence was inevitable. Each official during his tenure of office expected to

recover his initial outlay, and amass a small fortune besides. So not only were the bribes of interlopers acceptable, but the officials often themselves bought and sold the contraband articles.

37.   Froude: History of England, viii. p. 436 *ff.*

38.   1585, August 12th. Ralph Lane to Sir Philip Sidney. Port Ferdinando, Virginia. —He has discovered the infinite riches of St. John (Porto Rico?) and Hispaniola by dwelling on the islands five weeks. He thinks that if the Queen finds herself burdened with the King of Spain, to attempt them would be most honourable, feasible and profitable. He exhorts him not to refuse this good opportunity of rendering so great a service to the Church of Christ. The strength of the Spaniards doth altogether grow from the mines of her treasure. Extract, C.S.P. Colon., 1574-1660.

39.   Scelle, *op. cit.*, ii. p. xiii.

40.   Scelle, *op. cit.*, i. p. ix.

41.   1611, February 28. Sir Thos. Roe to Salisbury. Port d'Espaigne, Trinidad. —He has seen more of the coast from the River Amazon to the Orinoco than any other Englishman alive. The Spaniards here are proud and insolent, yet needy and weak, their force is reputation, their safety is opinion. The Spaniards treat the English worse than Moors. The government is lazy and has more skill in planting and selling tobacco than in erecting colonies and marching armies. Extract, C.S.P. Colon., 1574-1660. (Roe was sent by Prince Henry upon a voyage of discovery to the Indies.)

42.   "An historical account of the rise and growth of the West India Colonies." By Dalby Thomas, Lond., 1690. (Harl. Miscell., 1808, ii. 357.)

43.   Oviedo: Historia general de las Indias, lib. xix. cap. xiii.; Coleccion de documentos ... de ultramar, tom. iv. p. 57 (deposition of the Spanish captain at the Isle of Mona); Pacheco, etc.: Coleccion de documentos ... de las posesiones espanoles en America y Oceania, tom. xl. p. 305 (cross-examination of witnesses by officers of the Royal Audiencia in San Domingo just after the visit of the English ship to that place); English Historical Review, XX. p. 115. The ship is identified with the "Samson" dispatched by Henry VIII. in 1527 "with divers cunning men to seek strange regions," which sailed from the Thames on 20th May in company with the "Mary of Guildford," was lost by her consort in a storm on the night of 1st July, and was believed to have foundered with all on board. (*Ibid.*)

44.   Hakluyt, *ed.* 1600, iii. p. 700; Froude, *op. cit.*, viii. p. 427.

45.   Scelle., *op. cit.*, i. pp. 123-25, 139-61.

46.   Colecc. de doc. ... de ultramar. tom. vi. p. 15.

47.   Froude, *op. cit.*, viii. pp. 470-72.

48.   Corbett: Drake and the Tudor Navy, i. ch. 3.

49.   Corbett: Drake and the Tudor Navy, ii. chs. 1, 2, 11.

50.   Corbett: The Successors of Drake, ch. x.

51.   Marcel: Les corsaires français au XVIe siècle, p. 7. As early as 1501 a royal ordinance in Spain prescribed the construction of carracks to pursue the privateers, and in 1513 royal *cedulas* were sent to the officials of the *Casa de Contratacion* ordering them to send two caravels to guard the coasts of Cuba and protect Spanish navigation from the assaults of French corsairs. (*Ibid.*, p. 8).

52. Colecc. de doc. ...de ultramar, tomos i., iv., vi.; Ducéré: Les corsaires sous l'ancien régime. Append. II.; Duro, *op. cit.*, i. Append. XIV.

53. Colecc. de doc. ...de ultramar, tom. vi. p. 22.

54. *Ibid.*, p. 23.

55. Marcel, *op. cit.*, p. 16.

56. Colecc. de doc. ...de ultramar, tom. vi. p. 360.

57. Colecc. de doc. ...de ultramar, tom. vi. p. 360.

58. Lucas: A Historical Geography of the British Colonies, vol. ii. pp. 37, 50.

59. Weiss, *op. cit.*, ii. p. 292.

60. Duro, *op. cit.*, iii. ch. xvi.; iv. chs. iii., viii.

61. Portugal between 1581 and 1640 was subject to the Crown of Spain, and Brazil, a Portuguese colony, was consequently within the pale of Spanish influence and administration.

62. Blok: History of the People of the Netherlands, iv. p. 36.

63. Blok: History of the People of the Netherlands, iv. p. 37; Duro, *op. cit.*, iv. p. 99; Gage, *ed.* 1655, p. 80.

64. Brit. Mus., Add. MSS., 36,325, No. 10.

65. Robert Rich, Earl of Warwick, was created admiral of the fleet by order of Parliament in March 1642, and although removed by Charles I. was reinstated by Parliament on 1st July.

66. Brit. Mus., Sloane MSS., 793 or 894; Add. MSS., 36,327, No. 9.

67. Winwood Papers, ii. pp. 75-77.

68. Brown: Genesis of the United States, i. pp. 120-25, 172.

69. C.S.P. Colon., 1574-1660.

70. C.S.P. Colon., 1574-1660.

71. Clarendon State Papers, ii. p. 87; Rymer: Fœdera, xx. p. 416.

72. Duro, *op. cit.*, ii. p. 462.

73. Duro, *op. cit.*, iii. pp. 236-37.

74. C.S.P. Venet., 1603-07, p. 199.

75. Winwood Papers, ii. p. 233.

76. Brit. Mus., Add. MSS., 36,319, No. 7; 36,320, No. 8; 36,321, No. 24; 36,322, No. 23.

77. C.S.P. Colon., 1574-1660: —1629, 5th and 30th Nov.; 1630, 29th July.

78. Gage saw at Cartagena about a dozen English prisoners captured by the Spaniards at sea, and belonging to the settlement on Providence Island.

79. C.S.P. Colon., 1574-1660: —1635, 19th March; 1636, 26th March.

80. Brit. Mus., Add. MSS., 36,323, No. 10.

81. Duro, Tomo., iv. p. 339; *cf.* also in Bodleian Library: —"A letter written upon occasion in the Low Countries, etc. Whereunto is added avisos from several places, of the taking of the Island of Providence, by the Spaniards from the English. London. Printed for Nath. Butter, Mar. 22, 1641. "I have letter by an aviso from Cartagena, dated the 14th of September, wherein they advise that the galleons were ready laden with the silver, and would depart thence the 6th of October. The general of the galleons, named Francisco Dias Pimienta, had beene formerly in the moneth of July with above 3000 men, and the least of his ships, in the island of S. Catalina, where he had taken and carried away with all the English, and razed the forts, wherein they found 600 negroes, much gold and indigo, so that the prize is esteemed worth above halfe a million."

82. Rawl. MSS., A. 32,297; 31, 121.

83. Bibl. Nat., Nouv. Acq., 9334, f. 48.

84. C.S.P. Colon., 1574-1660, p. 130. This company had been organised under the name of "The Governor and Company of Adventurers for the Plantations of the Islands of Providence, Henrietta and the adjacent islands, between 10 and 20 degrees of north latitude and 290 and 310 degrees of longitude." The patent of incorporation is dated 4th December 1630 (*ibid.*, p. 123).

85. *Ibid.*, p. 131.

86. Ibid.

87. This identity was first pointed out by Pierre de Vaissière in his recent book: "Saint Domingue (1629-1789). La societé et la vie créoles sous l'ancien régime," Paris, 1909, p. 7.

88. C.S.P. Colon., 1574-1660, pp. 131-33.

89. *Ibid.*, pp. 174, 175.

90. This was probably the same man as the "Don Juan de Morfa Geraldino" who was admiral of the fleet which attacked Tortuga in 1654. *Cf.* Duro, *op. cit.*, v. p. 35.

91. In 1642 Rui Fernandez de Fuemayor was governor and captain-general of the province of Venezuela. *Cf.* Doro, *op. cit.*, iv. p. 341; note 2.

92. Brit. Mus., Add. MSS., 13,977, f. 505. According to the minutes of the Providence Company, a certain Mr. Perry, newly arrived from Association, gave information on 19th March 1635 that the island had been surprised by the Spaniards (C.S.P. Colon., 1574-1660, p. 200). This news was confirmed by a Mrs. Filby at another meeting of the company on 10th April, when Capt. Wormeley, "by reason of his cowardice and negligence in losing the island," was formally deprived of his office as governor and banished from the colony (*ibid.*, p. 201).

93. Brit. Mus., Add. MSS., 13,977, pp. 222-23.

94. *Ibid.*, pp. 226-27, 235.

95. *Ibid.*, pp. 226, 233, 235-37, 244.

96. Charlevoix: Histoire de. …Saint Domingue, liv. vii. pp. 9-10. The story is repeated by Duro (*op. cit.*, v. p. 34), who says that the Spaniards were led by "el general D. Carlos Ibarra."

97. Charlevoix, *op. cit.*, liv. vii. p. 10; Bibl. Nat. Nouv. Acq., 9334, p. 48 *ff.*

98. Charlevoix, *op. cit.*, liv. vii. pp. 10-12; Vaissière., *op. cit.*, Appendix I ("Mémoire envoyé aux seigneurs de la Compagnie des Isles de l'Amérique par M. de Poincy, le 15 Novembre 1640"). According to the records of the Providence Company, Tortuga in 1640 had 300 inhabitants. A Captain Fload, who had been governor, was then in London to clear himself of charges preferred against him by the planters, while a Captain James was exercising authority as "President" in the island. (C.S.P. Colon., 1574-1660. pp. 313, 314.) Fload was probably the "English captain" referred to in de Poincy's memoir. His oppressive rule seems to have been felt as well by the English as by the French.

99. Dutertre: Histoire générale des Antilles, tom. i. p. 171.

100. Charlevoix: *op. cit.*, liv. vii. pp. 12-13.

101. In this monograph, by "buccaneers" are always meant the corsairs and filibusters, and not the cattle and hog killers of Hispaniola and Tortuga.

102. Labat: Nouveau voyage aux isles de l'Amerique, *ed.* 1742, tom. vii. p. 233.

103. Le Pers, printed in Margry, *op. cit.*

104. Le Pers, printed in Margry, *op. cit.*

105. Dampier writes that "Privateers are not obliged to any ship, but free to go ashore where they please, or to go into any other ship that will entertain them, only paying for their provision." (Edition 1906, i. p. 61).

106. Labat, *op. cit.*, tom. i. ch. 9.

107. Labat, *op. cit.*, tom. vii. ch. 17.

108. *Ibid.*, tom. ii. ch. 17.

109. Gibbs: British Honduras, p. 25.

110. A Spaniard, writing from S. Domingo in 1635, complains of an English buccaneer settlement at Samana (on the north coast of Hispaniola, near the Mona Passage), where they grew tobacco, and preyed on the ships sailing from Cartagena and S. Domingo for Spain. (Add. MSS., 13,977, f. 508.)

111. A piece of eight was worth in Jamaica from 4s. 6d. to 5s.

112. Exquemelin, *ed.* 1684, Part I. pp. 21-22.

113. Dutertre, *op. cit.*, tom. i. ch. vi.

114. Charlevoix, *op. cit.*, liv. vii. p. 16.

115. Charlevoix, *op. cit.*, liv. vii. pp. 17-18.

116. According to a Spanish MS., there were in Tortuga in 1653 700 French inhabitants, more than 200 negroes, and 250 Indians with their wives and children. The negroes and Indians were all slaves; the former seized on the coasts of Havana and Cartagena, the latter brought over from Yucatan. In the harbour the platform had fourteen cannon, and in the fort above were forty-six cannon, many of them of bronze (Add. MSS., 13,992, f. 499 *ff.*). The report of the amount of ordnance is doubtless an exaggeration.

117. Add. MSS., 13,992, f. 499.

118. According to Dutertre, one vessel was commanded by the assassins, Martin and Thibault, and contained the women and children. The latter, when provisions ran low, were marooned on one of the Caymans, north-west of Jamaica, where they

would have perished had not a Dutch ship found and rescued them. Martin and Thibault were never heard of again.

119. Venables was not bound by his instructions to any definite plan. It had been proposed, he was told, to seize Hispaniola or Porto Rico or both, after which either Cartagena or Havana might be taken, and the Spanish revenue-fleets obstructed. An alternative scheme was to make the first attempt on the mainland at some point between the mouth of the Orinoco and Porto Bello, with the ultimate object of securing Cartagena. It was left to Venables, however, to consult with Admiral Penn and three commissioners, Edward Winslow (former governor of Plymouth colony in New England), Daniel Searle (governor of Barbadoes), and Gregory Butler, as to which, if any, of these schemes should be carried out. Not until some time after the arrival of the fleet at Barbadoes was it resolved to attack Hispaniola. (Narrative of Gen. Venables, edition 1900, pp. x, 112-3.)

120. Gardiner: Hist. of the Commonwealth and Protectorate, vol. iii. ch. xlv.; Narrative of Gen. Venables.

121. Gardiner: *op. cit.*, iii. p. 368.

122. *Cf.* the "Commission of the Commissioners for the West Indian Expedition." (Narrative of Gen. Venables, p. 109.)

123. *Cf.* American Hist. Review, vol. iv. p. 228; "Instructions unto Gen. Robt. Venables." (Narrative of Gen. Venables, p. 111.)

124. *Cf.* Narrative of Gen. Venables, pp. 3, 90; "Instructions unto Generall Penn," etc., *ibid.*, p. 107. After the outbreak of the Spanish war, Cromwell was anxious to clear his government of the charges of treachery and violation of international duties. The task was entrusted to the Latin Secretary, John Milton, who on 26th October 1655 published a manifesto defending the actions of the Commonwealth. He gave two principal reasons for the attempt upon the West Indies: —(1) the cruelties of the Spaniards toward the English in America and their depredations on English colonies and trade; (2) the outrageous treatment and extermination of the Indians. He denied the Spanish claims to all of America, either as a papal gift, or by right of discovery alone, or even by right of settlement, and insisted upon both the natural and treaty rights of Englishmen to trade in Spanish seas.

125. The memory of the exploits of Drake and his contemporaries was not allowed to die in the first half of the seventeenth century. Books like "Sir Francis Drake Revived," and "The World encompassed by Sir Francis Drake," were printed time and time again. The former was published in 1626 and again two years later; "The World Encompassed" first appeared in 1628 and was reprinted in 1635 and 1653. A quotation from the title-page of the latter may serve to illustrate the temper of the times: —

Drake, Sir Francis. The world encompassed. Being his next voyage to that to Nombre de Dios, formerly imprinted ... offered ... especially for the stirring up of heroick spirits, to benefit their country and eternize their names by like bold attempts. Lon. 1628.
Cf. also Gardiner, *op. cit.*, iii. pp. 343-44.

126. Gardiner, *op. cit.*, iii. p. 346; *cf.* also "Present State of Jamaica, 1683."

127. Long: "History of Jamaica," i. p. 260; C.S.P. Colon., 1675-76. Addenda, No. 274.

128. Long, *op. cit.*, i. p. 272 *ff.*

129. *Ibid.*; Thurloe Papers, VI. p. 540; vii. p. 260; "Present State of Jamaica, 1683"; C.S.P. Colon., 1675-76. Addenda, Nos. 303-308.

130. Long, *op. cit.*, i. p. 245; C.S.P. Colon., 1675-76. Addenda, Nos. 236, 261, 276, etc. The conditions in Jamaica directly after its capture are in remarkable contrast to what might have been expected after reading the enthusiastic descriptions of the island, its climate, soil and products, left us by Englishmen who visited it. Jackson in 1643 compared it with the Arcadian plains and Thessalien Tempe, and many of his men wanted to remain and live with the Spaniards. See also the description of Jamaica contained in the Rawlinson MSS. and written just after the arrival of the English army: —"As for the country ... more than this." (Narrative of Gen. Venables, pp. 138-9.)

131. C.S.P. Colon., 1675-76. Addenda, Nos. 229, 232; Lucas: Historical Geography of the British Colonies, ii. p. 101, and note.

132. Lucas, *op. cit.*, ii. p. 109.

133. C.S.P. Colon., 1675-76. Addenda, Nos. 230, 231. Fortescue was Gen. Venables' successor in Jamaica.

134. *Ibid.*, No. 218; Long, *op. cit.*, i. p. 262.

135. C.S.P. Colon., 1675-76. Addenda, Nos. 218, 252; Thurloe Papers, IV. pp. 451, 457.

136. Thurloe Papers, IV. pp. 152, 493.

137. C.S.P. Colon., 1675-76. Addenda, No. 236.

138. Thurloe Papers, IV. p. 604.

139. *Ibid.*, pp. 454-5, 604.

140. Thurloe Papers, IV. p. 452.

141. *Ibid.*, v. pp. 96, 151.

142. This was the treasure fleet which Captain Stayner's ship and two other frigates captured off Cadiz on 9th September. Six galleons were captured, sunk or burnt, with no less than £600,000 of gold and silver. The galleons which Blake burnt in the harbour of Santa Cruz, on 20th April 1657, were doubtless the Mexican fleet for which Admiral Goodson vainly waited before Havana in the previous summer.

143. C.S.P. Colon., 1675-76, Addenda, Nos. 260, 263, 266, 270, 275; Thurloe Papers, V. p. 340.

144. *Cf.* Brit. Mus., Add. MSS., 12,430: Journal of Col. Beeston. Col. Beeston seems to have harboured a peculiar spite against Doyley. For the contrary view of Doyley, *cf.* Long, *op. cit.*, i. p. 284.

145. C.S.P. Colon., 1675-76. Addenda., Nos. 309, 310. In these letters the towns are called "Tralo" and "St. Mark." *Cf.* also Thurloe Papers, VII. p. 340.

146. Captain Christopher Myngs had been appointed to the "Marston Moor," a frigate of fifty-four guns, in October 1654, and had seen two years' service in the West Indies under Goodson in 1656 and 1657. In May 1656 he took part in the sack of Rio de la Hacha. In July 1657 the "Marston Moor" returned to England and was ordered to be refitted, but by 20th February 1658 Myngs and his frigate were again at Port Royal (C.S.P. Colon., 1675-76, Addenda, Nos. 295, 297). After Admiral Goodson's return to England (*Ibid.*, No. 1202) Myngs seems to have been the chief naval officer

in the West Indies, and greatly distinguished himself in his naval actions against the Spaniards.

147. Tanner MSS., LI. 82.

148. C.S.P. Colon., 1675-76, Addenda, Nos. 315, 316. Some figures put it as high as £500,000.

149. C.S.P. Colon., 1675-76, Addenda, Nos. 315, 318. Captain Wm. Dalyson wrote home, on 23rd January 1659/60, that he verily believed if the General (Doyley) were at home to answer for himself, Captain Myngs would be found no better than he is, a proud-speaking vain fool, and a knave in cheating the State and robbing merchants. *Ibid.*, No. 328.

150. *Ibid.*, Nos. 327, 331.

151. C.S.P. Colon., 1675-76, Addenda, No. 326.

152. S.P. Spain, vol. 44, f. 318.

153. C.S.P. Colon., 1661-68, Nos. 17, 61.

154. C.S.P. Colon., 1661-68, No. 20.

155. *Ibid.*, No. 145.

156. *Ibid.*, Nos. 259, 278. In Lord Windsor's original instructions of 21st March 1662 he was empowered to search ships suspected of trading with the Spaniards and to adjudicate the same in the Admiralty Court. A fortnight later, however, the King and Council seem to have completely changed their point of view, and this too in spite of the Navigation Laws which prohibited the colonies from trading with any but the mother-country.

157. Art. ix. of the treaty. *Cf.* Dumont: Corps diplomatique, T.V., pt. ii. p. 625. *Cf.* also C.S.P. Venetian, 1604, p. 189: —"I wished to hear from His Majesty's own lips" (wrote the Venetian ambassador in November 1604), "how he read the clause about the India navigation, and I said, 'Sire, your subjects may trade with Spain and Flanders but not with the Indies.' 'Why not?' said the King. 'Because,' I replied, 'the clause is read in that sense.' 'They are making a great error, whoever they are that hold this view,' said His Majesty; 'the meaning is quite clear.'"

158. S.P. Spain, vol. 35.

159. C.S.P. Colon., 1661-68, No. 61.

160. *Ibid.*, No. 259.

161. *Ibid.*, No. 355.

162. *Ibid.*, No. 364.

163. Thurloe Papers, IV. p. 154.

164. Thurloe Papers, IV. p. 457.

165. Beeston's Journal.

166. Calendar of the Heathcote MSS. (pr. by Hist. MSS. Commiss.), p. 34.

167. Calendar of the Heathcote MSS., p. 34. *Cf.* also C.S.P. Colon., 1661-68, No. 384: — "An act for the sale of five copper guns taken at St. Jago de Cuba."

168. Beeston's Journal.

169.   S.P. Spain, vol. 46.

170.   *Ibid.*, vol. 47.

171.   C.S.P. Colon., 1661-68, Nos. 294, 375.

172.   Brit. Mus., Add. MSS., 11,410, f. 16.

173.   *Ibid.*, f. 6.

174.   Dampier also says of Campeache that "it makes a fine show, being built all with good stone ... the roofs flattish after the Spanish fashion, and covered with pantile." —*Ed.* 1906, ii. p. 147.

175.   However, the writer of the "Present State of Jamaica" says (p. 39) that Myngs got no great plunder, neither at Campeache nor at St. Jago.

176.   Beeston's Journal; Brit. Mus., Add. MSS., 13,964, f. 16: —"Original letter from the Licentiate Maldonado de Aldana to Don Francisco Calderon y Romero, giving him an account of the taking of Campeache in 1663"; dated Campeache, March 1663. According to the Spanish relation there were fourteen vessels in the English fleet, one large ship of forty-four guns (the "Centurion"?) and thirteen smaller ones. The discrepancy in the numbers of the fleet may be explained by the probability that other Jamaican privateering vessels joined it after its departure from Port Royal. Beeston writes in his Journal that the privateer "Blessing," Captain Mitchell, commander, brought news on 28th February that the Spaniards in Campeache had notice from St. Jago of the English design and made elaborate preparations for the defence of the town. This is contradicted by the Spanish report, in which it appears that the authorities in Campeache had been culpably negligent in not maintaining the defences with men, powder or provisions.

177.   S.P. Spain, vol. 46. Fanshaw to Sec. Bennet, 13th-23rd July 1664.

178.   *Ibid.*, vol. 45. Letter of Consul Rumbold, 31st March 1663.

179.   *Ibid.*, 4th May 1663.

180.   C.S.P. Colon., 1661-68, No. 443. Dated 28th April 1663.

181.   *Ibid.*, Nos. 441, 442.

182.   Rawlinson MSS., A. 347, f. 62.

183.   Beeston's Journal.

184.   C.S.P. Colon., 1661-68, No. 571; Beeston's Journal.

185.   S.P. Spain, vol. 46, ff. 94, 96, 108, 121, 123, 127, 309 (April-August 1664).

186.   C.S.P. Colon., 1661-68, Nos. 697, 744, 812.

187.   S.P. Spain, vol. 46, f. 280.

188.   S.P. Spain, vol. 46, f. 311.

189.   Dutertre, t. iii. p. 126; Add. MSS., 13,992, f. 499. On 26th February 1656 there arrived at Jamaica a small vessel the master of which, touching at Tortuga, had found upon the deserted island two papers, one in Spanish, the other in "sorrie English" (Thurloe Papers, IV. p. 601). These papers were copies of a proclamation forbidding settlement on the island, and the English paper (Rawl. MSS., A. 29, f. 500) is printed in Firth's "Venables" as follows: — "The Captane and Sarginge Mager Don Baltearsor Calderon and Spenoso, Nopte to the President that is now in the sity of

Santo-domingo, and Captane of the gones of the sitye, and Governor and Lord Mare of this Island, and stranch of this Lland of Tortogo, and Chefe Comander of all for the Khinge of Spaine. "Yoo moust understand that all pepell what soever that shall com to this Iland of the Khinge of Spaine Catholok wich is name is Don Pilep the Ostere the forth of this name, that with his harmes he hath put of Feleminge and French men and Englesh with lefee heare from the yeare of 1630 tell the yeare of thurty fouer and tell the yeare of fifte fouer in wich the Kinge of Spane uesenge all curtyse and given good quartell to all that was upon this Iland, after that came and with oute Recepet upon this Iland knowinge that the Kinge of Spane had planted upon it and fortified in the name of the Kinge came the forth time the 15th of Augost the last yeare French and Fleminges to govern this Iland the same Governeore that was heare befor his name was Themeleon hot man De founttana gentleman of the ourder of Guresalem for to take this Iland put if fources by se and land and forsed us to beate him oute of this place with a greate dale of shame, and be caues yoo shall take notes that wee have puelld doune the Casill and carid all the gonenes and have puelld doune all the houes and have lefte no thinge, the same Captane and Sargint-mager in the name of the Kinge wich God blesh hath given yoo notis that what souer nason souer that shall com to live upon this Iland that thare shall not a man mother or children cape of the sorde, thare fore I give notiss to all pepell that they shall have a care with out anye more notis for this is the order of the Kinge and with out fall you will not want yooer Pamente and this is the furst and second and thorde time, and this whe leave heare for them that comes hear to take notis, that when wee com upon you, you shall not pleate that you dod not know is riten the 25 of August 1656."

Baltesar Calderon y Espinosa

Por Mandado de Senor Gou[or].

Pedro Fran[co] de riva deney xasuss.

190. In Dutertre's account the name is Eliazouard (Elias Ward).

191. According to a Spanish account of the expedition the date was 1661. Brit. Mus., Add. MSS., 13,992, f. 499.

192. Dutertre, tom. iii. pp. 130-34.

193. Rawl. MSS., A. 347, ff. 31 and 36; S.P. Spain, vol. 47: —Deposition of Sir Charles Lyttleton; Margry, *op. cit.*, p. 281.

194. Charlevoix, *op. cit.*, liv. vii. p. 36; Vaissière, *op. cit.*, p. 10.

195. According to Dutertre, Deschamps' commission extended only to the French inhabitants upon Tortuga, the French and English living thereafter under separate governments as at St. Kitts. Dutertre, t. iii. p. 135.

196. Rawl. MSS., A. 347, f. 36. According to Dutertre's version, Watts had scarcely forsaken the island when Deschamps arrived in the Road, and found that the French inhabitants had already made themselves masters of the colony and had substituted the French for the English standard. Dutertre, t. iii. p. 136.

197. Rawl. MSS., A. 347, f. 36.

198. C.S.P. Colon., 1661-68, No. 648.

199. Dutertre, t. iii. p. 138; Vaissière, *op. cit.*, p. 11, note 2.

200. C.S.P. Colon., 1661-68, No. 233.

201. *Ibid.*, No. 364.

202. *Ibid.*, No. 390; *cf.* also No. 474 (1).

203. *Ibid.*, No. 475.

204. Beeston's Journal, 1st March 1663. According to Dutertre, some inhabitants of Tortuga ran away to Jamaica and persuaded the governor that they could no longer endure French domination, and that if an armed force was sent, it would find no obstacle in restoring the English king's authority. Accordingly Col. Barry was despatched to receive their allegiance, with orders to use no violence but only to accept their voluntary submission. When Barry landed on Tortuga, however, with no other support than a proclamation and a harangue, the French inhabitants laughed in his face, and he returned to Jamaica in shame and confusion. Dutertre, t. iii. pp. 137-38.

205. C.S.P. Colon., 1661-68, Nos. 817-21.

206. C.S.P. Colon., 1661-68, No. 635.

207. *Ibid.*, Nos. 656 and 664. Dated 15th and 18th February respectively.

208. *Ibid.*, No. 739.

209. C.S.P. Colon., 1661-68, Nos. 739 and 744.

210. *Ibid.*, Nos. 762 and 767.

211. *Ibid.*, No. 746; Beeston's Journal.

212. S.P. Spain, vol. 46, f. 192; C.S.P. Colon., 1661-68, No. 753.

213. C.S.P. Colon., 1661-68, No. 744; *cf.* also No. 811, and Lyttleton's Report, No. 812.

214. *Ibid.*, No. 789.

215. *Ibid.*, Nos. 859, 964; Beeston's Journal. For disputes over the cargo of the Spanish prize captured by Williams, *cf.* C.S.P. Colon., 1661-68, Nos. 1140, 1150, 1177, 1264, 1266.

216. *Ibid.*, No. 767.

217. Add. MSS., 11,410, pp. 16-25.

218. C.S.P. Colon., 1661-68, No. 786; *cf.* also Add. MSS., 11,410, f. 303: —"Mr. Worseley's discourse of the Privateers of Jamaica."

219. Charlevoix, *op. cit.*, liv. vii. pp. 57-65.

220. For the biography of Jean-David Nau, surnamed l'Olonnais, *cf.* Nouvelle Biographie Générale, t. xxxviii. p. 654.

221. C.S.P. Colon., 1661-68, Nos. 744, 812.

222. *Ibid.*, Nos. 744, 765, 786, 812.

223. C.S.P. Colon., 1574-1660, pp. 363, 421, 433.

224. *Ibid.*, pp. 419, 427, 428.

225. *Ibid.*, p. 447; Egerton MSS., 2395, f. 167.

226. C.S.P. Colon., 1661-68, No. 101; *cf.* also Nos. 24, 32, 122. From orders contained in the MSS. of the Marquis of Ormonde issued on petitions of convicted prisoners, we find that reprieves were often granted on condition of their making arrangements for their own transportation for life to the West Indies, without expense to the government. The condemned were permitted to leave the gaols in which they were confined

and embark immediately, on showing that they had agreed with a sea-captain to act as his servant, both during the voyage and after their arrival. The captains were obliged to give bond for the safe transportation of the criminals, and the latter were also to find security that they would not return to the British Isles without license, on pain of receiving the punishment from which they had been originally reprieved. (Hist. MSS. Comm. Rept. X., pt. 5, pp. 34, 42, 85, 94). *Cf.* also C.S.P. Colon., 1661-68, No. 1268.

227.   C.S.P. Colon., 1661-68, Nos. 331, 769-772, 790, 791, 798, 847, 1720.

228.   *Ibid.*, No. 866.

229.   C.S.P. Colon., 1661-68, Nos. 839, 843.

230.   *Ibid.*, No. 786.

231.   *Ibid.*, No. 943.

232.   *Ibid.*, Nos. 910, 919, 926.

233.   *Ibid.*, Nos. 942, 976.

234.   *Ibid.*, No. 944.

235.   C.S.P. Colon., 1661-68, No. 979. There were really nine ships and 650 men. Cf. *ibid.*, No. 1088.

236.   *Ibid.*, Nos. 980, 983, 992.

237.   *Ibid.*, No. 1088.

238.   C.S.P. Colon., 1661-68, Nos. 1073, 1088.

239.   *Ibid.*, No. 1042, I. Lieutenant-Colonel Thomas Morgan (not to be confused with Colonel Edward Morgan), who was left in command of St. Eustatius and Saba, went in April 1666 with a company of buccaneers to the assistance of Governor Watts of St. Kitts against the French. In the rather shameful defence of the English part of the island Morgan's buccaneers were the only English who displayed any courage or discipline, and most of them were killed or wounded, Colonel Morgan himself being shot in both legs. (*Ibid.*, Nos. 1204, 1205, 1212, 1220, 1257.) St. Eustatius was reconquered by a French force from St. Kitts in the early part of 1667. (*Ibid.*, No. 1401.)

240.   C.S.P. Colon., 1661-68, No. 1082.

241.   *Ibid.*, No. 1125. Stedman was later in the year, after the outbreak of war with France, captured by a French frigate off Guadeloupe. With a small vessel and only 100 men he found himself becalmed and unable to escape, so he boldly boarded the Frenchman in buccaneer fashion and fought for two hours, but was finally overcome. (*Ibid.*, No. 1212.)

242.   *Ibid.*, No. 1085; Beeston's Journal. Mansfield was the buccaneer whom Exquemelin disguises under the name of "Mansvelt."

243.   C.S.P. Colon., 1661-68, Nos. 1130, 1132-37.

244.   C.S.P. Colon., 1661-68, Nos. 1129, 1263.

245.   *Ibid.*, Nos. 1144, 1264.

246.   *Ibid.*, Nos. 1138, 1144.

247.   C.S.P. Colon., 1661-68, No. 1264, slightly condensed from the original.

248. C.S.P. Colon., 1661-68, Nos. 1142, 1147. The Governor of Havana wrote concerning this same exploit, that on Christmas Eve of 1665 the English entered and sacked the town of Cayo in the jurisdiction of Havana, and meeting with a vessel having on board twenty-two Spaniards who were inhabitants of the town, put them all to the sword, cutting them to pieces with hangers. Afterwards they sailed to the town of Bayamo with thirteen vessels and 700 men, but altering their plans, went to Sancti Spiritus, landed 300, plundered the town, cruelly treated both men and women, burnt the best houses, and wrecked and desecrated the church in which they had made their quarters. (S.P. Spain, vol. 49, f. 50.) Col. Beeston says that Mansfield conducted the raid; but according to the Spanish account to which Duro had access, the leader was Pierre Legrand. (Duro, *op. cit.*, v. p. 164).

249. C.S.P. Colon., 1661-68, No. 1147; Beeston's Journal. Beeston reports that after a six weeks' search for Mansfield and his men he failed to find them and returned to Jamaica.

250. C.S.P. Colon., 1661-68, No. 1213.

251. Exquemelin, however, says that he had 500 men. If he attacked Providence Island with only 200 he must have received reinforcements later.

252. Duro, *op. cit.*, v. p. 167; S.P. Spain, vol. 49, f. 50. The accounts that have come down to us of this expedition are obscure and contradictory. Modyford writes of the exploit merely that "they landed 600 men at Cape Blanco, in the kingdom of Veragua, and marched 90 miles into that country to surprise its chief city, Cartago; but understanding that the inhabitants had carried away their wealth, returned to their ships without being challenged." (C.S.P. Colon., 1661-68, No. 1213.) According to Exquemelin the original goal of the buccaneers was the town of Nata, north of Panama. The Spanish accounts make the numbers of the invaders much greater, from 800 to 1200.

253. C.S.P. Colon., 1661-68, No. 1263.

254. *Ibid.*, Nos. 1309, 1349. The capture of Providence Island was Mansfield's last exploit. According to a deposition found among the Colonial papers, he and his ship were later captured by the Spaniards and carried to Havana where the old buccaneer was put in irons and soon after executed. (*Ibid.*, No. 1827.) Exquemelin says that Mansfield, having been refused sufficient aid by Modyford for the defence of Providence, went to seek assistance at Tortuga, when "death suddenly surprised him and put a period to his wicked life."

255. Exquemelin refers to a voyage of Henry Morgan to Campeache at about this time, and says that he afterwards accompanied Mansfield as his "vice-admiral." There were at least three Morgans then in the West Indies, but Colonel Edward and Lieutenant-Colonel Thomas were at this time doubtless busy preparing the armament against Curaçao.

256. "Villa de Mosa is a small Town standing on the Starboard side of the River ... inhabited chiefly by Indians, with some Spaniards....Thus far Ships come to bring Goods, especially European Commodities....They arrive here in November or December, and stay till June or July, selling their Commodities, and then load chiefly with Cacao and some Sylvester. All the Merchants and petty Traders of the country Towns come thither about Christmas to Traffick, which makes this Town the chiefest in all these Parts, Campeache excepted." —Dampier, *ed.* 1906, ii. p. 206. The town was twelve leagues from the river's mouth.

257. C.S.P. Colon., 1661-68, No. 1142; Beeston's Journal, 20th August 1665. The viceroy of New Spain, in a letter of 28th March 1665, reports the coming, in February, of

150 English in three ships to Tabasco, but gives the name of the plundered town as Santa Marta de la Vitoria. According to his story, the buccaneers seized royal treasure amounting to 50,000 pieces of eight, besides ammunition and slaves. (S.P. Spain, vol. 49, f. 122.)

258. C.S.P. Colon., 1661-68, Nos. 1826, 1827, 1851; Exquemelin, *ed.* 1684, Part II. pp. 65-74.

259. S.P. Spain, vols. 46-49. Correspondence of Sir Richard Fanshaw.

260. *Ibid.*, vol. 46, f. 192.

261. *Ibid.*, vol. 49, f. 212.

262. *Ibid.*, vol. 52, f. 138; Record Office, Treaties, etc., 466.

263. C.S.P. Colon., 1661-68, No. 1276.

264. *Ibid.*, No. 1264.

265. *Ibid.*, No. 1537.

266. *Ibid.*, No. 1264. There was probably some disagreement in the Council in England over the policy to be pursued toward the buccaneers. On 21st August 1666 Mody-ford wrote to Albemarle: "Sir James Modyford will present his Grace with a copy of some orders made at Oxford, in behalf of some Spaniards, with Lord Arlington's letter thereon; in which are such strong inculcations of continuing friendship with the Spaniards here, that he doubts he shall be highly discanted on by some persons for granting commissions against them; must beg his Grace to bring him off, or at least that the necessity of this proceeding may be taken into serious debate and then doubts not but true English judges will confirm what he has done." On the other hand he writes to Arlington on 30th July 1667: "Had my abilities suited so well with my wishes as the latter did with your Lordship's, the privateers' attempts had been only practised on the Dutch and French, and the Spaniards free of them, but I had no money to pay them nor frigates to force them; the former they could not get from our declared enemies, nothing could they expect but blows from them, and (as they have often repeated to me) will that pay for new sails and rigging?... (but) will, suit-able to your Lordship's directions, as far as I am able, restrain them from further acts of violence towards the Spaniards, unless provoked by new insolences." Yet in the following December the governor tells Albemarle that he has not altered his posture, nor does he intend until further orders. It seems clear that Arlington and Albemarle represented two opposite sets of opinion in the Council.

267. On 21st December 1671, Morgan in a deposition before the Council of Jamaica gave his age as thirty-six years. (C.S.P. Colon., 1669-74, No. 705.)

268. C.S.P. Colon., 1661-68, No. 1838; Exquemelin, *ed.* 1684, Part II., pp. 79-88. Accord-ing to Exquemelin the first design of the freebooters had been to cross the island of Cuba in its narrowest part and fall upon Havana. But on receiving advice that the gov-ernor had taken measures to defend and provision the city, they changed their minds and marched to Puerto Principe.

269. The city of Porto Bello with its large commodious harbour afforded a good anchorage and shelter for the annual treasure galleons. The narrow entrance was secured by the two forts mentioned in the narrative, the St. Jago on the left entering the harbour, and the San Felipe on the right; and within the port was a third called the San Miguel. The town lay at the bottom of the harbour bending round the shore like a half-moon. It was built on low swampy ground and had no walls or defences on the land side.

(*Cf.* the descriptions of Wafer and Gage.) The garrison at this time probably did not exceed 300 men.

270. This statement is confirmed by one of the captains serving under Morgan, who in his account of the expedition says: "After remaining some days ... sickness broke out among the troops, of which we lost half by sickness and fighting." (C.S.P. Colon., 1669-74, No. 1.) And in "The Present State of Jamaica, 1683," we read that Morgan brought to the island the plague "that killed my Lady Modyford and others."

271. Morgan reported, however, that the ransom was offered and paid by the President of Panama. (C.S.P. Colon., 1661-68, No. 1838.)

272. Exquemelin, *ed.* 1684, Part II. pp. 89-103. The cruelties of the buccaneers at Porto Bello are confirmed by a letter from John Style to the Secretary of State, complaining of the disorder and injustice reigning in Jamaica. He writes: "It is a common thing among the privateers, besides burning with matches and such like slight torments, to cut a man in pieces, first some flesh, then a hand, an arm, a leg, sometimes tying a cord about his head and with a stick twisting it till the eyes shot out, which is called 'woolding.' Before taking Puerto Bello, thus some were used, because they refused to discover a way into the town which was not, and many in the town because they would not discover wealth they knew not of. A woman there was by some set bare upon a baking stone and roasted because she did not confess of money which she had only in their conceit; this he heard some declare with boasting, and one that was sick confess with sorrow." (C.S.P. Colon., 1669-74, No. 138.) Modyford writes concerning the booty got at Porto Bello, that the business cleared each privateer £60, and "to himself they gave only £20 for their commission, which never exceeded £300." (C.S.P. Colon., 1669-74, No. 103.) But it is very probable that the buccaneers did not return a full account of the booty to the governor, for it was a common complaint that they plundered their prizes and hid the spoil in holes and creeks along the coast so as to cheat the government of its tenths and fifteenths levied on all condemned prize-goods.

273. C.S.P. Colon., 1661-68, No. 1838.

274. C.S.P. Colon., 1661-68, Nos. 1863, 1867, 1892.

275. *Ibid.*, No. 1867; Beeston's Journal, 15th October 1668.

276. *Ibid.*, C.S.P. Colon., 1674-76, Addenda, No. 1207.

277. Exquemelin gives a French version of the episode, according to which the commander of the "Cour Volant" had given bills of exchange upon Jamaica and Tortuga for the provisions he had taken out of the English ship; but Morgan, because he could not prevail on the French captain to join his proposed expedition, used this merely as a pretext to seize the ship for piracy. The "Cour Volant," turned into a privateer and called the "Satisfaction," was used by Morgan as his flagship in the expedition against Panama.

278. According to Exquemelin the booty amounted to 250,000 crowns in money and jewels, besides merchandise and slaves. Modyford, however, wrote that the buccaneers received only £30 per man.

279. C.S.P. Colon., 1669-74, No. 1; S.P. Spain, vol. 54, f. 118; vol. 55, f. 177.

280. C.S.P. Colon., 1669-74, Nos. 227, 578.

281. C.S.P. Colon., 1669-74, No. 129.

282.   *Ibid.*, No. 149. In 1666 the Consejo de Almirantazgo of Flanders had offered the government to send its frigates to the Indies to pursue and punish the buccaneers, and protect the coasts of Spanish America; and in 1669 similar proposals were made by the "armadores" or owners of corsairing vessels in the seaport towns of Biscay. Both offers were refused, however, because the government feared that such privileges would lead to commercial abuses infringing on the monopoly of the Seville merchants. Duro, *op. cit.*, V. p. 169.

283.   C.S.P. Colon., 1669-74, Nos. 113, 161, 162, 172, 182, 264, 280.

284.   *Ibid.*, Nos. 207, 211, 227, 240.

285.   C.S.P. Colon., 1669-74, Nos. 207, 209-212, 226.

286.   *Ibid.*, No. 194.

287.   *Ibid.*, No. 237.

288.   C.S.P. Colon., 1669-74; Nos. 310, 359, 504; Exquemelin, *ed.* 1684, Pt. III. pp. 3-7; Add. MSS., 13,964, f. 24.

289.   C.S.P. Colon., 1669-74, Nos. 293, 310.

290.   S.P. Spain, vol. 57, ff. 48, 53.

291.   C.S.P. Colon., 1669-74, Nos. 293, 310; Add. MSS., 13,964, f. 26. The Spaniards estimated their loss at 100,000 pieces of eight. (Add. MSS. 11,268, f. 51.)

292.   C.S.P. Colon., 1669-74, Nos. 310, 359, 504. In a report sent by Governor Modyford to England (*ibid.*, No. 704, I.) we find a list of the vessels under command of Henry Morgan, with the name, captain, tonnage, guns and crew of each ship. There were twenty-eight English vessels of from 10 to 140 tons and from zero to 20 guns, carrying from 16 to 140 men; the French vessels were eight in number, of from 25 to 100 tons, with from 2 to 14 guns, and carrying from 30 to 110 men.

293.   *Ibid.*, No. 504. According to Exquemelin, before the fleet sailed all the officers signed articles regulating the disposal of the booty. It was stipulated that Admiral Morgan should have the hundredth part of all the plunder, "that every captain should draw the shares of eight men, for the expenses of his ship, besides his own; that the surgeon besides his ordinary pay should have two hundred pieces of eight, for his chest of medicaments; and every carpenter above his ordinary salary, should draw one hundred pieces of eight. As to recompenses and rewards they were regulated in this voyage much higher than was expressed in the first part of this book. For the loss of both legs they assigned one thousand five hundred pieces of eight or fifteen slaves, the choice being left to the election of the party; for the loss of both hands, one thousand eight hundred pieces of eight or eighteen slaves; for one leg, whether the right or left, six hundred pieces of eight or six slaves; for a hand as much as for a leg, and for the loss of an eye, one hundred pieces of eight or one slave. Lastly, unto him that in any battle should signalize himself, either by entering the first any castle, or taking down the Spanish colours and setting up the English, they constituted fifty pieces of eight for a reward. In the head of these articles it was stipulated that all these extraordinary salaries, recompenses and rewards should be paid out of the first spoil or purchase they should take, according as every one should then occur to be either rewarded or paid."

294.   Sir James Modyford, who, after the capture of Providence by Mansfield in 1666, had been commissioned by the king as lieutenant-governor of the island, now bestirred himself, and in May 1671 appointed Colonel Blodre Morgan (who commanded the rear-guard at the battle of Panama) to go as deputy-governor and take possession.

Modyford himself intended to follow with some settlers shortly after, but the attempt at colonization seems to have failed. (C.S.P. Colon., 1669-74, Nos. 494, 534, 613.)

295.   Add. MSS., 11,268, f. 51 *ff.*; *ibid.*, 13,964, f. 24-25.

296.   *Ibid.*, 11,268, f. 51 *ff.*; S.P. Spain, vol. 58, f. 156.

297.   Exquemelin, *ed.* 1684, Part III. pp. 23-27.

298.   C.S.P. Colon., 1669-74, No. 504. Exquemelin says that there were 1200 men, five boats with artillery and thirty-two canoes.

299.   Morgan's report makes it 200 men. (C.S.P. Colon., 1669-74, No. 504.)

300.   Morgan says: "The enemy had basely quitted the first entrenchment and set all on fire, as they did all the rest, without striking a stroke." The President of Panama also writes that the garrisons up the river, on receiving news of the fall of Chagre, were in a panic, the commanders forsaking their posts and retiring in all haste to Venta Cruz. (C.S.P. Colon., 1669-74, No. 547.)

301.   Exquemelin makes the buccaneers arrive at Venta Cruz on the seventh day. According to Morgan they reached the village on the sixth day, and according to Frogge on the fifth. Morgan reports that two miles from Venta Cruz there was "a very narrow and dangerous passage where the enemy thought to put a stop to our further proceeding but were presently routed by the Forlorn commanded by Capt. Thomas Rogers."

302.   Frogge says that after leaving Venta Cruz they came upon an ambuscade of 1000 Indians, but put them to flight with the loss of only one killed and two wounded, the Indians losing their chief and about thirty men. (S.P. Spain, vol. 58, f. 118.) Morgan reports three killed and six or seven wounded.

303.   "Next morning drew up his men in the form of a tertia, the vanguard led by Lieutenant-Colonel Lawrence Prince and Major John Morris, in number 300, the main body 600, the right wing led by himself, the left by Colonel Edw. Collyer, the rearguard of 300 commanded by Colonel Bledry Morgan." —Morgan's Report. (C.S.P. Colon., 1669-74, No. 504.)

304.   The close agreement between the accounts of the battle given by Morgan and Exquemelin is remarkable, and leads us to give much greater credence to those details in Exquemelin's narrative of the expedition which were omitted from the official report. Morgan says of the battle that as the Spaniards had the advantage of position and refused to move, the buccaneers made a flanking movement to the left and secured a hill protected on one side by a bog. Thereupon "One Francesco de Harro charged with the horse upon the vanguard so furiously that he could not be stopped till he lost his life; upon which the horse wheeled off, and the foot advanced, but met with such a warm welcome and were pursued so close that the enemies' retreat came to plain running, though they did work such a stratagem as has been seldom heard of, viz.: —attempting to drive two droves of 1500 cattle into their rear." (C.S.P. Colon., 1669-74, No. 504.)

305.   Morgan gives the number of Spaniards at 2100 foot and 600 horse, and Frogge reports substantially the same figures. The President of Panama, however, in his letter to the Queen, writes that he had but 1200 men, mostly negroes, mulattos and Indians, besides 200 slaves of the Assiento. His followers, he continues, were armed only with arquebuses and fowling-pieces, and his artillery consisted of three wooden guns bound with hide.

306. According to Frogge the Spaniards lost 500 men in the battle, the buccaneers but one Frenchman. Morgan says that the whole day's work only cost him five men killed and ten wounded, and that the loss of the enemy was about 400.

307. "In the city they had 200 fresh men, two forts, all the streets barricaded and great guns in every street, which in all amounted to thirty-two brass guns, but instead of fighting commanded it to be fired, and blew up the chief fort, which was done in such haste that forty of their own soldiers were blown up. In the market-place some resistance was made, but at three o'clock they had quiet possession of the city...." —Morgan's Report.

308. S.P. Spain, vol. 58, f. 156.

309. C.S.P. Colon., 1669-74, No. 547.

310. After the destruction of Panama in 1671, the old city was deserted by the Spaniards, and the present town raised on a site several miles to the westward, where there was a better anchorage and landing facilities.

311. The incident of Morgan and the Spanish lady I have omitted because it is so contrary to the testimony of Richard Browne (who if anything was prejudiced against Morgan) that "as to their women, I know or ever heard of anything offered beyond their wills; something I know was cruelly executed by Captain Collier in killing a friar in the field after quarter given; but for the Admiral he was noble enough to the vanquished enemy." (C.S.P. Colon., 1669-74, No. 608.)

312. The President had retired north to Nata de los Santos, and thence sent couriers with an account of what had happened over Darien to Cartagena, whence the news was forwarded by express boat to Spain. (S.P. Spain, vol. 58, f. 156). That the president made efforts to raise men to oppose the retreat of the buccaneers, but received no support from the inhabitants, is proved by Spanish documents in Add. MSS., 11,268, ff. 33, 37, etc.

313. The President of Panama in his account contained in Add. MSS. 11,268, gives the date as 25th February. Morgan, however, says that they began the march for Venta Cruz on 14th February; but this discrepancy may be due to a confusion of the old and new style of dating.

314. The buccaneers arrived at Chagre on 26th February. —Morgan's account.

315. Exquemelin, *ed.* 1684, Part III. pp. 31-76.

316. C.S.P. Colon., 1669-74, No. 608. Wm. Frogge, too, says that the share of each man was only £10.

317. Add. MSS., 11,268.

318. C.S.P. Colon., 1669-74, No. 542, I.

319. *Ibid.*, No. 542, II.

320. S.P. Spain, vol. 57, f. 76; vol. 58, f. 27.

321. C.S.P. Colon., 1669-74, Nos. 513, 531, 532, 544; Beeston's journal.

322. S.P. Spain, vol. 58, f. 30.

323. *Cf.* Memorial of the Conde de Molina complaining that a new governor had not been sent to Jamaica, as promised, nor the old governor recalled, 26th Feb. 1671 (S.P. Spain, vol. 58, f. 62).

324. C.S.P. Colon., 1669-74, No. 272.

325. *Ibid.*, No. 331.

326. C.S.P. Colon., 1669-74, Nos. 377, 424.

327. *Ibid.*, Nos. 405, 441, 452, 453, 552, 587.

328. *Ibid.*, Nos. 600, 604, 608, 655.

329. *Ibid.*, Nos. 653, 654.

330. S.P. Spain, vol. 58, f. 156.

331. S.P. Spain, vol. 58, f. 156.

332. C.S.P. Colon., 1669-74, No. 367.

333. *Ibid.*, Nos. 604, 608, 729; Beeston's Journal.

334. *Ibid.*, Nos. 552, 602.

335. C.S.P. Colon., 1669-74, Nos. 608, 633.

336. *Ibid.*, No. 604.

337. *Ibid.*, Nos. 638, 640, 663, 697. This may be the Diego Grillo to whom Duro (*op. cit.*, V. p. 180) refers —a native of Havana commanding a vessel of fifteen guns. He defeated successively in the Bahama Channel three armed ships sent out to take him, and in all of them he massacred without exception the Spaniards of European birth. He was captured in 1673 and suffered the fate he had meted out to his victims.

338. *Ibid.*, Nos. 697, 709, 742, 883, 944.

339. C.S.P. Colon., 1669-74, Nos. 733, 742, 796.

340. *Ibid.*, No. 729.

341. *Ibid.*, Nos. 742, 777, 785, 789, 794, 796.

342. C.S.P. Colon., 1669-74, Nos. 742, 945, 1042.

343. C.S.P. Colon., 1669-74, Nos. 733, 742, 779, 796, 820, 1022.

344. *Ibid.*, Nos. 650, 663, 697. Seventeen months later, after the outbreak of the Dutch war, the Jamaicans had a similar scare over an expected invasion of the Dutch and Spaniards, but this, too, was dissolved by time into thin air. (C.S.P. Colon., 1669-74, Nos. 887, 1047, 1055, 1062). In this connection, *cf.* Egerton MSS., 2375, f. 491: — Letter written by the Governor of Cumana to the Duke of Veragua, 1673, seeking his influence with the Council of the Indies to have the Governor of Margarita send against Jamaica 1500 or 2000 Indians, "guay quies," as they are valient bowmen, seamen and divers.

345. C.S.P. Colon., 1669-74, Nos. 697, 789, 794, 900, 911; Beeston's Journal.

346. *Ibid.*, Nos. 697, 789.

347. *Ibid.*, Nos. 1212, 1251-5.

348. *Ibid.*, No. 1259, *cf.* also 1374, 1385, 1394.

349. *Ibid.*, No. 1379.

350. *Ibid.*, 1675-76, Nos. 458, 467, 484, 521, 525, 566.

351. S.P. Spain, vol. 63, f. 56.

352. C.S.P. Colon., 1669-74, No. 1389; *ibid.* 1675-76, No. 564; Add. MSS., 36,330, No. 28.

353. C.S.P. Colon., 1669-74, Nos. 888, 940.

354. C.S.P. Colon., 1669-74, Nos. 1178, 1180, 1226; *ibid.*, 1675-76, No. 579.

355. *Ibid.*, 1669-74, No. 1423; *ibid.*, 1675-76, No. 707.

356. *Ibid.*, 1675-76, No. 520.

357. Ibid.

358. *Ibid.*, 1669-74, Nos. 1335, 1351, 1424; S.P. Spain, vols. 60, 62, 63.

359. C.S.P. Colon., 1675-76, No. 643.

360. *Ibid.*, Nos. 639-643.

361. *Ibid.*, Nos. 633-635, 729.

362. *Ibid.*, Nos. 693, 719, 720.

363. C.S.P. Colon., 1669-74, Nos. 310, 704, iv. It was a very profitable business for the wood then sold at £25 or £30 a ton. For a description of the life of the logwood-cutters *cf.* Dampier, Voyages, *ed.* 1906, ii. pp. 155-56. 178-79, 181 *ff.*

364. *Ibid.*, No. 580.

365. *Ibid.*, Nos. 587, 638.

366. *Ibid.*, Nos. 777, 786.

367. C.S.P. Colon., 1669-74. No. 825.

368. *Ibid.*, Nos. 819, 943.

369. *Ibid.*, Nos. 954, 1389. Fernandez Duro (t.v., p. 181) mentions a Spanish ordinance of 22nd February 1674, which authorized Spanish corsairs to go out in the pursuit and punishment of pirates. Periaguas, or large flat-bottomed canoes, were to be constructed for use in shoal waters. They were to be 90 feet long and from 16 to 18 feet wide, with a draught of only 4 or 5 feet, and were to be provided with a long gun in the bow and four smaller pieces in the stern. They were to be propelled by both oars and sails, and were to carry 120 men.

370. C.S.P. Colon., 1669-74, Nos. 950, 1094; Beeston's Journal, Aug. 1679.

371. *Ibid.*, 1675-76, No. 566.

372. C.S.P. Colon., 1675-76, No. 673.

373. *Ibid.*, No. 526. In significant contrast to Lord Vaughan's praise of Lynch, Sir Henry Morgan, who could have little love for the man who had shipped him and Modyford as prisoners to England, filled the ears of Secretary Williamson with veiled accusations against Lynch of having tampered with the revenues and neglected the defences of the island. (*Ibid.*, No. 521.)

374. *Ibid.*, No. 912. In testimony of Lord Vaughan's straightforward policy toward buccaneering, *cf.* Beeston's Journal, June 1676.

375. C.S.P. Colon., 1675-76, No. 988.

376. Leeds MSS. (Hist. MSS. Comm., XI. pt. 7, p. 13) —Depositions in which Sir Henry Morgan is represented as endeavouring to hush up the matter, saying "the privateers

were poore, honest fellows," to which the plundered captain replied "that he had not found them soe."

377.   C.S.P. Colon., 1675-76; Nos. 860, 913.

378.   Statutes at Large, vol. ii. (Lond. 1786), pp. 210, 247.

379.   C.S.P. Colon., 1675-76; Nos. 993-995, 1001.

380.   *Ibid.*, No. 1093.

381.   C.S.P. Colon., 1677-80, Nos. 500, 508.

382.   *Ibid.*, 1675-76, No. 916.

383.   *Ibid.*, No. 1126.

384.   *Ibid.*, Nos. 998, 1006.

385.   *Ibid.*, No. 1129.

386.   *Ibid.*, No. 1129 (vii., viii.); *cf.* also No. 657.

387.   C.S.P. Colon., 1675-76, No. 1129 (xiv., xvii.).

388.   C.S.P. Colon., 1675-76, Nos. 656, 741.

389.   *Ibid.*, 1677-80, No. 313; *cf.* also Nos. 478, 486.

390.   *Ibid.*, No. 368. A similar proclamation was issued in May 1681; *cf. Ibid.*, 1681-85, No. 102.

391.   *Ibid.*, No. 375.

392.   C.S.P. Colon., 1677-80, Nos. 243, 365, 383; Egerton MSS., 2395, f. 591.

393.   In a memoir to Mme. de Montespan, dated 8th July 1677, the population of French San Domingo is given as between four and five thousand, white and black. The colony embraced a strip of coast 80 leagues in length and 9 or 10 miles wide, and it produced 2,000,000 lbs. of tobacco annually. (Bibl. Nat., Nouv. Acq., 9325, f. 258).

394.   C.S.P. Colon., 1677-80, Nos. 347, 375, 383, 1497; S.P. Spain, vol. 65, f. 102.

395.   A small island east of Curaçao, in latitude 12° north, longitude 67° 41' west.

396.   Saint Yves, G. Les campagnes de Jean d'Estrées dans la mer des Antilles, 1676-78; *cf.* also C.S.P. Colon., 1677-80, Nos. 604, 642, 665, 687-90, 718, 741 (xiv., xv.), 1646-47. According to one story, the Dutch governor of Curaçao sent out three privateers with orders to attend the French fleet, but to run no risk of capture. The French, discovering them, gave chase, but being unacquainted with those waters were decoyed among the reefs.

397.   C.S.P. Colon., 1677-80, Nos. 1646-47.

398.   Dampier says of this occasion: "The privateers … told me that if they had gone to Jamaica with £30 a man in their Pockets, they could not have enjoyed themselves more. For they kept in a Gang by themselves, and watched when the Ships broke, to get the Goods that came from them; and though much was staved against the Rocks, yet abundance of Wine and Brandy floated over the Riff, where the Privateers waited to take it up. They lived here about three Weeks, waiting an Opportunity to transport themselves back again to Hispaniola; in all which Time they were never without two or three Hogsheads of Wine and Brandy in their Tents, and Barrels of Beef and Pork." —Dampier, *ed.* 1906, i. p. 81.

399.   Charlevoix, *op. cit.*, liv. viii. p. 120.

400.   Bibl. Nat., Nouv. Acq., 9325, f. 260; Charlevoix, *op. cit.*, liv. viii. p. 122.

401.   *Ibid.*, p. 119; C.S.P. Colon., 1677-80, Nos. 815, 869; Beeston's Journal, 18th October 1678.

402.   C.S.P. Colon., 1677-80, Nos. 569, 575, 618.

403.   *Ibid.*, No. 770.

404.   *Ibid.*, Nos. 622, 646.

405.   C.S.P. Colon., 1677-80, Nos. 770, 815, 1516: Beeston's Journal, 18th October 1678.

406.   The Spanish ambassador, Don Pedro Ronquillo, in his complaint to Charles II. in September 1680, placed the number at 1000. (C.S.P. Colon., 1677-80, No. 1498.)

407.   C.S.P. Colon., 1677-80, Nos. 1150, 1188, 1199, 1516; Beeston's Journal, 29th September and 6th October 1678. Lord Carlisle, in answer to the complaints of the Spanish ambassador, pretended ignorance of the source of the indigo thus admitted through the customs, and maintained that it was brought into Port Royal "in lawful ships by lawful men."

408.   Sloane MSS., 2752, f. 29; S.P. Spain, vol. 65, f. 121. According to the latter account, which seems to be derived from a Spanish source, the loss suffered by the city amounted to about 100,000 pieces of eight, over half of which was plunder carried away by the freebooters. Thirteen of the inhabitants were killed and four wounded, and of the buccaneers thirty were killed. Dampier writes concerning this first irruption of the buccaneers into the Pacific: —"Before my first going over into the South Seas with Captain Sharp ... I being then on Board Captain Coxon, in company with 3 or 4 more Privateers, about 4 leagues to the East of Portobel, we took the Pacquets bound thither from Cartagena. We open'd a great quantity of the Merchants Letters, and found ... the Merchants of several parts of Old Spain thereby informing their Correspondents of Panama and elsewhere of a certain Prophecy that went about Spain that year, the Tenour of which was, That there would be English Privateers that Year in the West Indies, who would ... open a Door into the South Seas; which they supposed was fastest shut: and the Letters were accordingly full of Cautions to their Friends to be very watchful and careful of their Coasts. "This Door they spake of we all concluded must be the Passage over Land through the Country of the Indians of Darien, who were a little before this become our Friends, and had lately fallen out with the Spaniards, ... and upon calling to mind the frequent Invitations we had from these Indians a little before this time, to pass through their Country, and fall upon the Spaniards in the South Seas, we from henceforward began to entertain such thoughts in earnest, and soon came to a Resolution to make those Attempts which we afterwards did, ... so that the taking these Letters gave the first life to those bold undertakings: and we took the advantage of the fears the Spaniards were in from that Prophecy ... for we sealed up most of the Letters again, and sent them ashore to Portobel." —*Ed.* 1906, I. pp. 200-201.

409.   C.S.P. Colon., 1677-80, No. 1199.

410.   *Ibid.*, No. 1188.

411.   Sloane MSS., 2572, f. 29.

412.   C.S.P. Colon., 1677-80, Nos. 1344, 1370.

413.   *Ibid.*, No. 1516.

414. *Cf.* Archives Coloniales-Correspondance générale de St Domingue, vol. i.; Martinique, vol. iv.

415. C.S.P. Colon., 1677-80, Nos. 1420, 1425; Sloane MSS., 2724, f. 3.

416. Sloane MSS., 2724, f. 198. Coxon probably did not submit, for Dampier tells us that at the end of May 1681, Coxon was lying with seven or eight other privateers at the Samballas, islands on the coast of Darien, with a ship of ten guns and 100 men. — *Ed.* 1906, i. p. 57.

417. *Ibid.*, f. 200; C.S.P. Colon., 1681-85, Nos. 16, 51, 144, 431. Everson was not shot and killed in the water, as Morgan's account implies, for he flourished for many years afterwards as one of the most notorious of the buccaneer captains.

418. Ringrose's Journal. *Cf.* also S.P. Spain, vol. 67, f. 169; C.S.P. Colon., 1681-85, No. 872.

419. C.S.P. Colon., 1681-85, Nos. 431, 632, 713; Hist. MSS. Commiss., VII., 405 b.

420. C.S.P Colon., 1677-80, Nos. 1425, 1462.

421. *Ibid.*, No. 1361.

422. C.S.P. Colon., 1677-80, Nos. 601, 606, 607, 611; *ibid.*, 1681-85, No. 160; Add. MSS., 22, 676; Acts of Privy Council, Colonial Series I. No. 1203.

423. C.S.P. Colon., 1681-85, Nos. 501, 552. *Cf.* also Nos. 197, 227.

424. C.S.P. Colon., 1681-85, Nos. 364-366, 431, 668.

425. *Ibid.*, Nos. 476, 609, 668. Paine was sent from Jamaica under arrest to Governor de Cussy in 1684, and thence was shipped on a frigate to France. (Bibl. Nat., Nouv. Acq., 9325, f. 334.)

426. *Ibid.*, Nos. 668, 769, 963.

427. C.S.P. Colon., 1681-85, Nos. 769, 963, 993.

428. *Ibid.*, Nos. 1065, 1313.

429. *Ibid.*, No. 1313.

430. *Ibid.*, Nos. 1190, 1216.

431. C.S.P. Colon., 1681-85, No. 1173.

432. *Ibid.*, Nos. 1168, 1190, 1223, 1344; *cf.* also Nos. 1381, 1464, 1803. In June 1684 we learn that "Hamlin, captain of La Trompeuse, got into a ship of thirty-six guns on the coast of the Main last month, with sixty of his old crew and as many new men. They call themselves pirates, and their ship La Nouvelle Trompeuse, and talk of their old station at Isle de Vaches." (*Ibid.*, No. 1759.)

433. C.S.P. Colon., 1681-85, Nos. 777, 1188, 1189, 1223, 1376, 1471-1474, 1504, 1535, 1537, 1731.

434. *Ibid.*, Nos. 1222, 1223, 1676, 1678, 1686, 1909; *cf.* also Nos. 1382, 1547, 1665.

435. *Ibid.*, Nos. 552, 599, 668, 712. Coxon continued to vacillate between submission to the Governor of Jamaica and open rebellion. In October 1682 he was sent by Sir Thos. Lynch with three vessels to the Gulf of Honduras to fetch away the English logwood-cutters. "His men plotted to take the ship and go privateering, but he valiently resisted, killed one or two with his own hand, forced eleven overboard, and brought three here (Port Royal) who were condemned last Friday." (*Ibid.*, No. 769.

Letter of Sir Thos. Lynch, 6th Nov. 1682.) A year later, in November 1683, he had again reverted to piracy (*ibid.*, No. 1348), but in January 1686 surrendered to Lieut.-Governor Molesworth and was ordered to be arrested and tried at St. Jago de la Vega (*ibid.*, 1685-88, No. 548). He probably in the meantime succeeded in escaping from the island, for in the following November he was reported to be cutting logwood in the Gulf of Campeache, and Molesworth was issuing a proclamation declaring him an outlaw (*ibid.*, No. 965). He remained abroad until September 1688 when he again surrendered to the Governor of Jamaica (*ibid.*, No. 1890), and again by some hook or crook obtained his freedom.

436. C.S.P. Colon., 1681-85, Nos. 660, 673.

437. *Ibid.*, Nos. 627, 769.

438. He is not to be confused with the Peter Paine who brought "La Trompeuse" to Port Royal. Thomas Pain, a few months before he arrived in the Bahamas, had come in and submitted to Sir Thomas Lynch, and had been sent out again by the governor to cruise after pirates. (C.S.P. Colon., 1681-85, Nos. 769, 1707.)

439. C.S.P. Colon., 1681-85, Nos. 1509, 1540, 1590, 1924, 1926.

440. *Ibid.*, Nos. 1927, 1938.

441. *Ibid.*, Nos. 1540, 1833.

442. Charlevoix, *op. cit.*, liv. viii. p. 130. In 1684 there were between 2000 and 3000 filibusters who made their headquarters in French Hispaniola. They had seventeen vessels at sea with batteries ranging from four to fifty guns. (C.S.P. Colon., 1681-85, No. 668; Bibl. Nat., Nouv. Acq., 9325, f. 336.)

443. Charlevoix, *op. cit.*, liv. viii. pp. 128-30.

444. C.S.P. Colon., 1681-85, Nos. 963, 998, 1065.

445. C.S.P. Colon., 1681-85, Nos. 709, 712.

446. C.S.P. Colon., 1681-85, No. 1163; Charlevoix, liv. viii. p. 133; Narrative contained in "The Voyages and Adventures of Captain Barth, Sharpe and others in the South Sea." Lon. 1684. Governor Lynch wrote in July 1683: "All the governors in America have known of this very design for four or five months." Duro, quoting from a Spanish MS. in the Coleccion Navarrete, t. x. No. 33, says that the booty at Vera Cruz amounted to more than three million reales de plata in jewels and merchandise, for which the invaders demanded a ransom of 150,000 pieces of eight. They also carried away, according to the account, 1300 slaves. (*Op. cit.*, v. p. 271.) A real de plata was one-eighth of a peso or piece of eight.

447. S.P. Spain, vol. 69, f. 339.

448. *Ibid.*, vol. 70, f. 57; C.S.P. Colon., 1681-85, No. 1633.

449. During de Franquesnay's short tenure of authority, Laurens, driven from Hispaniola by the stern measures of the governor against privateers, made it understood that he desired to enter the service of the Governor of Jamaica. The Privy Council empowered Lynch to treat with him, offering pardon and permission to settle on the island on giving security for his future good behaviour. But de Cussy arrived in the meantime, reversed the policy of de Franquesnay, received Laurens with all the honour due to a military hero, and endeavoured to engage him in the services of the government (Charlevoix, *op. cit.*, liv. viii. pp. 141, 202; C.S.P. Colon., 1681-85, Nos. 1210, 1249, 1424, 1461, 1649, 1718 and 1839).

450.   Charlevoix, *op. cit.*, liv. viii. pp. 139-145; C.S.P. Colon., 1685-88, No. 378.

451.   Charlevoix, *op. cit.*, liv. ix. pp. 197-99; Duro., *op. cit.*, v. pp. 273-74; C.S.P. Colon., 1685-88, Nos. 193, 339, 378, 778.

452.   According to Charlevoix, de Grammont was a native of Paris, entered the Royal Marine, and distinguished himself in several naval engagements. Finally he appeared in the West Indies as the commander of a frigate armed for privateering, and captured near Martinique a Dutch vessel worth 400,000 livres. He carried his prize to Hispaniola, where he lost at the gaming table and consumed in debauchery the whole value of his capture; and not daring to return to France he joined the buccaneers.

453.   "Laurens-Cornille Baldran, sieur de Graff, lieutenant du roi en l'isle de Saint Domingue, capitaine de frégate légère, chevalier de Saint Louis" —so he was styled after entering the service of the French king (Vaissière, *op cit.*, p. 70, note). According to Charlevoix he was a native of Holland, became a gunner in the Spanish navy, and for his skill and bravery was advanced to the post of commander of a vessel. He was sent to American waters, captured by the buccaneers, and joined their ranks. Such was the terror inspired by his name throughout all the Spanish coasts that in the public prayers in the churches Heaven was invoked to shield the inhabitants from his fury. Divorced from his first wife, whom he had married at Teneriffe in 1674, he was married again in March 1693 to a Norman or Breton woman named Marie-Anne Dieu-le-veult, the widow of one of the first inhabitants of Tortuga (*ibid.*). The story goes that Marie-Anne, thinking one day that she had been grievously insulted by Laurens, went in search of the buccaneer, pistol in hand, to demand an apology for the outrage. De Graff, judging this Amazon to be worthy of him, turned about and married her (Ducéré, *op. cit.*, p. 113, note). In October 1698 Laurens de Graff, in company with Iberville, sailed from Rochefort with two ships, and in Mobile and at the mouths of the Mississippi laid the foundations of Louisiana (Duro, *op. cit.*, v. p. 306). De Graff died in May 1704. *Cf.* also Bibl. Nat., Nouv. Acq., 9325 f. 311.

454.   C.S.P. Colon., 1681-85, Nos. 1958, 1962, 1964, 1991, 2000. Dampier writes (1685) that "it hath been usual for many years past for the Governor of Petit Guaves to send blank Commissions to Sea by many of his Captains, with orders to dispose of them to whom they saw convenient.... I never read any of these French Commissions ... but I have learnt since that the Tenor of them is to give a Liberty to Fish, Fowl and Hunt. The Occasion of this is, that ... in time of Peace these Commissions are given as a Warrant to those of each side (*i.e.*, French and Spanish in Hispaniola) to protect them from the adverse Party: But in effect the French do not restrain them to Hispaniola, but make them a pretence for a general ravage in any part of America, by Sea or Land." —Edition 1906, I. pp. 212-13.

455.   C.S.P. Colon., 1681-85, Nos. 668, 769, 942, 948, 1281, 1562, 1759; *ibid.*, 1685-88, No. 558. In a memoir of MM. de St. Laurent and Begon to the French King in February 1684, they report that in the previous year some French filibusters discovered in a patache captured from the Spaniards a letter from the Governor of Jamaica exhorting the Spaniards to make war on the French in Hispaniola, and promising them vessels and other means for entirely destroying the colony. This letter caused a furious outburst of resentment among the French settlers against the English (*cf.* also C.S.P. Colon., 1681-85, No. 1348). Shortly after, according to the memoir, an English ship of 30 guns appeared for several days cruising in the channel between Tortuga and Port de Paix. The sieur de Franquesnay, on sending to ask for an explanation of this conduct, received a curt reply to the effect that the sea was free to everyone. The French governor thereupon sent a barque with 30 filibusters to attack the Englishman, but the filibusters returned well beaten. In despair de Franquesnay asked

Captain de Grammont, who had just returned from a cruise in a ship of 50 guns, to go out against the intruder. With 300 of the corsairs at his back de Grammont attacked the English frigate. The reception accorded by the latter was as vigorous as before, but the result was different, for de Grammont at once grappled with his antagonist, boarded her and put all the English except the captain to the sword. —Bibl. Nat., Nouv. Acq., 9325 f. 332. No reference to this incident is found in the English colonial records.

456. C.S.P. Colon., 1681-85, No. 963.

457. *Ibid.*, Nos. 1844, 1852.

458. C.S.P. Colon., 1681-85, Nos. 1246, 1249, 1250, 1294, 1295, 1302, 1311, 1348, 1489, 1502, 1503, 1510, 1562, 1563, 1565.

459. *Ibid.*, No. 1938; *ibid.*, 1685-88, Nos. 33, 53, 57, 68, 128, 129, 157.

460. *Ibid.*, 1681-85, Nos. 668, 769; *ibid.*, 1685-88, No. 986.

461. C.S.P. Colon., 1681-85, Nos. 1163, 1198; Bibl. Nat., Nouv. Acq., 9325, f. 332.

462. C.S.P. Colon., 1681-85, Nos. 1796, 1854, 1855, 1943; *ibid.*, 1685-88, Nos. 218, 269, 569, 591, 609, 706, 739.

463. *Ibid.*, 1681-85, Nos. 1163, 1198, 1249, 1630.

464. *Ibid.*, Nos. 963, 992, 1938, 1949, 2025, 2067.

465. *Ibid.*, Nos. 963, 992, 1759.

466. *Ibid.*, Nos. 1259, 1563.

467. C.S.P. Colon., 1681-85, Nos. 1845, 1851, 1862, 2042. His ship is called in these letters "La Trompeuse." Unless this is a confusion with Hamlin's vessel, there must have been more than one "La Trompeuse" in the West Indies. Very likely the fame or ill-fame of the original "La Trompeuse" led other pirate captains to flatter themselves by adopting the same name. Breha was captured in 1686 by the Armada de Barlovento and hung with nine or ten of his companions (Charlevoix, *op. cit.*, liv. ix. p. 207).

468. *Ibid.*, Nos. 1299, 1862.

469. *Ibid.*, No. 1249.

470. C.S.P. Colon., 1681-85, Nos. 1560, 1561.

471. *Ibid.*, Nos. 1605, 1862.

472. *Ibid.*, Nos. 1634, 1845, 1851, 1862.

473. *Ibid.*, 1685-88, Nos. 363, 364, 639, 1164.

474. *Ibid.*, Nos. 1029, 1161; Hughson: Carolina Pirates, p. 24.

475. *Ibid.*, 1681-85, No. 1165.

476. Hughson, *op. cit.*, p. 22.

477. C.S.P. Colon., 1685-88, Nos. 1277, 1278.

478. *Ibid.*, No. 1411.

479. *Ibid.*, No. 1463.

480. *Ibid.*, No. 1602; *cf.* also *ibid.*, 1693-96, No. 2243.

481. C.S.P. Colon., 1685-88, Nos. 116, 269, 805.

482. *Ibid.*, Nos. 1066, 1212.

483. *Ibid.*, Nos. 965, 1066, 1128.

484. *Ibid.*, 1681-85, Nos. 1759, 1852, 2067; *ibid.*, 1685-88, No. 1127 and *cf.* Index. For the careers of John Williams (*alias* Yankey) and Jacob Everson (*alias* Jacobs) during these years *cf.* C.S.P. Colon., 1685-88, Nos. 259, 348, 897, 1449, 1476-7, 1624, 1705, 1877; Hist. MSS. Comm., xi. pt. 5, p. 136 (Earl of Dartmouth's MSS.).

485. C.S.P. Colon., 1685-88, Nos. 1406, 1656, 1670, 1705, 1723, 1733; *ibid.*, 1689-92, Nos. 52, 515; Hist. MSS. Commiss., xi. pt. 5, p. 136.

486. C.S.P. Colon., 1685-88, No. 1959.

487. *Ibid.*, No. 433.

488. *Ibid.*, Nos. 706, 1026.

489. *Ibid.*, No. 1567.

490. *Ibid.*, Nos. 758, 920, 927, 930, 1001, 1187, 1210.

491. C.S.P. Colon., 1685-88, Nos. 1567, 1646, 1655, 1656, 1659, 1663, 1721, 1838, 1858.

492. Dict. of Nat. Biog.

493. C.S.P. Colon., 1685-88, No. 1941; *cf.* also 1906.

494. *Ibid.*, No. 1940.

495. *Ibid.*, 1689-92, Nos. 6, 29, 292.

496. *Ibid.*, No. 299.

497. *Ibid.*, No. 493.

498. *Ibid.*, Nos. 7, 50, 52, 54, 85, 120, 176-178, 293, 296-299, 514, 515, 874, 880, 980, 1041.

499. C.S.P. Colon., 1689-92, Nos. 293, 467; *Ibid.*, 1693-96, Nos. 1931, vii., 1934.

500. *Ibid.*, 1689-92, Nos. 515, 616, 635, 769.

501. C.S.P. Colon., 1689-92, Nos. 873, 980, 1021, 1041.

502. *Ibid.*, No. 714.

503. *Ibid.*, Nos. 2034, 2043, 2269, 2496, 2498, 2641, 2643.

504. *Ibid.*, Nos. 72-76, 2034.

505. *Ibid.*, Nos. 2034, 2044, 2047, 2052, 2103.

506. *Ibid.*, Nos. 2278, 2398, 2416, 2500.

507. *Ibid.*, 1693-96, Nos. 634, 635, 1009, 1236.

508. C.S.P. Colon., 1693-96, Nos. 778, 876; Archives Coloniales, Corresp. Gen. de St. Dom. III. Letter of Ducasse, 30 March 1694.

509. C.S.P. Colon., 1693-96, Nos. 1109, 1236 (i.).

510. *Ibid.*, Nos. 1074, 1083, 1106, 1109, 1114, 1121, 1131, 1194, 1236; Charlevoix, I. x. p. 256 *ff.*; Stowe MSS., 305 f., 205 b; Ducéré: Les corsaires sous l'ancien regime, p. 142.

511. The number of white men on the island at this time was variously estimated from 2000 to 2400 men. (C.S.P. Colon., 1693-96, Nos. 1109 and 1258.)

512. C.S.P. Colon, 1693-96, No. 1516.

513. *Ibid.*, Nos. 207, 876, 1004.

514. C.S.P. Colon., 1693-96, Nos. 1946, 1973, 1974, 1980, 1983, 2022. According to Charlevoix, it was the dalliance and cowardice of Laurens de Graff, who was in command at Cap François, and feared falling into the hands of his old enemies the English and Spaniards, which had much to do with the success of the invasion. After the departure of the allies Laurens was deprived of his post and made captain of a light corvette. (Charlevoix, I. x. p. 266 *ff.*)

515. Ducéré, *op. cit.* p. 148.

516. Narrative of de Pointis.

517. Narrative of de Pointis; C.S.P. Colon., 1696-97, No. 824.

518. Narrative of de Pointis; C.S.P. Colon., 1696-97, No. 868.

519. Narrative of de Pointis.

520. C.S.P. Colon., 1696-97, Nos. 373-376, 413, 661, 769.

521. *Ibid.*, Nos. 715, 868.

522. C.S.P. Colon., 1696-97, Nos. 375, 453.

523. *Ibid.*, 944. 978.

524. The mouth of the harbour, called Boca Chica, was defended by a fort with 4 bastions and 33 guns; but the guns were badly mounted on flimsy carriages of cedar, and were manned by only 15 soldiers. Inside the harbour was another fort called Santa Cruz, well-built with 4 bastions and a moat, but provided with only a few iron guns and without a garrison. Two other forts formed part of the exterior works of the town, but they had neither garrison nor guns. The city itself was surrounded by solid walls of stone, with 12 bastions and 84 brass cannon, to man which there was a company of 40 soldiers. Such was the war footing on which the Spanish Government maintained the "Key of the Indies." (Duro, *op. cit.*, v. p. 287.)

525. Narrative of de Pointis. *Cf.* Charlevoix, *op cit.*, liv. xi., for the best account of the whole expedition.

526. Charlevoix, *op. cit.*, liv. xi. p. 352. In one of the articles of capitulation which the Governor of Cartagena obtained from de Pointis, the latter promised to leave untouched the plate, jewels and other treasure of the churches and convents. This article was not observed by the French. On the return of the expedition to France, however, Louis XIV. ordered the ecclesiastical plate to be sequestered, and after the conclusion of the Peace of Ryswick sent it back to San Domingo to be delivered to the governor and clergy of the Spanish part of the island. (Duro, *op. cit.*, v. pp. 291, 296-97).

527. Duro, *op. cit.*, v. p. 310.

528. C.S.P. Colon., 1669-74, No. 697.

529. *Ibid.*; *cf.* C.S.P. Colon., 1669-74, No. 138: "The number of tippling houses is now doubly increased, so that there is not now resident upon the place ten men to every house that selleth strong liquors. There are more than 100 licensed houses, besides sugar and rum works that sell without licence."

530.   Crawford: Bibliotheca Lindesiana. Handlist of Proclamations.

531.   Firth: Naval Songs and Ballads, pp. l.-lii.; *cf.* also Archives Coloniales, Corresp. Gén. de St Dom., vols. iii.-ix.; *Ibid.*, Martinique, vols. viii.-xix.

532.   Archives Coloniales, Corresp. Gén. de Martinique, vol. xvi.

www.ingramcontent.com/pod-product-compliance
Lightning Source LLC
Chambersburg PA
CBHW071759120626
46550CB00002B/856